THE WEIGHT OF LOVE

The Weight of Love

Affect, Ecstasy, and Union
in the Theology of Bonaventure

Robert Glenn Davis

FORDHAM UNIVERSITY PRESS

New York 2017

The author and publisher are grateful to the Arts and
Sciences Deans of Fordham University for providing
funding toward production costs of this book.

Visit us online at www.fordhampress.com.

Library of Congress Cataloging-in-Publication Data

Names: Davis, Robert Glenn, author.
Title: The weight of love : affect, ecstasy, and union in the
theology of Bonaventure / Robert Glenn Davis.
Description: New York : Fordham University Press, [2017] |
Includes bibliographical references and index.
Identifiers: LCCN 2016013982 | ISBN 9780823272129
(cloth : alk. paper) | ISBN 9780823274536 (pbk. : alk. paper)
Subjects: LCSH: Bonaventure, Saint, Cardinal, approximately
1217–1274. | Love—Religious aspects—Christianity—
History of doctrines—Middle Ages, 600–1500.
Classification: LCC B765.B74 D38 2017 | DDC 241/.4—dc23
LC record available at https://lccn.loc.gov/2016013982

Printed in the United States of America
19 18 17   5 4 3 2 1
First edition

for Ben

CONTENTS

THE WEIGHT OF LOVE

Introduction: Weighing Affect in Medieval Christian Devotion

"Take a corpse, and place it where you like. You will see that it puts up no resistance to motion, nor does it grumble about its position, or complain when it is put aside. If it is propped up on a throne, it does not raise its head up, but rather looks down. If it is clothed in purple, it will look twice as pale. This is the truly obedient one, who does not judge why he is moved, and does not care where he is placed." According to his thirteenth-century hagiographers, the Umbrian saint Francis of Assisi responded with these words to a group of followers asking for spiritual instruction by offering, as an example of true obedience, a dead body (*exanime corpus*, literally, a body without a soul).[1]

This story, especially in the context of the *vitae* of St. Francis, illustrates what students of medieval Christianity have long known: The saintly body, in its wonderful and pitiful conformity to Christ's body, played an exemplary role in the Passion-centered piety of late-medieval Europe. But this curious pedagogical scene, which is found throughout the early Franciscan hagiographical tradition, presents the holy body as something more (or less) than simply a vehicle for cruciform suffering. Why was a dead body a spiritual exemplar? What else were holy bodies capable of besides (alongside of) suffering? As this episode demonstrates, the body, in its most fundamental capacity to be moved by an external force, served as a source of instruction and site of desire for the late-medieval Christian devotional imagination. The pliant body of Francis's macabre exemplum is no particular body—a nameless corpse—but in the *vita* of Francis, the corpse casts its shadow forward over Francis's own body. The earliest legends of Francis's holiness recount his angelic vision near the end of his life that left him branded with the wounds of Christ's passion. In what became the official account of Francis's life, Bonaventure of Bagnoregio's longer *Life of St. Francis* (the *Legenda Maior*) depicts Francis's body transformed by the ardor of his love, pierced by joy and grief at the sight of a six-winged Seraph affixed to a cross. But he is not just transformed by the vision—he is incapacitated by it. Unable to walk, Francis has to be carried through the streets, while still living, like the corpse he would soon become. By the end of his life, Francis has become the yielding body that he had earlier offered to his followers as an example.

Another pedagogical scene, framing and reflecting the first: this time Francis himself is the exemplum, and Bonaventure is the teacher. In a sermon given at the Franciscan house in Paris on the feast day of Francis of Assisi in 1262,[2] Bonaventure explains the significance of the figure of the Seraph that appeared to Francis shortly before his death and branded him with the marks of Christ's passion:

> Why do we, being so wretched, have such cold hearts that we will not endure anything for the sake of our Lord? Our hearts do not burn or boil with love. For just as heat is a property of the heart, and when this heat is greater a person's actions are stronger and more robust, so too one who has more of the heat of love or charity in their heart is for this reason able to perform more virtuous deeds. Do you want to imprint Christ crucified in your heart? Do you wish to transform yourself into him so much that you burn with charity? Just as iron, when it is heated to the point of melting, can be imprinted with any form or image, so too a heart burning with the love of Christ crucified is imprinted with the crucified Christ or the cross, and the lover is carried over or transformed into the Crucified, just as the blessed Francis was. Some people are amazed that a Seraphim was sent to him when the stigmata of Christ's passion were to be imprinted upon him. Surely, they say, no Seraphim was crucified! No, but the Seraphim is the spirit whose name means "ardor," which signifies that Francis was burning with charity when the Seraphim was sent to him. And the cross or the sign of the cross imprinted upon his body signifies the affection which he had for

the crucified Christ, and that, from the ardor of his love, he was wholly transformed into Christ.[3]

The sermon is an exegesis both of Francis's vision and Matthew 24:30: "Then the sign of the Son of Man will appear in heaven." In the moral sense, Bonaventure explains, the verse refers to stigmata that Francis received; he is the "heavens" upon which the sign of the Son of Man appears. Through this tropological identification, Francis's stigmatized flesh becomes the scriptural text of the homily: An eschatological and cosmic message is legible on his branded body.[4] The sermon takes the form of an extended comparison of Francis to the celestial sphere—its beauty is reflected in Francis's purity, its orderly movement is modeled in Francis's obedience, its universal expanse is measured in Francis's limitless love, and its mysteries are intimated in Francis's ecstatic contemplation. In this context, the appearance of the Seraph is not out of place. The heavens are not a void dotted with spinning orbs, but a dynamic hierarchy of angelic presences. The figure of the Seraph indicates that Francis's love is as expansive as the heavens and as ardent, even self-immolating, as the fiery creatures who flank God's throne. But if the celestial body of Francis suggests cosmic splendor, the image of a softened heart evokes a more intimate devotion. Inflamed with love, Francis's heart is supple.[5] The marks on his body bear witness to a heart melted by love, whose receptivity to divine wounding made possible the physical impression. Love makes the body pliable, and a pliable body is the physical manifestation of love.

This scene, like the first, addresses the question of what the devotional body can do. Here, pliability, imprintability, and mobility are capacities of the ardent body—that is, a body inflamed with love. *Amor* as fire is both spiritual and corporeal, the substance that effects the transfer of spiritual ardor into bodily marks, and Bonaventure's sermon presents two embodiments of this love: the impressionable body of Francis and the pliable body of iron. The latter becomes the example of the former, and both exemplify the quality of *amor* that is the focal point of the sermon. *Amor* is the principle of pious devotion to the Passion and of purifying and perfecting union with God: The warm, tender love that Bonaventure urges his audience to feel for the sufferings of the crucified Christ is at the same time the angelic charity that lifts up and divinizes. In his sermon, Bonaventure registers the shock of this coincidence of opposites in the third person: "Surely, they say, no Seraphim was crucified!" The Incarnation itself—Word made flesh—is the ultimate and paradigmatic coincidence of opposites, but the image of the Seraph dying on a cross is represented as a further scandal, an

impossible violation of the cosmic hierarchy. If literally impossible, however, this image nonetheless organizes the affections proper to Franciscan
devotion: compassion for the pathetic body of Christ crucified and wonder
at the grandeur of the divinely ordered cosmos. Reflection on the crucified Seraph intensifies and perfects the soul's affective capacity—that is, its
capacity to be moved, transformed, and united to God.

These two images—the pliable corpse and the cruciform Seraph—ad-
umbrate the central argument of this book: that the medieval devotional
techniques aimed at inciting and intensifying affective response (usually of
compassion, pity, and grief) to Christ's passion found their complement in
scholastic reflection on the nature of the *affectus* and its relationship to the
space and time of the soul's return to God. As has been well-studied, another affective turn was taking place in the Parisian schools in the twelfth
and thirteenth centuries: a revival of theological interest in the sixth-
century Syrian ascetic known as Dionysius the Areopagite, whose brief
but extremely influential corpus detailed, among other things, the ninefold
angelic structure of the heavens and the means by which the mind could
ascend this cosmic ladder to a union with God beyond knowledge. For a
number of commentators, notably the Victorines Hugh of St. Victor and
Thomas Gallus, the Dionysian itinerary of mystical ascent to unknowing
was the realization of an affective union higher than and exclusive of the
activities of the intellect. As I will discuss in Chapter 1, Bonaventure found
in this reading of Dionysius not simply an affirmation of love's superiority to knowledge, but a conception of psychic and celestial hierarchy that
revealed the cosmic significance of Francis's affective transformation.

Each of these two "affective turns"—devotional programs based on
compassionate identification with Jesus's suffering and the "affective" interpretation of Dionysian mystical theology—has been well-observed by
historians, literary scholars, and theologians. But the question of their
coincidence and coimplication has remained largely unexamined. This
book takes up that question by examining a figure who was, more than any
other medieval author, central to both of these developments, and argues
that a common theory of the nature and role of *affectus* animates both of
these "turns." As regent master of the Franciscan school at Paris beginning in 1254 and then minister general of the order from 1257 until his
death in 1274, Bonaventure of Bagnoregio produced university texts such
as commentaries and disputed questions as well as meditations intended
for broader mendicant audiences of men and women. Across these genres,
Bonaventure developed a program of ascent to divinizing union rooted in
and realized through the soul's innate affective orientation toward God.

For him, the Passion-centered piety of Francis of Assisi and the cosmic speculations of Dionysius were intertexts that interpret one another and together inform the soul's natural affective inclination toward God.

The nature of this innate affective inclination (which Bonaventure identifies variously as the natural *affectus* or the scholastic concept of synderesis), and its role and fate in the soul's union with God, are at the heart of this book's inquiry. While the chapters that follow attend closely to these issues within Bonaventure's own writings, they aspire to an argument with a more far-reaching application: that meditational techniques and writings that scholars identify as "affective" must be examined in conversation with medieval theological sources on the nature and significance of *affectus*. Making this argument does not require subscribing to the limiting interpretive model, critiqued by Thomas Bestul and others, that sees clerical Latin works as a theoretically inexhaustible "background" that guarantees the meaning and import of popular vernacular texts.[6] Nor does it require, for that matter, much faith in the difference between "scholastic" and "devotional" literature. To be sure, a commentary on Peter Lombard's *Sentences* arose out of and answered to different generic and institutional demands than a *vita* of a popular saint. But in the case of a figure like Bonaventure, whose work spans these and other popular genres, it is possible to see the working out, in diverse textual forms, of a set of related theological and practical questions regarding the nature and destiny of the cosmos and the place of human beings within it. As Bonaventure himself has it, the Dionysian universe not only provides a scheme for understanding the spiritual significance of Francis; but Francis's own life interprets the corpus of Dionysius as well. Understanding the role of affect in Bonaventure or any other medieval thinker requires navigating these intertextual dynamics in multiple directions.

These dynamics are evident in Bonaventure's treatment of the climactic episode of Francis's life, his vision of the cruciform Seraph on Mount La Verna. As I will argue in Chapter 1, while Bonaventure is not the first to introduce the image of the Seraph into the legend of Francis's reception of the stigmata, he exploits its Dionysian resonance in a new way. The Seraph is of the highest rank of angels flanking the divine. Dionysius associates the Seraphim with fire and warmth, and later commentators associate them further with ardent love. In Bonaventure's writings, the Seraph of Francis's vision alludes to the drama of the soul's hierarchical ascent to affective union with God beyond the intellect. And yet, at the same time, the scene of Francis being moved to ecstatic joy, pity, and desire by the sight of the crucified Seraph is itself a scene of affective piety. Bonaventure depicts

Francis as the exemplary (and extraordinary) Passion meditant, his gaze fixed on the awful sight of Jesus's suffering, his affections excited with the appropriate responses, and his body overwhelmed by the experience.

Scholars of medieval history and literature typically use the term "affective piety" or "affective devotion" to refer to a family of meditational texts that explicitly seek to stimulate the reader's affections through vivid depiction of Jesus's human sufferings at the events of his crucifixion. The narrative of a broad shift in European Christian devotional practice (at the hands of Anselm of Canterbury and twelfth-century Cistercian authors, above all) toward the cultivation of self-knowledge on the one hand and tender compassion toward Jesus on the other received its classic formulation in Richard Southern's 1953 *The Making of the Middle Ages*: "The theme of tenderness and compassion for the sufferings and helplessness of the Saviour of the world was one which had a new birth in the monasteries of the eleventh century, and every century since then has paid tribute to the monastic inspiration of this century by some new development of the theme."[7] Textual witnesses of this new birth include both the emotionally performative (and performable) first-person prayers of authors such as John of Fécamp and Anselm of Canterbury, and also graphic guided meditations on the scenes of Christ's life and death intended to stimulate compassion for his pains and for Mary's sorrow. Canonical examples of the latter genre include the fourteenth-century *Meditations on the Life of Christ*, James of Milan's *Stimulus of Love*, and Bonaventure's *On the Perfection of Life Addressed to the Sisters*.

Pliable as it is, the coherence of "affective piety" as a category describing a historical shift or movement in the later middle ages is debatable; Anglo-Saxonist scholars have amply demonstrated that Anselm and his contemporaries had a long tradition of highly wrought, affective prayers and devotions to draw on.[8] Moreover, the characterization of particular forms of devotion as "affective" risks both redundancy (what would non-affective devotion look like?) and question-begging, leading us to ignore or de-emphasize aspects and functions of devotional texts other than those aiming at the intensification or direction of affective response.[9] Yet few would argue with Southern's basic premise that a change—in style, emphasis, and sheer volume—occurred in the devotional literature and practices of Western Christian devotion sometime around the eleventh century.

Scholarly treatments of affective piety, in fact, often open onto larger questions about historical change. The development of affective meditation has long been crucial to the way historians and literary scholars have narrated the development of lay piety, vernacular spirituality, women's religiosity, and even the very emergence of late medieval society out of feudal Europe.[10] It is as if *affectus* marks in medievalist historiography the privileged site of transformation that it represented on a spiritual level for many medieval writers. For medieval writers and their modern interpreters, affect is axial.

In her monumental study of the change in devotional attitudes from the ninth through the twelfth centuries, Rachel Fulton warns against a tendency to discuss this shift as an "emergence" in the historiographical ether of cultural mentalities, and seeks instead to trace the development of Passion devotion through specific historical catalysts and actors (even as she also addresses herself to "a whole imaginative and emotional climate").[11] Fulton tells a complex story involving the development of Eucharistic theology, post-millenial apocalyptic disappointment, and bridal mysticism. Key actors for Fulton are the Benedictines John of Fécamp and Anselm of Canterbury, and twelfth-century Cistercians, especially Bernard of Clairvaux, figures long central to the narrative of affective devotion emerging from new monastic technologies of the self developed in eleventh- and twelfth-century religious reform movements and spreading, via the Franciscans above all, to the laity. As Southern puts it, "With St. Francis and his followers, the fruits of the experiences of St. Anselm and St. Bernard were brought to the market place, and became the common property of the lay and clerical world alike."[12] Sarah Beckwith follows the lineaments of this narrative in her study of the role of Christ's body as social medium in late medieval Europe. In the anguished, excited meditations on Christ's human and divine body of Anselm and Bernard, Beckwith sees tools for the fashioning of a new, reflexive subjectivity whose self-reformation aims both to intensify and resolve the divisions of flesh and spirit, human and divine, desire and fulfillment, within the self. These new disciplinary practices organized around Christ's body had far-reaching implications: "The reformist understandings of affective theology developed a set of interpretive strategies which disciplined the way in which they were utilized and understood within the institutional setting of the monastery. But the influence of these texts was felt far beyond the walls of the monastery."[13] Crucial to the extension of this influence, Beckwith argues, were the Franciscan devotional texts that opened the reform program of subjective formation around the body of Christ to lay audiences.[14] As she writes, "Franciscanism described the gestural techniques of *affectus* in its development of imitative and meditational schema for the production of contrition."[15] Thus, whether as innovators or popularizers, the Franciscans have long held a preeminent place in narratives of the development of affective piety.

Thomas Bestul claims that Franciscans "carried devotion to the suffering humanity of Christ to new heights."[16] For Bestul, Bonaventure's works
represented the highest of these new heights and a model for later Passion
meditation literature, much of which circulated under Bonaventure's authority in the fourteenth century.[17]

In a thorough revision of this standard Anselmian-Cistercian-Franciscan
narrative of affective devotion, Sarah McNamer contends that the genre of
Passion meditation and its techniques for the literary production of affect
were not the innovation of a handful of male theologians, but rather in the
first instance developed in women's religious communities. Like Fulton,
McNamer seeks to ground the narrative of affective devotion in specific
historical actors and motives. For McNamer, this motive was less theological than social and legal: Passion meditation was a technique for the production of compassion, the presence of which functioned as a guarantee of
religious women's status as brides of Christ (*sponsae Christi*).[18] In particular,
McNamer disputes claims for Bonaventure's originality and significance
for the tradition of Passion meditation, and even seeks to distinguish his
devotional writings from the affective meditations that circulated in his
name. For example, she argues, in contrast to the Pseudo-Bonaventuran
Meditations on the Life of Christ, in Bonaventure's *Lignum vitae* "affective
response is assertively situated within a framework of speculative theology;
thus the texts seek to engage the reader's intellect more than the heart, and
the apprehension of theological truth is the ultimate aim."[19] In both the
Lignum vitae and the *Itinerarium mentis in Deum*, then, the elaborate theological allegorizations work against affective response, mediating and con-
taining it. The allegorical layering of the Passion narrative in these works
obscures, in McNamer's view, the human, suffering body of Christ, as con-
fronted so frankly in texts that reflect women's meditational practices.

In her study of the role of imagination in Passion meditations, Michelle
Karnes offers a very different construal of the relationship between theological reflection and corporeal sensation. Like Bestul, she sees Bonaventure as determinative for the tradition of meditation on Jesus's suffering
humanity, but for different reasons. Correcting the tendency of scholars
to overemphasize affect and neglect other stylistic features and theological
functions of meditations on the life and death of Christ, Karnes argues that
these texts should be seen as tools for the cultivation of the imagination.
As the cognitive bridge between sensory perception and intellection, medieval imagination was positioned on the boundary of flesh and spirit, and
thus served as path by which the meditant progressed from meditation on
the human, bodily sufferings of Jesus to contemplation of Christ's divin-

ity. Indeed, for Bonaventure, who, Karnes argues, "first applied scholastic philosophy of imagination to medieval meditations on Christ," every act of intellect is incarnational, insofar as it unites the sensory with the spiritual.[20] In Bonaventure's hands (and also in the literary tradition he influenced) the purpose of imagining Jesus's sufferings was not simply to produce emotional fervor, but to be united, in contemplation, to Christ.

Karnes skillfully and persuasively traces the intimate link that Bonaventure's works draw between devotion to Christ's humanity and the soul's union to God. Yet her deliberate focus on the more recognizably Aristotelian aspects of Bonaventure's psychology leaves a sustained consideration of his mystical theology outside the purview of her study. While Karnes recognizes that Neoplatonic and Aristotelian philosophy are "interwoven" in scholastic thought, she maintains that "the fault lines between them are always visible. They never merge into syncretic union."[21] I do not wish to argue the contrary. Yet even the disavowed possibility of syncretism suggests a boundedness to both Neoplatonism (which is, from the first instance, already "Aristotelian") and medieval Aristotelianism that risks an overly schematic reading of scholastic texts—a risk nevertheless avoided in Karnes's own lucid and nuanced readings of Bonaventure and the meditational texts he inspired. Tracing the Augustinian and Aristotelian influences in Bonaventure's thought, Karnes illuminates the devotional and theological goals of his account of imagination and cognition, and in turn offers a convincing account of the theological complexity and depth of medieval devotional literature and practices.

The present book seeks to build especially on this aspect of Karnes's work, by giving sustained attention to the complex theorizations of *affectus* that animate the context of late-medieval devotional practices studied under the banner of "affective devotion." In particular, I suggest that the place of affect in medieval Christian devotion cannot be understood outside of its role in the Neoplatonic cosmos and the program of ascent that medieval theologians in the twelfth and thirteenth centuries found—and substantially expanded and reimagined—in the writings of Pseudo-Dionysius.

What follows, however, is not a comprehensive study or survey of the concept of *affectus* in the Bonaventuran corpus.[22] Nor is it an attempt to define the boundaries of affective piety or re-narrate its history. Instead, this book advances an interpretation of Bonaventure's writings on the soul's capacity for and path to affective union with God that sees the cosmic and mystical dimensions of *affectus* as crucial for the practice of affective meditation. In particular, I focus on Bonaventure's account of the innate *affectus* that inclines the human person to God. Referring variously to *apex affectus*, synderesis, a natural instinct, or, most revealingly, the weight (*pondus*) of the soul or will (concepts I will discuss at length in what follows), Bonaventure works out an incarnational understanding of the soul's affective capacity in the context of a mystical itinerary that is profoundly—and paradoxically—embodied. In other words, I argue that for Bonaventure, devotion is essentially an ecstatic enterprise, integrally involving but ultimately abandoning intellect as the soul moves toward affective ecstasy in God. This enterprise is organized around and oriented toward the body of Christ and the body of Francis. As I will argue, the itinerary of ascent begins in the soul's innate affective orientation toward God and culminates in the becoming-body of the soul—its transformation as exemplified by the Christic body of Francis.

The present book is organized according to this same trajectory. Chapter 1 begins with a historical and theological reflection on the Seraph, the image through which Bonaventure connects the exemplary love of St. Francis with the Dionysian program of ascent beyond knowledge. The figure of the Seraph—glossed according to its post-Dionysian association with fiery love—provides for Bonaventure an interpretive key through which to read the life of St. Francis as a Dionysian ascent toward affective transformation through an innate affective capacity in human beings in which is located the possibility of ecstatic union.

After exploring some of the explicitly Dionysian influences on Bonaventure in the first chapter—with special attention to the Victorine Thomas Gallus—Chapter 2 turns to another important and often overlooked source for understanding how affectivity works in Bonaventure's thought: the concept of synderesis, an infallible tendency of the soul toward the Good that he understands as affective. On his account, synderesis marks the place of the soul's most immediate and innate relationship to God. By locating that relationship in a capacity that is entirely exterior to cognition (i.e., synderesis), I show how Bonaventure offers a precise (though not uncomplicated) psychological account of the soul's capacity for affective ecstasy and union. Ecstasy (*ecstasis*) is an inherent tendency within the soul, a capacity for being drawn to the good that is neither truly active nor simply passive. Rather, ecstasy (dis)locates the soul's desire for the good outside of itself.

Furthermore, as I argue in Chapter 3, by identifying the natural motion of the will as the soul's "weight" (*pondus*), Bonaventure links the scholastic debates on synderesis both to an Augustinian motif of love as a spiritual force and to an Aristotelian physics of elemental motion and natural place. In Aristotelian physics, there is an ambiguity regarding the *agent* of natural motion: Is it a capacity inherent in bodies (a body's desire for its natural place) or a force that the object of desire exerts *on* simple bodies? Bonaventure, I argue, does not simply inherit this philosophical ambiguity. Rather, he exploits it so as to attribute the ascent of the soul to God's grace, while still locating this ascent in a natural capacity of human beings. Desire, then, holds a privileged place in Bonaventure's thought. It is the absolute coincidence of nature and grace in the creation of the cosmos and its consummation in the return of all things to God.

In two subsequent chapters, I read a pair of Bonaventure's works that were extremely influential for later medieval Christian piety: *The Soul's Journey Into God* (*Itinerarium mentis in Deum*) and the *Life of St. Francis* (*Legenda Maior*). I approach these two texts as works that, in Ann Astell's formulation, are mutually interpreting.[23] Thus, I argue in Chapter 4 that the *Itinerarium* charts the intensification of desire through a series of ecstatic transformations culminating in the abandonment of intellect. Likewise, Chapter 5 traces the transforming effects of that desire on and through the body of the saint in the *Legenda*. Just as the Seraphic progression of the *Itinerarium* ends in death, so too does Francis's Seraphic vision render him a living corpse. Through three series of *exempla* (the pliability of the inanimate body, the affection of the animals attracted to Francis, and the vulnerable compassion of the saint), the *Legenda* materializes the dynamics of *affectus* that Bonaventure elaborates more systematically in other genres. These *exempla* graphically illustrate the paradox of affectivity: As the soul is consumed progressively by desire for God, its activity is increasingly conceived in physical terms; spiritual progress is, ultimately, the becoming-body of the soul.

Therefore, as I argue in a brief Conclusion, Bonaventure's stages of ascent chart a transformation of soul into body—that is, into the body of Christ and the body of Francis, no longer possessed of intellect or will. As Bonaventure writes in the seventh chapter of the *Itinerarium*, this transformation is "mystical and most secret." That is, the natural inclination to the good that Bonaventure locates in synderesis and that is transformed into God, cannot *as such* be reduced to a cognition of God. This is clear both in the constitution of synderesis as simply innate and affective and in the final transfer of affect that takes place in the complete darkening of the intellect. Yet if the secret of affect cannot be told, *affectus* can be witnessed in the silent, stigmatized body, the *exanime corpus*, which offers no resistance to the movement of desire. The "spiritual martyrdom" of Francis is, paradoxically, the becoming-body of his desire.[24] Francis therefore embodies for Bonaventure the perfect example of this natural affective tendency in the soul. For Bonaventure, the ascent of the soul in union with

God is the becoming-body of spiritual desire. This entails not simply the exteriorization of an interior capacity, but the coincidence of absolute interior and absolute exterior that takes place, for essential reasons, beyond knowledge. Finally, I suggest, this same dynamic animates and organizes the devotional program of the extended treatise on Passion meditation that Bonaventure addressed a community of Poor Clares (*On the Perfection of Life Addressed to the Sisters*). Here it becomes evident that the program of meditating on the human sufferings of Christ and cultivating compassion is a mystical iterinary.

Becoming and Embodiment

A reader might well suspect that in this alignment of the middle ages, mysticism, affectivity, and the body, the outline of a familiar and stultifying caricature is taking shape—one that many would recognize as that of Teresa of Avila as depicted by Gian Lorenzo Bernini: passive, eyes closed, doubled over by affective ecstasy. The dichotomy of "speculative" and "affective mysticism" (wherein the latter is characterized by an ecstatic, desirous union with God in which the passive soul is stripped of its intellectual capacities) shaped early twentieth-century studies of mysticism and continues today to influence scholarly and popular conceptions of medieval Christian spirituality.[25] Most perniciously, affective mysticism has been associated with femininity, and the writings of medieval religious women such as Hadewijch and Marguerite Porete have far too often been assumed to be the unreflective and unmediated transcriptions of an embodied, affective experience (an unwholesome contrast to the more writerly theological expositions of, for example, Meister Eckhart or Jan Van Ruusbroec). Charlotte Radler's work on Meister Eckhart has forcefully challenged this dichotomy of speculative and affective mysticism by illuminating the centrality of love to the mystical theology of Eckhart—a theologian who has frequently been characterized as privileging the intellect and ontology over affective experience.[26] As Radler points out, characterizations of Eckhart's theology as rigorously intellectual are bound up with claims to his thoroughgoing Neoplatonism. The speculative-affective binary in studies of medieval mysticism, then, rests on a characterization of medieval Christian Neoplatonism itself as entirely intellectualizing, a characterization this book works to correct by examining the deeply Dionysian influences on Bonaventure's conception of natural *affectus*.

In examining the affective dimensions of Eckhart's theology, Radler builds on the work of Bernard McGinn and Amy Hollywood, who, in demonstrating the influences of beguine women on Eckhart's thought, undermine the caricature of women's spirituality as ecstatic and affective in contrast to the intellectual and speculative mysticism of university-trained male theologians. In the last twenty years, a number of feminist scholars, including Hollywood, have further complicated this caricature, and in the process have deepened and expanded our understanding of the rhetoric of gender and embodiment in medieval texts by both men and women.

In drawing attention to the complex and highly constructed relationships between the body, textuality, authorship, and experience in the writings of medieval religious women, feminist scholars have helped to illuminate the original theological interventions of texts whose disclaimers to any speculative intentions have too often been taken at face value.[27] And in the process, these scholars have developed a more complex understanding of the role of the body in mystical texts and devotional practices. Caroline Walker Bynum, whose wide-ranging studies of medieval women's spirituality defined a field, has argued that later medieval women authors were "more apt to somatize" their religious experiences than men.[28] However, Hollywood's work on figures such as Marguerite Porete, Angela of Foligno, Beatrice of Nazareth has demonstrated that medieval spiritual writers, female and male, held widely variant and highly complex views about the value and role of the body in devotional practice; thus what it means for religious experience to be somatized is not at all self-evident or straightforward.[29]

Patricia Dailey echoes Hollywood's claims when she cautions that "we cannot presume to know to what medieval mystical texts refer when they call attention to the body."[30] In her book *Promised Bodies*, Dailey compellingly demonstrates that the textual mediation of "bodily experience" in women's visionary and mystical writing is textually mediated not simply by virtue of its being written down; rather, mediation is integral to the complex theological poetics and incarnational hermeneutic the texts advance. Indeed, in the case of the thirteenth-century Flemish beguine Hadewijch, it is integral to experience as such, as it is fashioned in her texts. Therefore, Hadewijch's visions should not be read as reports of experience that has already taken place; rather, they articulate experience—at once textual and affective—as the suffering at, and desire for, the postponement of the full inhabitation of her body.[31]

My reading of Bonaventure affirms and seeks to build on Dailey's contention that embodiment in medieval Christian mystical texts was conceived and written not as a static given nor as an unmediated experience of the flesh, but as what she calls a "transformational process": The body of the medieval Christian mystic is always, in some sense, futural.[32] Dailey's elucidation of the poetics of *lichame* (the perfected or spiritual body) in Hadewijch's visions attests to the presence of the paradoxical "embodiment of the soul" in vernacular mystical texts that I examine in Bonaventure's corpus.[33] Where Dailey traces the development of what she sees as a Pauline and Augustinian thematic of "inner and outer persons," I suggest that for Bonaventure, an Aristotelian physics of natural motion undergirds a Dionysian dynamic of ascent that culminates in the coincidence of inner and outer, soul and body.

Far from recurring to a now dismantled caricature of medieval "affective mysticism," then, my own reading of Bonaventure is deeply indebted to, and seeks to build upon, the work of these scholars in a number of other ways. First, I provide further evidence, if any were needed, that any straightforward association of affective, excessive mystical experience with the feminine in medieval Christian texts is undercut by the complexity of the textual evidence. While Bonaventure wrote to communities of men and women, he did not restrict exhortations to affective devotion to women, nor did he go out of his way to code *ecstasis* or *desiderium* as a literally or figuratively feminine experience in the texts written for friars of his own order. Second, against the stubborn persistence of the dichotomy of affective experience and theological reflection, I demonstrate that the program of affective devotion leading to the death of the soul in union is rooted in a detailed scholastic psychology—though one not without its own internal tensions.

Affective experience was anything but unreflective in medieval mystical texts, a point that becomes abundantly clear when we read Bonaventure's scholastic commentaries alongside his devotional guides such as the *Itinerarium*. The language of *affectus* was a profound theological and rhetorical tool for describing the ineffable union of human and divine. Crucially, I am not claiming, however, that Bonaventure encouraged affective excess itself as a tool to be employed by the rational will, or that affect constituted for Bonaventure an alternative form of knowledge or cognition. On the contrary, *affectus* provides in Bonaventure's texts a means of describing an experience that is beyond description; it represents the unrepresentable, and so, for Bonaventure (the university master no less than the Franciscan hagiographer), *affectus* marks the place, textually, of an impossibility. Affect is thus the mode in which the human being exceeds herself in a union that is unknown to the structures of cognition, including deliberative rational thought, free choice, and speech. Accordingly, the language of affect provides a medium for testifying to that which is, fundamentally and finally, not an object of cognition. Drawing on terms whose medieval and modern resonances I will elaborate in the course of subsequent chapters, the affective marks for Bonaventure the place of a testimony in secret.

Yet such a place is foreclosed when we rush to assimilate *affectus* to the structures and aims of knowledge. To be sure, Bonaventure does theorize the relationship between *affectus* and *intellectus*, and much of what he writes on the subject traces their interpenetration. As Karnes notes, "affect and intellect are proportionate and interdependent, and the accord between them is well demonstrated by Bonaventure himself."[34] I am not insisting to the contrary on an absolute split between the affective and the intellective in Bonaventure's thought. However, I am calling attention to a distinction that Bonaventure himself appears to take very seriously and that forms the basis for his understanding of how the soul acts and is acted upon. I agree with Karnes that "to oppose affect to intellect entire is to distort the sources."[35] But it would also be a distortion to ignore the painstaking analytical effort that Bonaventure put into distinguishing them. Thus, we should not overlook the fact that differentiating affect and intellect was a worthwhile task for medieval Christian authors such as Bonaventure— that the difference, or differences, mattered. Understanding why requires more, not less, attention to the ways in which Bonaventure sought to distinguish them. As Dailey argues, warning against an uncritical association of affectivity with excess, "If affect is merely categorized as excessive and irrational, or a sign of 'feeling' without any theological connotation, we in turn become 'illiterate': unable to decipher the elaborate theological mechanism at work or to understand the subtle textures invoked in the mystic's text and life."[36] In many key texts of Bonaventure's corpus, I will argue, this elaborate theological mechanism functions precisely to dissociate affect from the structures of deliberative rationality—and this dissociation also needs to be understood in order to make affect legible in the texts of medieval devotion.

The Tropics of Affect

While the category of "affective devotion" may be so broad as to risk meaninglessness or redundancy, I nonetheless retain the term in discussing Bonaventure's writings to underscore the work certain texts do to highlight the affective aspect of the soul and the pedagogical strategies that pertain distinctively to that aspect. Though Bonaventure divides the powers of the soul in various ways, as discussed in this book, the most fundamental distinction he draws is between the soul's cognitive and affective parts.[37]

Though not essentially distinct, there are good pedagogical reasons for heeding the difference between them because these two parts represent two different capacities for being moved and for acting—and activating them requires rhetorical and argumentative strategies suited to each. As Bonaventure explains in his *Breviloquium*, or little compendium of theology, the aim of scripture is not to impart speculative knowledge but to bring about an affective inclination in the reader. This is why scripture does not read like a university textbook. Similar to Augustine's argument in *De trinitate* that the low style of scripture aims to humble the vanity of readers accustomed to the sophisticated literary and philosophical works of the pagans, Bonaventure's *accessus* to scripture works to demonstrate that the sacred writings fit their style perfectly to their aim, for "the affect (*affectus*) is moved more by example than by argument, more by promises than proofs, more through devotions than definitions."[38] If the phrase is redundant, the idea of "affective devotion" indicates what to Bonaventure is a distinct pedagogical strategy: Devotion stands alongside example and promise, orienting a whole spatio-temporality of affective transformation. As Francis's own *imitatio Christi* illustrates, devotion to the exemplar transforms the devotee into the example—thus likeness is the fulfillment of the promise. Such an orientation casts the spiritual journey itself, then, as the movement of the *affectus* through that time and space.

Ancient and Early Medieval Articulations of Affectus

The concept of *affectus* as the dynamic principle of movement within the soul has deep roots in early Christian thought and in the Latin and Greek rhetorical and philosophical traditions that influenced it. In his study of the roots of the twelfth-century Cistercian concept of *affectus*, Damien Boquet identifies two seemingly opposed but intertwined tendencies in early Christian elaborations of the concept. The first tendency treats *affectus* as a morally neutral term for the dispositions of the soul, something like what Quintilian identifies as the *qualitas mentis* that the rhetor seeks to influence or bring about through his art. At the same time, this sense of *affectus* could be used interchangeably with *amor* to denote in general the soul's attachment to an object.[39] In both cases, the ethical value of *affectus* is indeterminate.

The second tendency in ancient philosophical reflection on *affectus*, which Boquet finds especially in the writings of Cicero and Seneca, is to identify affect with the passions—the potential or actual susceptibility of the soul to the perturbations of grief, joy, fear, or desire. Out of this complex ancient semantic field, Boquet argues, a new Christian conception of *affectus* emerges in the fourth and fifth centuries, one that is neither morally neutral nor seen simply as a problem to overcome. For Lactantius, *affectus* refers to the inclinations that can either cause the soul to err or can lead the soul to the Good. For Ambrose, *affectus* is a natural power of the soul, counterposed and cooperating with reason, which innately tends toward the Good but is accidentally prone to disorder in its fallen state. As a principle of movement in the soul toward good or ill, *affectus* becomes the stage on which the drama of spiritual and moral transformation is enacted. Accordingly, late ancient theologians did not abandon the Stoic theory of the passions so much as they integrated it into a broader affective dynamic. With Augustine, all of the ancient valences of *affectus*—attachment, power, inclination, instinct, passion, perturbation—are drawn up into a scale of movements of the soul, more or less voluntary, but all subsumed under the category of the will. And yet, in linking *affectus* both with the movements of the rational will and with the unruly impulses of the sensitive appetite, Augustine doubly (and confusingly) determines *affectus* as both voluntary and corporeal. As Boquet summarizes, "In elaborating the concept of affect on the ruins of the ancient notion of passion, the Latin fathers of the fourth and fifth centuries imputed both the faintest and the most commanding impulses of the soul to the heart of the will."[40] Late ancient theologians thereby imparted to medieval Christianity a comprehensive if somewhat confused conception of *affectus*.

While the narrative Boquet tells of the "emancipation" of medieval affect from its ancient roots may at times be overly linear, his survey helpfully maps the semantic overdetermination of the term and its ambivalences. In early Christian usage, *affectus* may be involuntary or willed, rational or opposed to reason; it sometimes refers exclusively to love or attachment and sometimes to a whole range of affective states; it is both an active force within the soul and an external stimulus to which the soul is passive. These antinomies only become sharper in the later middle ages, and especially in the Cistercian writings of the twelfth century (what Jean Chatillon called the "siècle des *affectus*").[41] In his study of the spiritual senses, Gordon Rudy remarks on the range of meanings that Bernard of Clairvaux attaches to the term, meanings that resonate in Bonaventure's writings: *Affectus* "refers most basically to a transforming influence on the order of grace, and also the human capacity or faculty for that influence . . . Bernard usually uses it to refer to our active capacity to desire and love, and our passive capacity to receive love."[42] Bernard McGinn points out that Bernard, like Anselm of Canterbury and many ancient authors, makes a distinction between *affectio*

and *affectus*. For Bernard, *affectio* is an active stimulus that produces an effect (i.e. an *affectus*) in a passive recipient of that stimulus. But as McGinn
notes, there are sound theological reasons for the confusion between the
active and passive senses: "Because the *affectus* given us by God's prior love
is the source of our own various *affectiones*, Bernard, William of St. Thierry,
and other Cistercians often used the terms interchangeably."[43] As Michael
Casey observes, "Bernard used *affectus* equally for the fundamental dynamic principle within the human being and for the range of emotions and
activities in which this underlying reality finds expression."[44] Casey suggests that Bernard tended more toward descriptions of affective experience
than toward technical accounts of the psychological dynamics of the soul.
By contrast, many Cistercian authors devoted treatises to expounding the
nature and capacities of the soul. Bernard's friend William of St. Thierry
(d. 1148) wrote one of the several Cistercian treatises entitled *De anima*,
and there and in other works, he gives detailed attention to the nature and
dynamics of *affectus*. (I discuss one of these treatises, *On the Nature and
Dignity of Love*, in Chapter 3.) For William, *affectus* has both human and divine aspects: In human beings it tends toward goodness, while in its divine
aspects it is the Holy Spirit working within the soul. The transformation
of the soul into the *unitas spiritus* in which the human will is conformed to
God's is, as Thomas Davis notes, *affectus*.[45] Yet *affectus* can also refer to the
virtues or various faculties of the soul, "a movement of piety, or perception, or faith, or hope, or love, or thought, or will, and so on."[46]

Like the category of affective devotion, then, the medieval concept of
affectus may seem so elastic, so capable of covering even contradictory
psychic and spiritual phenomena, as to stretch beyond meaningfulness or
analytical value. For medieval Christian authors, however, the opposite
was true. The very ambiguities of the concept pointed to its dynamism
and thus placed it at the center of twelfth-century spiritual arts. Between
wickedness and beatitude, passion and action, the body and the intellect,
affectus provided an explanatory mechanism and a practical means for the
interior and communal transformations at the heart of twelfth-century religious reforms.

In this way, the semantic overdeterminations of medieval *affectus* witness the equally overdetermined ontology of the concept that the term
seeks to represent; but this may suggest the way to approach it as a subject
of historical and theological inquiry. In short, there is no simple answer to
what affect *is*. Not only will no single model or definition of affect cover
all cases, but any single definition will be inadequate to the ambiguities
involved in any particular instance of the concept in medieval Christian

literature. Rather than offering a singular definition, then, I instead want
to consider what work the discourse of *affectus* performed for medieval authors. What I will suggest is that from the thirteenth-century, for interpreters of Dionysius and authors of meditational treatises (and those who,
like Bonaventure, were both), *affectus* provided a means of representing the
limits of human agency, cognition, and representation itself. My reading of
Bonaventure contends that for medieval devotional and mystical texts, the
resistance of affect to definition is constitutive of the rhetorical, theoretical, and theological work that it does.

Modeling Affect in Medieval History

To approach medieval Christian articulations of *affectus* as resistant to definition is to quit the search for an appropriate "model" through which to
constitute affect and emotion as objects of historical inquiry. Historians
and anthropologists in the past twenty years have sought better models by
which to account for emotions not as transhistorical givens but as socially
and culturally contingent, learned habits that change over time. William
Reddy's 2001 study, *The Navigation of Feeling: A Framework for the History of
Emotions*, offers just such a model—a programmatic statement about how
to read expressions of emotion and analyze "emotional regimes" in their
historical and cultural specificity.[47] For Reddy, however, the ability to his-
toricize particular emotional regimes depends on recourse to "universal
features" of human emotion. He thus positions his framework as a corrective to what he sees as the excesses of social constructionist explanations
of emotion.[48] "If emotional change is to be something other than random
drift, it must result from interaction between our emotional capacities and
the unfolding of historical circumstances."[49] Those capacities include, according to the anthropological and psychological research that Reddy crit-
ically appropriates, the "overlearned cognitive habits" by which individuals
coordinate effort toward particular goals.[50] Crucial for Reddy's theoretical
model is an understanding of emotion as a domain of effort for individuals in any society: the management of emotions is central to the project
of the self. Identifying emotions as a project allows Reddy to distinguish
mental states and habits from the tools by which one manages those states.
Among those tools are what he terms "emotives"—speech acts that are
both descriptive and performative. This concept of emotives avoids both
a credulous expressionism (wherein textual and cultural traces are read as
self-interpreting expressions of interior states) and a flattening construc-
tionism that, in Reddy's view, surrenders the political ground from which

particular emotional regimes might be evaluated and critiqued. In other words, emotives are linguistic tools that describe emotions even as they produce and shape them.

In Reddy's hands, this framework for reading emotives and chronicling historical change proves to be a powerful and supple tool when employed in his analysis of Revolutionary France. An understanding of emotions as a domain of effort and cultivation would seem similarly well-suited to the study of medieval Christian mysticism, and in particular what Niklaus Largier has called (albeit according to a different theoretical framework) the art of sensory and emotional stimulation developed in medieval devotional literature.[51] Sarah McNamer's study discussed earlier, for example, follows the outlines of Reddy's approach. Compassion in the context of meditation on Christ's passion, McNamer argues, served a very specific social function, providing religious women with a tool for achieving recognition in their vocation. McNamer's intervention is therefore organized around the search for a motive for the cultivation of particular emotional complexes as a corrective to a historiographical naivety that accepts emotional utterances in texts as straightforward expressions of interiority.[52]

Analysis of the social, rhetorical, and performative dimensions of compassion in medieval texts is helpful insofar as a rigorous theorization of performativity offers a way in which to understand the means by which signs (here including emotions and devotional acts) may circulate without imputing those signs to intentional subjects or to an uncritical notion of rational agency. McNamer's phrase for the affective techniques of late medieval Passion devotion, "intimate scripts," suggests the ways in which religious emotions were both interiorly felt and simultaneously determined by a larger matrix of culture, language, and gender expectations in medieval European society.[53]

In her 2002 essay "Worrying About Emotions in History," the medievalist historian Barbara Rosenwein extends the cognitive and anthropological approaches on which Reddy draws in order to expose the persistence of what she calls the "hydraulic" model of emotions—a nineteenth-century view of emotions as a kind of undifferentiated substance that must be either released or repressed.[54] While acknowledging that this model has roots in medieval theories of the humors, she pins the persistence of the hydraulic model in modernity primarily on Freud, as well as on Darwin. In this programmatic essay and in her further research into what she calls "emotional communities" in medieval European culture, Rosenwein works to dismantle the stubborn characterization of the middle ages as an unenlightened age of unchecked emotion—the prejudice that medieval affect was both purer and more puerile than its modern counterpart.

The work of Reddy, Rosenwein, and others working within the paradigm of the "history of emotions" has initiated a greater critical awareness of the historical specificity of emotion—one that understands affectivity not as a physiological given, but as a contextually specific medium of social politics for the varied performance of gendered, cultural, and religious identifications. Yet in arguing for the historical specificity of particular emotional complexes, the "history of emotions" risks losing sight of the historical variability of the very concepts of "emotion" and "affectivity" themselves. A model that understands emotions as "among the tools with which we manage social life as a whole" has the advantage of analytical flexibility: These tools can function differently in different contexts, and as responses to particular social and historical exigencies.[55] But the assumption that emotions *are* tools or strategies may be primarily reflective of contemporary concerns about the rational efficacy of emotions, and may thus risk failing to attend to the complex ways that affectivity has been understood and embodied historically in different cultural situations. When a historical emotion is explained by way of concrete motive, the concept of *performativity* as a lens through which to understand the overdetermination and circulation of particular emotional regimes is in danger of collapsing into a simple notion of *performance*, wherein emotions become means of exercising rational agency toward a determinate goal.

Surveying and critiquing recent theoretical efforts to "recuperate" emotion as a valuable means of social and political intervention, Sara Ahmed writes, "Within contemporary culture, emotions may even be represented as good or better than thought, but only insofar as they are re-presented as a form of intelligence, as 'tools' that can be used by subjects in the project of life and career enhancement. If good emotions are cultivated, and are worked on and towards, then they remain defined against uncultivated or unruly emotions, which frustrate the formation of the competent self."[56] Bringing Ahmed's point to bear on the historiography of medieval emotion, we might ask if the project of exposing the social and political functions of historical emotions participates (albeit from a very different perspective) in the same framework of "good" and "bad" emotions by which earlier generations of scholarship disparaged the emotionalism of medieval cultures. Rosenwein's essay roundly rejects the enterprise of sorting out salubrious and destructive emotions in medieval history, and argues against the periodization of Western history on the basis of an emotional

maturation at a societal level. Nevertheless, distinguishing between good
and bad models of emotion (wherein the good model is informed by contemporary anthropology and cognitive science) would seem to recapitulate
the triumph of modern rationality over medieval emotionalism. Here, a
modern *theory* of emotion reveals a truth that medieval understandings of
affect obscure. Medieval emotions can accordingly be regarded as "good"
only when they are construed as rational, strategic, goal-oriented activity.

Yet, as Thomas Dixon has demonstrated in his history of the concept
of emotion, the English-language term is of relatively recent coinage.[57]
It emerged, Dixon argues, in the first half of the nineteenth century and
came into widespread use in the second half. For moral philosophers and,
later, evolutionary psychologists, the term "emotion" was useful as a properly secular alternative to a wide array of then-current terms such as "passions," "affections," "sentiments," and "appetites"—all of which, Dixon
maintains, carried religious and theological baggage that threatened the
scientificity of the emerging field of psychology in the late nineteenth
century. Similarly, Michel de Certeau traces the exile of the "passions"
from social and scientific discourses and their relegation to the literary
sphere in the same period.[58] If this historical genealogy is correct, then using "emotion" as the lens through which to analyze premodern Christian
texts in historical terms carries with it a number of disadvantages. In the
first place, we flatten a complex and highly developed vocabulary into a
single, imprecise term. And second, we run the risk of naturalizing "emotion" as a transhistorical given. As Kurt Danzinger observes with respect
to the historical use of psychological categories, "The use of contemporary
terms [to analyze premodern texts and practices] strongly suggests that
the objects of current psychological discourse are the real, natural objects
and that past discourse necessarily referred to the same objects in its own
quaint and subscientific way."[59] Moreover, taking the category of emotion
as the lens through which to examine premodern Christian texts and practices may participate in, or reinscribe, the secularization of affectivity that
Dixon traces. As a historiographical lens, emotion would then be a tool for
ignoring what is irreducibly religious about religious affects, functioning
as what Dipesh Chakrabarty analyzes as the scientific "higher language"
that is presumed in every case to mediate historically contingent and culturally specific idioms.[60]

If Dixon is right that the emergence of the category of emotion represented a secularizing strategy of the nineteenth century, then it is perhaps
especially ill-suited as an analytical category for the project of understanding medieval religiosity—or for understanding the theological genealogies

of secular scientific concepts. Late medieval Christian writers may have had nothing to say about "emotion" as such, but they wrote and reflected at length on "affectus"—a complex term with deep psychological, physical, and theological resonances that still sound in contemporary invocations and experiences of affect and emotion alike.

In its efforts to rehabilitate affectivity from the judgment of irrationality, the study of medieval emotion has disregarded an aspect of how affectivity has been conceived in most periods of Western thought—one that is often considered painfully obvious. For from the standpoint of medieval writers, no less than in the routine confessions of contemporary clichés (the now-inert distillations of centuries of experience and reflection), affections such as love and fear are what move us—they push and pull us to act, make us cling to what we love and flee from what we fear. Affection is a word that describes the way things are affected—not just the way we touch others but also the ways we are touched, acted, and impinged upon. To undertake the historiography of medieval affectivity from the assumption that emotions are only tools for managing individual, collective, and political life is not merely anachronistic; it misses what makes the affective so unsettling and so potent for medieval Christian practice and theological reflection on that practice.

Representing Affect

The perceived need to attend to the "more" of affect—affect as autotelic excess, non-conscious force, and asignifying intensity—has animated a number of philosophers and cultural and literary theorists over the past twenty years, often under the (suspiciously singular) banner of what is generally termed "affect theory." Writers taking up the mantle of affect theory position themselves variously as participating in a departure from several late-twentieth-century intellectual occupations: the arrest of play in structuralist analyses, the fixed and reductive narratives of psychoanalytic theory, the exhaustion of the humanities in the critique of ideology, and the supposed oblivion of materiality in poststructuralist critiques within which everything collapses into discourse.

In the two sprawling volumes of their *Capitalism and Schizophrenia* project, Gilles Deleuze and Félix Guattari seek to redeploy the Spinozist concept of affect as an increase or decrease in a body's capacity for action (or passion). Spinoza defines affect, at once corporeal and ideational, as that which is always determining anew (without closing) the question of what a body can do. For Brian Massumi (Deleuze and Guattari's English translator), attending to and reanimating this corporeal and dynamic concept of affect for cultural and literary studies means keeping it rigorously distinct (at least analytically) from the concept of emotion. If affect is a non-subjective, pre-personal intensity, by contrast, "an emotion is a subjective content, the sociolinguistic fixing of the quality of an experience which is from that point onward defined as personal."[61] Thus emotion is the qualification of—that is, the subjective appropriation of and assigning of signification to—intensity. As Massumi puts it, emotion is "intensity owned and recognized."[62] This distinction between affect and emotion is both real and analytical for Massumi, insofar as distinguishing the terms allows him to account more precisely for the emergence of emotion from that which always exceeds and escapes it.

In this way, for Massumi and the many theorists influenced by him, affect comes to mark the place of the immanent other of consciousness, cognition, and volition. As Gregory Seigworth and Melissa Gregg define it, "affect, at its most anthropomorphic, is the name we give to those forces—visceral forces beneath, alongside, or generally *other than* conscious knowing, vital forces insisting beyond emotion—that can serve to drive us toward movement, toward thought and extension, that can likewise suspend us (as if in neutral) across a barely registering accretion of force-relations, or that can even leave us overwhelmed by the world's apparent intractability."[63] In light of such declarations, it is not surprising that critics (most notably, Ruth Leys) have charged affect theory with depending on a crude dualism that pits cognition, signification, and language against affect, intensity, and viscerality—and that champions the latter set as somehow in itself politically and ethically salutary.[64] Such a move, it has been argued, reifies a disembodied notion of cognition and results, ironically, in a static and homogenous view of affect.

More recently, Eugenie Brinkema, while embracing "the passions of affect studies," criticizes the tendency of affect theory to flatten the varied and particular ways affects function at a formal level in film and texts, reducing this diversity to nothing more than a "vague, shuddering intensity."[65]

> There is a formula for work on affect, and it turns on a set of shared terms: speed, violence, agitation, pressures, forces, intensities. In other words, and against much of the spirit of Deleuze's philosophy, which celebrated the minor, the changeable, and the multiple, Deleuzian theories of affect offer all repetition with no difference. When affect is taken as a synonym for violence or force (or intensity or sensation), one

can only speak of its most abstract agitations instead of any particular textual workings.[66]

Responding to an anti-formalism in film theory that has styled itself as a "turn" to affect, Brinkema offers the sustained and persuasive rejoinder that turning to affect need not (and should not) mean turning away from careful attention to form. Her intervention extends itself beyond film studies to other fields within the humanities. At the outset, she poses a series of rhetorical questions: "Insofar as affect has been positioned as what resists systematicity and structure, has it in fact been able to recover notions of contingency, possibility, and play? Has the turning toward affect in the theoretical humanities engendered a more complex understanding of texts? Have accounts of affects produced more nuanced, delightful interpretations of forms in texts—and have they recovered the dimension of being *surprised* by representation?"[67]

The presumptive answer to each of these questions is no. Or, at least, not yet, as the rest of the book makes the case for (and productively employs) practices of close reading and formal analysis to nuance and inform theories of affect. The work of attending to specific affective forms, to accounting for the various permutations of particular affects and emotions, is no doubt ongoing, and we should expect it to be inexhaustible. In analyzing affects as something other than expressions of subjective interiority, Brinkema carries on the work that Massumi and others sought to initiate by way of positing a distinction between affect and emotion. However, her project also self-avowedly breaks with Massumi's, insofar as the latter remains dependent on a visceral embodied subject capable of registering affective intensities, whereas Brinkema seeks to attend to affects as themselves representational forms.

As in Leys's critique, then, for Brinkema, affect theory is errant insofar as it turns on an absolute separation of affect from signification, one that renders the theory incapable of providing textured accounts of particular affects. And indeed it is difficult to understand what Massumi's "asignifying philosophy of affect" would mean (presumably, it would mean nothing, or would prefer not to mean).[68] At the very least, there is surely a tension in the point at which Massumi, on a single page, both declares that "intensity is the unassimilable" and advises that "much could be gained by integrating the dimension of intensity into cultural theory."[69] Yet, while the integration of the unassimilable would seem to be a definitionally impossible task, the challenge has been taken up, more or less explicitly, by literary and cultural theorists such as Lauren Berlant and Kathleen Stewart—to take two of the most luminous examples.[70] In these works, affect theory becomes an occasion not for flights of theoretical fancy but for developing new modes of observation and description. For example, Stewart describes her "ficto-critical" experiment as an attempt "to slow the quick jump to representational thinking and evaluative critique long enough to find ways of approaching the complex and uncertain objects that fascinate because they literally hit us or exert a pull on us. My effort here is not to finally 'know' them—to collect them into a good enough story of what's going on—but *to fashion some form of address that is adequate to their form*; to find something to say about ordinary affects by performing some of the intensity and texture that makes them habitable and animate."[71] Stewart's book is a proleptic "yes" to Brinkema's questions as to the creative efficacy of affect theory. As if responding to Massumi's call for a "cultural-theoretical vocabulary specific to affect,"[72] Stewart seeks a new form of analysis for that which resists analysis. The wager is that the move to distinguish affect from signification might be generative of new forms of signification proper to affect. And as Stewart's textured and surprising vignettes demonstrate, if shifts in affective intensity are somehow unknowable per se, they nevertheless form part of the structure of everyday perception and action and thus may yield to properly attuned observation and description. The integration of affect into literary, cultural, and anthropological analysis begins with the recognition of a something that resists assimilation to knowledge even as that "something" is a condition of possibility for knowledge.

Likewise, a tactical distinction between affect and emotion, such as that which Massumi draws, may help to enrich explorations into the medieval representations of emotions by calling attention to the rhetorical dynamics of affect that are missed when one's analysis focuses narrowly on particular emotion-words or emotional presentations in medieval texts. And this is all the more the case when the concept of "emotion" in view assumes the unity of the cognizing and volitional self that mystical texts aim to disrupt and transform. Yet defining affect against emotion risks reforging the link between the latter term and subjectivity that the theorization of affect works to unseat. Rei Terada critiques modern instances of the assumption that emotion "requires"—i.e., can only be understood as a function of—the self-presence of conscious intentionality. Like Brinkema, Terada works to develop, through close readings of Jacques Derrida and Paul de Man, a theory of affectivity as a textual effect rather than as an expression of a subject. Though Terada takes up the term "emotion," she seeks to redraw its semantic scope in relation to its other, affect (or feeling). Noting the emphasis on the ideational and judicative functions of emotion in Anglo-American philosophy since 1950, Terada shows how the distinction between affect (the empirically observable, nonconscious effects of a stimulus in or on a body) and emotion (the intentional articulations of a subject) is in many ways a transposition of Edmund Husserl's distinction between indicative and expressive signs. Where indication is only an external mark or a trace—a pawprint in the sand, a scar on flesh—an expression is a meaningful, volitional utterance of an idea formed and intended in the interior nonspace of a self-present subject. As Terada notes, though Husserl does not develop a "theory of emotion" as such, "emotions appear to be exemplary inner contents" because theories of emotion have long relied on a concept of expression, "with the result that emotions have had to become 'cognitive' in order to fit those theories."[73] Terada thus extends Derrida's reading of Husserl in *Speech and Phenomena* to offer her own critique of expressive theories of emotion. In Derrida's reading of Husserl, soliloquy—the inner voice representing itself addressing itself—is the fable that embodies the reality of self-presence: The *experience* of subjective interiority is an effect of the non-identity of the self to itself. Feeling (or emotion) is possible only because of the impossibility of immediate self-presence: "Emotion demands virtual self-difference—an extra 'you.'"[74] As an effect of representation, emotion can therefore never be simply an object of representation. Through a reading of Derrida's reading of Rousseau (too intricate to retrace here), Terada develops a conception of emotion as "the difference between subjective ideality and the external world, appearing within experience."[75] Emotion is never just a mark, not simply or fully a corporeal effect; in Husserlian terms, emotion is no more an indication than it is an expression. Terada thus rejects the dichotomy between affect (as external, nonconscious, corporeal trace) and emotion (as intentional, ideational content) in favor of an understanding of affective experience as difference. Terada's term for this Derridean account of emotion is "textuality"—the representation of emotion by "traces in a differential network."[76]

While Terada goes on to critique Deleuze's account of affect as dispensing altogether with experience, her reading of Derridean emotion-as-textuality has affinities with aspects of Massumi and Stewart—insofar as affect functions not so much as the proper name of an ineffable, visceral quantum, but rather to describe the play of differences between representation and its object, marking the inadequacy of representation. Yet where the post-Deleuzian celebration of affect as nonconscious intensity risks leaving intact the subjective concept of emotion (emotion as "intensity owned and recognized," to recur to Massumi's formulation), Terada's Derridean reading offers an alternative to the depth model in which affect is the corporeal substrate of a personal, subjective experience (emotion).

I contend that such an account of affective experience—one that does not assume a unified, self-transparent subject—is a useful interpretive idiom through which to approach the seemingly paradoxical experience of dispossession that medieval mystical texts describe. The analyses of the following chapters draw on this idiom to offer an interpretation of Bonaventure's place within the history of Christian mysticism. The school of mystical theology associated with Bonaventure has sometimes been seen as an attempt to domesticate the radicality of Dionysian *apophasis* by reintroducing knowledge, under a different name, into the darkness of union. This book advances a different view: *affectus* for Bonaventure structures a rhetorical strategy of unsaying that marks the place of an immanent excess in language and thereby attempts to account for human beings' capacity to experience an unknowable God.

CHAPTER I

The Seraphic Doctrine:
Love and Knowledge
in the Dionysian Hierarchy

Contemporary debates about the autonomy of affect resurrect medieval questions about the relationship of the faculties of intellect and affect. Then as now, thinking people disagreed about the degree to which affect operated independently of cognition, and the relative value of each to the examined life. Then as now, the disagreements could become acrimonious.[1] The nature of affect and its relationship to the intellectual faculty was a primary concern for the medieval interpreters of the corpus of Pseudo-Dionysius the Areopagite, whose writings were formative for medieval mystical thought and practice. Dionysius's small but influential corpus discusses the inadequacy of all forms of address to the divine beyond being and language, describes the ascent of the mind beyond knowledge in union with God, and advances a hierarchical cosmology of nine ranks of angels mirrored in the ranks of ecclesiastical offices. The twelfth- and thirteenth-century Latin interpretations of these works, especially the program of ascent in the *Mystical Theology* and the angelic speculations of the *Celestial Hierarchy*, are rich sources for examining the place of affect in later medieval Western Christian devotion and mysticism. Yet these sources have been largely neglected in recent studies of late medieval affective meditation, the literary and spiritual practices of popular Christian devotion seemingly far removed from the esoteric mystical theology and angelology of Dionysius. But it was through this theological framework that devotional writers theorized the practices that their texts prescribed. Because the celestial hierarchy was understood to be mirrored in the visible realm, Dionysius's seemingly obscure speculations on the ranks of angels in fact revealed for medieval Christians the nature of the material world and humans' place within it. For the Dionysian interpreters of the twelfth and thirteenth centuries, above all Bonaventure, the Seraph, the six-winged angel who occupied the highest and most intimate place in the hierarchy and who came to be associated with ardent love, was a crucial interpretive topos in debates about the value of affect and intellect in the devotional life and path to union with God.

This chapter provides historical context for the readings of Bonaventure to follow in subsequent chapters by narrating Bonaventure's role in the development of what has been referred to as the affective misreading of Dionysius—an understanding of mystical theology based on the writings of Dionysius the Areopagite that privileges unitive love over intellectual activity through an association of the Seraph with love. Though Bonaventure's debts to Dionysius are frequently noted, he receives surprisingly little attention in broader histories of medieval Latin Dionysius scholarship.[2] Unlike Hugh of St. Victor, Thomas Gallus, Robert Grosseteste, Albert the Great, and Thomas Aquinas, Bonaventure did not produce commentaries on the Dionysian texts. Yet the cosmology and mystical theology of Dionysius (as refracted chiefly through the commentaries of the Victorine Thomas Gallus) were so integral to Bonaventure's thought that he deserves to be counted among the most important proponents of Dionysian theology in the thirteenth century. And if, as I will argue in Chapter 5, Bonaventure's *vita* of Francis itself is thoroughly marked by his understanding of Dionysian ascent, then, given the widespread influence of that text for later medieval mysticism, Bonaventure occupies a crucial place in the history of later medieval piety, translating a program of mystical ascent through unknowing into an embodied example of ecstatic piety in imitation of Christ. Placing Bonaventure within this interpretive tradition allows us to see Bonaventure's account of the soul's movement toward and union with God as a theologically rigorous claim about the nature of love. This requires not simply parsing the relevant terms (*affectus, intellectus, cognitio*, et al.) but also asking what work the distinctions between various modes of union and aspects of the soul perform.

The Seraph in the Dionysian Hierarchy

While the writings of Dionysius were not entirely unknown to Latin theologians in the early middle ages, they were not available in Latin until the ninth century, when the abbot Hilduin translated the corpus given by the Byzantine emperor to Louis the Pious in 827. In the translation and commentary of the ninth-century theologian John Scotus Eriugena, and again in the twelfth- and thirteenth-century schools through the translation of the Victorine John Sarrazen, the Dionysian corpus exercised a profound influence on medieval Christian thought in the West. Drawing deeply on the language of scripture and the fifth-century Neoplatonist philosopher Proclus, Dionysius describes the ascent of the mind to God and the drawing of all things into God by the means of a hierarchy of ecclesial and celestial ranks. Of particularly wide influence was Dionysius's conception of a ninefold angelic hierarchy by which all things are purified, illumined, and perfected so that they come to resemble God as closely as possible.

By the thirteenth century, many readers would find in the Latin translations of Dionysius's writings a program of ascent through contemplation that culminated in a loving intimacy with God that penetrates deeper than knowledge. Such a conception is not to be found explicitly in the Dionysian corpus. But the traditional association of the Seraphim (who occupy the most intimate position to God in the Dionysian celestial hierarchy) with love or affection provided a crucial exegetical hinge. With this post-Dionysian association of the Seraphim with love, the Dionysian ascent to a state beyond knowing could be seen to culminate in a divine union characterized by the sharing of love between God and the soul.

Dionysius's own writings, however, never associate the Seraph specifically with love. In the *Celestial Hierarchy*, Dionysius gives the etymology of the term "Seraphim" as "carriers of warmth" (*thermainontēs*) and explains that the name signifies

> a perennial circling around the divine things, penetrating warmth, the
> overflowing heat of a movement which never falters and never fails,
> a capacity to stamp their own image on subordinates by arousing and
> uplifting in them too a like flame, the same warmth. It means also the
> power to purify by means of the lightning flash and the flame. It means
> the ability to hold unveiled and undiminished both the light they have
> and the illumination they give out. It means the capacity to push aside
> and to do away with every obscuring shadow.[3]

For Dionysius, the fire that characterizes the Seraphim is the dynamism of hierarchy: Burning, it purifies; flashing, it illuminates; and heating, it unites and perfects. All three of these Seraphic operations are ordered toward the goal of every hierarchy: "to enable beings to be as like as possible to God and to be at one with him."[4] The Seraphim, who with the Cherubim and the Thrones enjoy the closest likeness and proximity to God, conform and unite beings to God in the manner of a purifying and elevating fire.

Though all orders of angels purify, illumine, and perfect (and in this way unite all beings to God), Dionysius suggests that the characteristics of Seraphic fire are somehow exemplary of the hierarchic operations as a whole. The properties of fire, at least, provide a fitting solution to the exegetical problem presented by the biblical appearance of the Seraph in Isaiah 6:6. In this passage, the Seraph is depicted as touching the prophet's lips with a live coal plucked from the burning altar. It was on the basis of this passage that the Seraph was understood to purify, and the live coal helped to cement the association of the Seraph's purifying activity with fire. But at the same time, the scene seems to violate the hierarchic order, insofar as the highest order of intermediaries, rather than one of the lower ranks of angels, appears to a human being.

The author considers a number of credible solutions to the problem. It is possible, he writes, that by the term "Seraphim" the scriptures mean only to signify the purifying operation by means of fire—and that the angel who visited the prophet was in fact of a lower order. He goes on then to consider another, more profound explanation. In this case, the qualities of Seraphic fire are taken to explain the nature of the entire celestial hierarchy. What a hierarchy *is*, according to this explanation, is a series of reflections and transmissions of the light and warmth of the highest order, just as "the rays of the sun pass easily through the front line of matter since it is more translucent than all the others." But the subsequent layers of matter are more opaque and thus transmit less and less of the sun's light: "Similarly, the heat of fire passes more easily into those entities which are good conductors, more receptive and in fact quite like it."[5]

Yet this is not a mere simile for Dionysius, but an instance of the "harmonious law that operates throughout nature" and that reigns in the celestial hierarchy just as it does in the material realm. What every intermediary mediates is, in fact, the light and warmth of God.[6] Because this light and warmth is most fully reflected and absorbed in the highest order of the Seraphim, its manifestation in the lower orders of the hierarchy is identified most fully with those beings of the highest ranks. In an extraordinary ascent of contemplation, then, Isaiah was able to see, in a manner of speaking, the highest orders of angels through the transparency of the hierarchy and the immediate presence of God throughout that hierarchy. And Isaiah's "vision" occurred both because of the self-diffusive nature of the light and warmth of God *and* the uplifting power of fire—whereby the Seraphim make all things godlike through an "endless, marvelous upward thrust toward God," signified by the beating of their intermediate wings. Thus, in Dionysius's own cosmology, the Seraphim enjoy a preeminent position not just in the angelic ranks but in the deifying thermodynamics of hierarchy. For Dionysius, the prophet's uplifting is intellectual: "the sacred theologian was uplifted to a conceptual knowledge [*noētēn*] of the things seen."[7] Explicitly connecting this seraphic uplifting to Dionysius's erotic cosmology would be the work of later interpreters.

Dionysius in the West

As Paul Rorem has shown, the increasing emphasis on the role of affectivity in Dionysian union among a number of twelfth- and thirteenth-century theologians was not the result of a single interpretive decision.[8] The association of the Seraphim not only with fire broadly conceived, but more specifically with the fire of love, appears in Christian literature throughout late ancient and early medieval Christian writings. Long before the Dionysian corpus found its way to the Frankish court and into Latin translation, theologians in the west already knew the name of Dionysius and had some exposure to his celestial hierarchy. Though he likely had no direct knowledge of the corpus,[9] Gregory the Great's homily 34 on Luke 15 includes a discussion of the angelic ranks—and a nod to Dionysius—that exercised a great influence in later medieval angelology. There Gregory gives an extended reflection on the fiery and desirous nature of the Seraphim.[10] However, he does not impute love to the Seraphim to the exclusion of the other orders. The distinction between Seraphim and Cherubim is not based on the distinction between love and knowledge (a distinction that Gregory took pains to complicate), but rather on different modes of love. Citing Romans 13:10 ("love is the fullness of the law"), Gregory offers an etymology for the term "Cherubim" as meaning "fullness of knowledge" (*plenitudo scientiae*) and notes that the Cherubim are "full of love [*dilectione*] for God and their neighbor."[11]

This passage would seem to be the source for Bernard of Clairvaux's discussion of the angels in his nineteenth sermon on the Song of Songs. Concerning the Seraphim, Bernard writes:

> God, who is love, has so drawn and absorbed them into himself, and so seized for himself their ardor of holy affection, that they seem to be one spirit with God, just as, when fire inflames the air and imprints all of its own heat, the air assumes the color of the fire so that it appears not just to be ignited, but to be fire itself. The Cherubim love especially to contemplate God's knowledge which is without limit, but the Seraphim love the charity that never passes away. Hence they derive their names from that in which they are seen to be preeminent: "Cherubim" denotes the fullness of knowledge, but those called "Seraphim" are burning or enkindled.[12]

The association of the Seraphim with ardent love echoes Gregory's homily, and Bernard's list of the nine angelic ranks is identical to the one Gregory supplies. Yet with Bernard's homily, the distinction between the Seraphim and the Cherubim begins to harden along the axis of love and knowledge. Of the Cherubim, Bernard mentions only their self-sufficiency in gazing on the wisdom and knowledge of Christ. Where the Cherubim look upon God with knowledge, the Seraphim adhere to God as one spirit in love.[13]

Even so, it would be easy to overstate the distinction Bernard makes here between knowledge and love, as the lesson of the sermon is that the righteous love of the angels of every rank is grounded in knowledge. He glosses the "young maidens" (*adulescentulae*) of Song of Songs 1:2 as those human beings who are filled with love for God, because they have just begun to receive God's "outpouring" or infusion of love. By contrast, the nine angelic orders love God according to their modes of understanding and according to their more perfect knowledge of him. Far from a hymn to Seraphic love beyond knowing, Bernard's sermon draws a reproachful contrast between well-ordered angelic love based on knowledge and the misguided zeal of effusive love that causes new recruits to religious life, the *adulescentulae*, to err in intemperate self-sacrifice. Thus his description of the Seraphic "ardor of affection" is put to the service of cooling the fires of ecstatic love in his listeners. Yet Bernard, too, would be cited in support of the "affective reading" of Dionysius intent on stoking those same fires. It is a witness to the complexity and the fluidity of the medieval Christian concept of *affectus* that Bernard's use of Seraphic imagery to condemn intemperate fervor among spiritual beginners became an *auctoritas* for a description of loving union with God from which knowledge was excluded.

The Dionysian Revival at St. Victor

If there was a Dionysian renaissance in twelfth- and thirteenth-century Paris, the abbey school of St. Victor was its cradle. Among the works on Dionysius by figures associated with the school, none were perhaps as fateful as Hugh of St. Victor's commentary on Eriugena's translation of the *Celestial Hierarchy*. Hugh offers an explication of Dionysius's anagogy according to a scholastic organization of knowledge that recalls his own *Didascalicon*. And he interprets Dionysius's reflections on clothing of divine truth in symbols according to his own distinction between the work of creation (*opus conditionis*) and the work of restoration (*opus restaurationis*).[14] In discussing the ranks of angels, Hugh interprets the preeminence of the Seraphim over the Cherubim as an affirmation of the superiority of love to knowledge in union. Hugh so orders love and knowledge hierarchically on the basis of Eriugena's comment that the motion of the Seraphim is warm because it is inflamed with charity.[15] Around the same time as Hugh produced his gloss on the *Celestial Hierarchy*, John Sarrazen, also a Victorine, made a new and complete translation of the Greek corpus, upon which the commentaries of Thomas Gallus (d. 1246)—a regular canon who taught at St. Victor in the first quarter of the thirteenth century—are based.[16] Though Gallus did not produce his commentaries while in Paris, the school of St. Victor was a major center of textual production for the reception of Dionysius in the West, and Gallus's study of Dionysius surely began there.[17]

Whether all of these works bear enough in common theologically to qualify as a discretely "Victorine" phenomenon is another question. Csaba Németh argues that Gallus's take is sufficiently different from Hugh and Richard's as to constitute a new tradition of Latin Dionysian thought rather than a development of the first.[18] Yet however one carves up the terrain, Gallus is a central figure in the intellectual landscape of thirteenth-century mystical theology. New research on and editions of Gallus's work continue to revise our understanding of his significance for later medieval mysticism and readings of Dionysius in particular. In 1219, Gallus left St. Victor to found the Abbey of St. Andrew at Vercelli in northern Italy—of which he would later become abbot and where he would, in the last decade of his life, produce his most important commentaries on the Dionysian corpus. At a minimum, these include the *Extractio* (an abridgment and paraphrase that Gallus composed in 1238 and which was subsequently included in most of the manuscripts of the Dionysian corpus that circulated in thirteenth-century Paris[19]) and the longer *Explanatio*, an extensive gloss on Sarrazen's translation of the corpus that Gallus produced between 1241 and 1244.[20] The sheer breadth of Gallus's work secures his singular place in the history of Dionysian scholarship, but it is the depth and novelty of his reading of Dionysian ascent as an affective transformation toward union that left a decisive mark on later Christian mystical theology, a mark perhaps nowhere more clearly legible than in the writings of Bonaventure. In the concept of an innate affective power by which the soul exceeds its own capacities (which Gallus and Bonaventure call *synderesis*), and in the association of this power with the rank of the Seraphim, Thomas Gallus furnished Bonaventure with the hermeneutical key to reading the exemplary life, vision, and embodied piety of Francis of Assisi.

Though the association of the Seraphim with ardor and with charity long preceded Thomas Gallus, he was, nevertheless, the first to gloss the Dionysian state of unknowing explicitly as affective. As Boyd Coolman has observed, with the *Extractio*, "the very text of *The Mystical Theology* acquires an affective dimension" when Gallus writes that Moses was united to God through a union of love (*per unitionem dilectionis*).[21] Yet Gallus is not attempting to deprecate knowledge as such. Ironically, by glossing the state of unknowing as affective, Gallus reintroduces knowledge into the Dionysian darkness, calling this loving union "effective of true cognition."

In his *Explanatio* on the *Mystical Theology*, Gallus brings further specificity to the ascent toward God by describing the capacity in the human soul for affective union—what he calls the *principalis affectio*, or the "spark of synderesis [*scintilla synderesis*] which alone is able to be united to the divine spirit."[22] He explains the spark of synderesis or the "principalis affectio" to be higher than the intellect, the highest cognitive force (*summam uim cognitiuam*). Gallus refers the reader to his gloss on Isaiah 6—where he identifies the highest part of the soul, synderesis, with the figure of the Seraph. As the next chapter discusses more fully, Gallus's notion of synderesis as an affective capacity for ecstatic union plays an important role in Bonaventure's psychology and account of union, even as Bonaventure sets this conception within a somewhat different context of ethical questions about *conscientia* and the will.

The affective associations of the Dionysian Seraph were crucial to the new interpretations of his corpus developed in the twelfth and thirteenth centuries. But interest in the Seraph was by no means limited to the Dionysian commentary tradition. Jacques de Vitry's *vita* of the early Beguine Marie D'Oignies recounts that the holy woman, hating the wretchedness of her flesh, cut out a piece of her body: "She had been so inflamed by an overwhelming fire of love that she had risen above the pain of her wound and, in this ecstasy of mind, she had seen one of the seraphim standing close by her."[23] Almost twenty years before Francis's death, this episode from the life of Marie D'Oignies associates ecstasy, wounds, burning love, and a vision of the Seraph. While there is no firm evidence of influence on the Franciscan tradition, this episode clearly anticipates not only the later legend of Francis's wounding, but also Bonaventure's interpretation of it in terms of the branding "fire of love."[24]

Though Bonaventure—known since the first half of the fourteenth century as *Doctor Seraphicus*[25]—does more to exploit the image of the Seraph as a model of Franciscan devotion than anyone before him, he was not the first to do so.[26] The association of the Seraph with Francis's stigmata has a long history in the legends of Francis's life prior to Bonaventure's account. It has traditionally been held that Francis's vision was attested as early as the announcement of his death. However, as this source cannot be reliably dated to the year of Francis's death in 1226, Wayne Hellmann has argued convincingly that Thomas of Celano's *Vita Prima* (completed in 1229) provides the earliest known mention of the Seraph's appearance in Franciscan legend.[27] Unlike later versions of the story, however, Thomas's does not make the Seraph the agent of Francis's wounds. In fact, the figure he describes is not really a Seraph, but a man with six wings "like a Seraph."[28] In a later passage, Thomas returns to the six-winged figure of the Seraph, this time as a model of Franciscan piety: "We too can undoubtedly reach these things, if we extend two wings over our heads, as the Seraph did; that is to say, by having a pure intention and right conduct in all good works, according to the example of the blessed Francis . . ."[29] The middle wings, outstretched, are the "twofold duty of charity" to one's neighbor—"refreshing his soul with the word of God and . . . sustaining his body with earthly help."[30] The lower wings, contrition and confession, clothe the body with restored innocence. In all of this, Thomas writes, the Seraphic model is Francis, who "bore the image and form of the Seraph" and "merited to fly away to the sublime order of the spirits."[31]

In the twelfth and thirteenth centuries, a number of treatises on contemplation found in the six-winged Cherub a convenient organizational scheme for the stages of ascent. These include Richard of St. Victor's *Beniamin Maior* and the anonymous *De sex aliis cherubim*, traditionally attributed to Alan of Lille. Thomas's transposition of the allegory from the Cherub onto the Seraph has little significance insofar as the creature functioned simply as a mnemonic or organizing device for a six-fold spiritual lesson.[32] But by invoking the Seraphim, Thomas introduced into the story of Francis's vision a Dionysian vision that Thomas himself left unexplored,

and which Bonaventure is the first to fully develop. By making explicit the
Dionysian resonances of Francis's Seraphic vision (and the particular ways
the Dionysian Seraph resonated in thirteenth-century Paris), Bonaventure
gives flesh to Dionysius's mystical itinerary through love (*eros, amor*) to a
union beyond knowledge in the exemplary life of the saint. While Bonaventure was not the first to understand Dionysian union as a function of
the *affectus*, he deploys and develops a conception of *affectus* that grounds
Dionysian anagogy within the faculty psychology of the thirteenth-century schools and provides the rationale for a program of imitation of and
ascent to Christ through the exemplar of Francis.

   At the culmination of that program of imitation and ascent, as Bonaventure describes it in the *Itinerarium mentis in Deum*, the relationship
between the intellect and affect emerges most pointedly as a problem. As
I discuss further in Chapter 4, Bonaventure positions the *Itinerarium* as a
kind of exegesis of Francis of Assisi's vision of the Seraph, and describes
six ascending illuminations on the way to divine union, a progression that
mirrors the six wings of the Seraph. The *Itinerarium* becomes, then, for
its reader, a visitation of the very Seraph who appeared to Francis. The
final, seventh chapter of the *Itinerarium* attempts to describe the union that
succeeds the six illuminations, and reads, in part, as a gloss of Dionysius's
Mystical Theology. Here Bonaventure scripts his reader to pray, "with Dionysius," his prayer to the unknowable Trinity. Bonaventure then follows
Dionysius's change of address, from God in prayer to his friend Timothy
in spiritual instruction, advising the reader directly through the words of
Dionysius: "having completed the journey, abandon both the senses and
intellectual operations, both sensible and invisible things, all that exists
and does not exist, and, insofar as it is possible, be restored, unknowing
(*inscius*), to the unity of the one who is beyond all essence and knowledge
(*essentiam et scientiam*)."[33]

   To the reader who wants to achieve this state ("If you ask how this
comes about . . . ") Bonaventure offers an explanation of what he calls the
soul's *transitus* ("passing over," and also, literally, "death") and *excessus mentis* (ecstasy or exceeding of the soul) into God: "For this passing over to be
complete, all intellectual operations must be abandoned, and the height of
the affect [*apex affectus*] must be completely carried over and transformed
into God. This is mystical and very secret; no one knows [*novit*] it but the
one who receives it, and no one receives it but the one who desires [*deside-
rat*] it, and no one desires it unless they are inflamed to the marrow with
the fire of the Holy Spirit."[34]

No other single passage of Bonaventure's writings has inspired so much scholarly commentary and debate. At stake, it seems, is how to classify Bonaventure with respect to the intellectual changes taking place in the thirteenth and fourteenth century—does Bonaventure represent the culmination of an older monastic tradition in which intellectual speculation and affective fervor are intertwined? Or is he the forerunner of the so-called affective mysticism of late-thirteenth- and fourteenth-century authors, such as Hugh of Balma and the anonymous author of *The Cloud of Unknowing*, who grow increasingly suspicious of intellectual effort in the devotional life? On the one hand, Bonaventure makes some kind of claim for union as a state of knowing when he states, in language drawn from the book of Revelation, that "no one knows [*novit*] it [this mystery] except one who receives it." Whatever Bonaventure is describing, *notitia* and *experientia*—knowledge and experience—are not entirely inappropriate terms for it (though, at least in the *Itinerarium*, the term *scientia*—certain knowledge—is rejected). And yet he draws a sharp contrast between the darkness of the soul's final *excessus mentis* and the illuminations that preceded it. The *transitus* of the soul in divine union is the death of the soul: What kind of knowledge could take place here?[35] The question, rather, is what the love that characterizes ecstatic union *is* in the soul, and why it is privileged in the *excessus mentis*.

In his 1924 study of Bonaventure's thought, Etienne Gilson insists that the abandonment of knowledge is the essential point of Bonaventure's mysticism, affirming that the soul cannot fully grasp or see God in this life. But where the intellect cannot by its very nature go, he writes, the faculty of love pursues further, to touch and know God experientially.[36] In doing so, the intellect is not so much abandoned as drawn up into and concentrated in the faculty of love because for Bonaventure the faculties are ultimately identical to the soul itself in substance. Thus on Gilson's reading, the *mens* is exceeded in a way that includes the intellect within the faculty of affect. To say that intellect is abandoned simply means that the soul has no representation of God, but instead enjoys immediate contact with its object.

Gilson's reminder of the essential identity of the faculties with the soul is apposite because for Bonaventure mental ecstasy occurs at a point beyond the ordinary functioning of the faculties. Yet this alone does not explain why Bonaventure insists that the intellect is abandoned while the affect is transformed and carried into God. George Tavard, by contrast, convincingly argues that ecstasy in Bonaventure exceeds *all* faculties of the soul because it occurs beyond the distinction of the faculties in the undifferentiated substance of the soul. Thus, he concludes, ecstasy may be considered either in terms of love or knowledge. Nevertheless, Tavard concludes, love is the more appropriate term since synderesis is affective.[37]

Joseph Ratzinger is less equivocal, suggesting that in Bonaventure's vision, ecstatic union with God is totally free of knowledge. This view was conditioned, he writes, not only by Bonaventure's Dionysian influences but also by a "Franciscan view which attributed a higher value to the *affectus* rather than to the *intellectus*."[38] Yet because Bonaventure not only received but also helped to create the "Franciscan view" in question, Ratzinger's explanation would seem only to defer the question of what Bonaventure means by the abandonment of intellectual operations in ecstasy. And even if one wished to speak of a more or less unified "Franciscan view," the characterization of this view as valuing *affectus* over *intellectus* is too simple. Affective and intellectual operations are crucial for the formation and spiritual progress of the believer. The question here is precisely what role affect plays in the *excessus mentis*. Is it possible to give a positive characterization of this state as something other than a deeper form of knowing?

Desire (*desiderium*), Bonaventure explains, can be activated even in the absence of certain knowledge.[39] It is not a consequence of or response to *scientia*, but a receptive capacity for spiritual movement, cohesion, and transformation. Thus, when it is a question of union, affect serves better than intellect as an explanatory mechanism for the relationship between God and the soul. For Bonaventure, affect is not simply the other of intellect, nor is it a modification or deepened form of knowledge (where that term is determined by analogy to intellectual activity). Rather, affect is privileged as the highest point of encounter possible in this life—not because it is more powerful than or superior to knowledge, or more like God than intellect, but because the nature of affection is to cleave and unite: affection is movement and touch. And the *affectus* names the capacity for that movement and contact in the soul. This is evident in the movements of physical objects, and it is no less literally true for spiritual beings. Natural motion is not a convenient metaphor for ascent; it is a divinely implanted means of return to God. When Bonaventure writes that at the highest stage, all intellectual operations are abandoned and the height of the affect is carried over into God, he is working out more fully the implications of a theological anthropology and cosmology derived from Thomas Gallus's reading of the Dionysian corpus.

As Coolman writes, reflection on the role of *affectus* in the interpretation of Dionysian ascent "is not merely an interpolation of love into *The Mystical Theology*, but also a conviction regarding how human beings are most basically constituted and how they relate most fundamentally to God."[40] These convictions about the constitution of human beings in relation to God carried with them related assumptions about how creation as a whole was ordered by and to its Creator. According to Gallus in the *Explanatio* to the *Divine Names*, love (*amor*) names the "ineffable, harmonious compact between the creator and the created universe," evident throughout all levels of being, known in part even to the pagan philosophers, but perfected in the Incarnate Word.[41] For Bonaventure, too, the constitution of affectivity—by which all things revert to their source—is more basic than the distinction between humans and nonhumans or animate and inanimate beings. Concomitant with the analogical structure of the universe (a structure that is more fundamental than the distinction between the bodily and the spiritual) is a similarly continuous understanding of affect—a single principle of movement that orders the physical world and governs the soul's wayfaring through the sensible and intelligible worlds and its journey into God.

It is a mistake to characterize the privileging of affect in Gallus's and Bonaventure's readings of Dionysius as "anti-intellectual." But it is equally misleading to attempt to rescue these theologians from the charge of anti-intellectualism by hastening to understand affect as only another form of knowledge. To reduce affect to knowledge is to miss the force of affect in a spiritual and corporeal economy. Bonaventure's development of the concept of *affectus* itself is deeply embedded in the Dionysian universe, and draws, implicitly and explicitly, on the conception of *eros/amor* as a capacity to effect a unity that Dionysius describes in the *Divine Names*.[42] Bonaventure, while heavily indebted especially to Gallus's interpretive interventions, carries through these insights about the force of *eros* into a program of Christian devotion organized around the exemplary body of Francis.

In Denys Turner's formulation, *eros* is the key to Dionysius's ecstatic metaphysics: God's ecstasy of *eros* creates the cosmos and through ecstatic *eros* all creation returns to God.[43] For Dionysius, *eros* is the affirmation that all things are in God, for "all things must desire, must yearn for, must love, the Beautiful and the Good."[44] And in this way the Beautiful and the Good are the source of all movement, both the movement of the soul and the movement in the "realm of what is perceived." *Eros* is that which "binds the things of the same order in a mutually regarding union. It moves the superior to provide for the subordinate, and it stirs the subordinate in a return toward the superior."[45] In other words, *eros* orders the cosmos to

God and holds it together in hierarchy. And since it is hierarchy through which all things flow from God, return to God, and are ultimately united with God, *eros* is ecstatic union.[46] As Dionysius writes, "The divine *eros* brings ecstasy so that the lover belongs not to self but to the beloved."[47] This conception of *eros*—God's providence for creation, the movement of creation toward its end, and the dispossession of the soul in God— resonates with Bonaventure's understanding of the place of *affectus* in the soul and in the role of *desiderium* in the consummation of creation in God. As I will discuss in Chapter 3, Bonaventure cites the *Divine Names* on this very point: "We call love the unitive force."[48] And he places *amor* at the heart of Dionysius's theology in his *Commentary on the Gospel of Luke*: "For, as Dionysius says, the whole of mystical theology, 'what is hidden in mystery,' consists in excessive love according to a threefold hierarchic force: purgative, illuminative, and perfective."[49] What Bonaventure derives from Dionysius's corpus—and not only from the identification of the Seraph with charity—is that love means a modality of union, one that is the end of the soul in its relation to her Beloved and the end of all things in relation to their creative source.

The abandonment of intellectual operations that Bonaventure describes in the final stage of the *itinerarium*, however, is not a simple passage from knowledge to love. In the first place, the force of *amor* is present throughout the journey as that by which each stage exceeds itself, and by which the soul is drawn into and out of itself. In addition, to describe the mystical *transitus* as a passage from knowledge to love is to miss what is for Bonaventure a more fundamental transformation. To put it in the simplest terms—terms whose inadequacy will become evident throughout the rest of my analysis—it is a transformation from moving to being moved. This distinction is more fundamental than the distinction between love and knowledge; or rather, it is on the basis of the distinction between moving and being moved that Bonaventure's use of love and knowledge terminology must be understood.

In the seventh of his *Disputed Questions on the Knowledge of Christ*, Bonaventure makes this distinction between modes of movement explicit. There he argues that Christ's (human) soul had a comprehensive knowledge of the finite created things which were in the Exemplar. But the infinity of things expressed in the Exemplar could not be comprehended by any finite soul. Therefore, Bonaventure concludes, Christ knew the infinity of the expressive exemplar not with a comprehensive knowledge, but by an "excessive" or "ecstatic" knowledge—one that, rather than grasping things completely, is instead "taken captive [*capitur*] by them." So he explains,

"I call this an ecstatic mode of knowing [*excessivum modum cognoscendi*], not because the knower exceeds what it knows, but because the knower is drawn toward an object that exceeds it in an ecstatic way that raises the soul above itself."[50] This kind of knowing, Bonaventure notes, is what Dionysius describes in the *Mystical Theology* as a union exceeding the nature of the intellect. This capacity for knowledge was perfect in Christ, but it is also possible for all souls, both *in via* and in heaven, depending on the measure of grace they receive.

Bonaventure distinguishes these two modes of knowledge in a number of ways. First, "in the comprehensive mode, the knower takes captive what it knows, but in the ecstatic mode what is known takes the knower captive." Second, comprehensive knowledge "terminates in the gaze [*aspectus*] of the intelligence, while ecstatic knowledge finds its goal in an appetite of the intelligence."[51] When the soul knows something finite, it takes in the object and conforms it to itself. But when the soul knows the infinite, it is the soul which is drawn up and transformed into the object. As Bonaventure explains, the fulfillment of this latter type of knowledge is not vision, but desire. Though classed here as a mode of knowledge, this transformation, which "totally deifies" the soul, is described just as the mystical *excessus mentis* of the *Itinerarium*. Whether or not it goes by the name of knowledge, the movement of ecstasy is a movement and transformation of the soul into God. Ecstatic knowledge is nothing the soul does, but something that happens to the soul. And the language for this kind of movement is the language of affectivity, not cognition. Ecstatic knowing is realized in *appetitus*, not *aspectus*.

This passage suggests that the transformation that occurs in the soul's exceeding of itself is, most fundamentally, a transformation of the soul's mode of moving. To know God ecstatically means to be drawn out of oneself and into God. Another name for the soul's motion toward its object is *amor*. Thus, one could say that to love God is to know God in an ecstatic way—or, conversely, that to know God ecstatically is love. The crucial distinction is that union with God is a state in which the soul is seized, taken captive, and transformed into its object. This is why ordinary knowledge—in which the soul takes hold of its object—can have no place in the soul's intimacy with God, according to Bonaventure. In this way, *amor* names an even closer intimacy with God than *sapientia*, which Bonaventure characterizes as a movement of a thing toward the soul.[52] By a contrary motion, love carries the soul towards the thing it loves. Love is still defined here in opposition to knowledge, but in Bonaventure's distinction, *amor* is not simply a more perfect or deeper *cognitio*. Love and knowledge are two different forms of movement and contact between the soul and its object. As the next two chapters discuss, what here goes by the name of love or ecstatic knowledge operates in Bonaventure's other writings as natural motion. And following and building on Gallus, Bonaventure calls the capacity for this supremely simple motion *synderesis*: The apex of the soul is above intellect and unaffected by knowledge. The inclination by which the soul is moved in ascent belongs to the *affectus*.

CHAPTER 2

Affect, Cognition, and the
Natural Motion of the Will

As the highest point of the soul and the principle of mystical ascent, the now-obscure concept of "synderesis" provides a focused lens through which to view the interpenetration of scholastic theology and devotional practice. Medieval theologians held sharply divergent theories about the nature and operations of the *apex mentis*, divergences that were implicated in very different approaches to the devotional life and mystical theology. This chapter examines Bonaventure's account of synderesis as wholly affective, an interpretation that distinguished him from many of his scholastic predecessors and contemporaries and that presents a number of theoretical difficulties. Bonaventure's account of synderesis reveals the difficulties inherent in attempting to articulate affect as something that is at least theoretically distinct from language, cognition, and judgment. The fact that he attempted it suggests the importance of the distinction between affect and intellect for his understanding of Dionysian mystical theology and the devotional program that it organizes. For Bonaventure, humans' ability to be restored to their original rectitude and united with God depends on there being an aspect of the soul that desires God (at least theoretically) independently of the mind's cognitive deliberations.

The emergence in medieval theology of the concept of synderesis—the innate "spark of conscience" by which humans naturally apprehend or desire the good—was both fortuitous and overdetermined.[1] The scholastic debates about synderesis concerned fundamental theological questions about the original constitution of human nature, the corruption of the soul through sin, and the possibility and components of moral action in the state of fallenness. The question of synderesis was essentially the question of how humans were created to seek and to find righteousness. Such questions, of course, exceed the semantic field of the term "synderesis" and predate its emergence. A number of scriptural authorities, for example, refer to some kind of desire for the Good naturally implanted in the soul or to a natural and universal knowledge of the law.[2] Such ideas inevitably gave rise to speculation about the nature, operations, and limits of these innate endowments.

The converging of these questions around the concept of synderesis, however, appears to have been the result historically of what Jacques de Blic characterizes as a "happy accident."[3] In this case something was gained in the translation of the Greek *syneidesis* (as in, for example, 2 Corinthians 1:12) as *conscientia* in the Latin of the Vulgate, and particularly in Jerome's discussion of the term in his commentary on Ezekiel. In that commentary, Jerome considers a novel interpretation of the four figures of Ezekiel's vision (a man or angel, a lion, an ox, and an eagle), which already by the fourth century were commonly understood to refer allegorically to the four Evangelists. He reports that some commentators, "following Plato," read Ezekiel's vision as a reference to the *logikon* (the man), *thumikon* (the lion), and *epithumetikon* (the ox)—the rational, irascible, and concupiscible parts of the soul discussed in the fourth book of the *Republic*.[4] But Jerome is most interested in the way these Platonizing exegetes square the tripartite structure of the soul with the fourfold figure of Ezekiel's vision by positing a fourth power above the other three:

> The Greeks call it *syneidesin*—the spark of conscience [*scintilla conscientiae*], which, even in the sinner Cain, after he was thrown out of paradise, was not extinguished. Through it we feel ourselves to sin [*nos peccare sentimus*] when, deceived by a likeness of reason, we are conquered by pleasures and furor. And they properly consider it to be the eagle, since it is not mixed up with the other three but corrects them when they err. And meanwhile, we read in scriptures that it is called the spirit which "intercedes for us with ineffable groans." For no one knows [*scit*] what is in human beings except the spirit within them, which Paul,

writing to the Thessalonians, implored them to preserve together with body and soul. And yet, following what is written in Proverbs ("The wicked one esteems it lightly when he goes to the depths of sin"), we can see that in the wicked it falls and loses its place, since they have no embarrassment or shame in their delights, and thus deserve to hear: "Your face has become that of a prostitute, for you do not even know that you should blush."[5]

This already enigmatic passage, here translated from the modern critical edition, was further complicated for medieval readers by the subsequent fate of Jerome's text. Medieval manuscripts of Jerome's commentary rendered the Greek term in question as *synderesis* or *synteresis*. This mistranscription left medieval readers with an entirely unattested term that eventually came to be regarded as distinct from *conscientia*.[6] The strange term, which Jerome's commentary furnished with a sequence of interpretive problems, provided a fruitful locus of theological speculation for medieval Christians concerning the extent and nature of sin's corruption of the soul, the capacity of the soul to recognize this corruption, and the presence in the soul of a motivation for moral action.

In other words, Jerome's commentary framed for theologians of the twelfth, thirteenth, and fourteenth centuries a nexus of questions about the relations between the intellectual and affective or motive parts of the soul. Jerome describes synderesis as that by which humans *feel* shame and embarrassment at their sin. But he also attributes to synderesis the power to correct, and calls it the spirit that knows the soul interiorly, suggesting a cognitive or intellectual faculty. Given the ambiguity of the passage on this point, then, it is no surprise that the question of the intellectual or affective nature of synderesis produced perhaps the greatest variance of opinion among the theologians and canon lawyers who gave accounts of this obscure concept. Theological reflection on synderesis thus generated complex, conflicting, and often highly nuanced explanations of the respective roles of cognition and affect in human beings' pursuit of the good.

When Bonaventure began lecturing on Peter Lombard's *Sentences* in 1250 or 1251, a tangle of conflicting opinions on the nature of synderesis preceded him. Bonaventure, like several of his Franciscan predecessors at Paris, advances a notion of synderesis as a wholly affective and inexorable tendency to motion toward the good. His account stands out in the history of discussions of synderesis, however, for the thoroughness of its attempt both to work out the implications of positing such a tendency in the soul and also to account for the relation of this affective capacity to conscience (*conscientia*), which he places in the cognitive part of the soul. Bonaventure's effort to account for this relationship, I argue, is significant above all for the difficulties he encounters in describing the function of synderesis in deliberative moral action—difficulties that his account does not fully resolve and which I believe echo throughout his later works. In Bonaventure's early account of synderesis, we see the productive tension between the soul's natural and inexorable affective movement toward the good and the circuitous paths traced by the deliberative motions of the soul acting as a whole. It is one of the central arguments of this book that this very tension reverberates throughout Bonaventure's subsequent writings on the spiritual life, and thus constitutes one of the animating forces of Bonaventure's "mystical theology"—that is, his interpretation of the Dionysian ascent to union with God as uniquely revealed through the life of Francis of Assisi.

My focus on the irresolvable difficulties that Bonaventure's account of synderesis produces is not an attempt to find fault, but rather to offer an alternative to the overwhelming emphasis on synthesis and integration as the primary hermeneutic lenses through which Bonaventure has been read by modern theologians and historians. In this vein, Douglas Langston highlights the cooperation and interpenetration of the cognitive and affective to be one of Bonaventure's signal contributions to the medieval theory of conscience and synderesis. "Bonaventure," Langston writes, "while placing synderesis and conscience in different parts of a human being, does not isolate them. On the contrary, he views conscience as driven by synderesis and at the same time directing synderesis."[7] Langston elaborates this view elsewhere: "Although some might see in this interpenetration of the rational and the affective orders untidiness, in fact it is a sign of sophistication for it escapes the tendency to identify particular human functions with particular parts of the human being."[8]

In regard to Bonaventure's broader aims in delineating the respective functions of conscience and synderesis, Langston's conclusion is entirely convincing and thoroughly supported by Bonaventure's text. Bonaventure does describe the interpenetration and mutual dependence of conscience and synderesis, and he frequently warns against overly reifying the distinctions among the soul's parts.[9] But despite Bonaventure's emphasis on integration, his attempt to reconcile this interpenetration with Jerome's claim that synderesis is "not mixed up in the errors" of the other faculties results in an ambiguous account of the nature of synderesis and its place and function in the execution of moral acts. How can synderesis be both inextricably involved in the operations of the other powers and remain aloof from their errors?

I am by no means the first to see such enduring tensions and ambiguities in this notion of synderesis. In his critical survey of medieval theories of conscience, Timothy Potts concludes that Bonaventure fails to adequately distinguish between conscience and synderesis, thereby rendering the latter concept useless as an explanatory mechanism for moral action, and thus unhelpful for a modern analytic approach to conscience.[10] And with regard to Christian conceptions of conscience more generally, Joseph Ratzinger has argued that the distinction between two levels of conscience is vital, but dismisses the particular concept of synderesis as "unclear in its exact meaning," and thus "a hindrance to a careful development of this essential aspect of the whole question of conscience."[11] The target of Ratzinger's critique is not medieval discussions of synderesis, but the modern notion of conscience as "subjective certitude," which would make the individual infallible.[12] For Ratzinger, what is needed is not a recovery of the medieval concept of synderesis, but a new way to articulate the notion of a higher level of conscience, for which he suggests the term *anamnesis*: the innate and universal ability to recognize the truth of authoritative teaching (thus undermining the notion of conscience as a resource for faithful dissent from the magisterium). Significantly, Ratzinger identifies *anamnesis* both as a "primordial knowledge" and as the natural love of God—both cognitive and affective—thereby sidestepping medieval debates about the precise nature of this "spark" in the soul and avoiding the difficulties of maintaining that synderesis is wholly affective.

I agree with Potts and Ratzinger that the concept of synderesis, especially as articulated by Bonaventure, is an ambiguous one. But I do not agree that this ambiguity is grounds for dismissal. On the contrary, as I will suggest, the difficulties raised by positing an inexorable affective tendency to the good are extremely useful for historians and theologians insofar as they throw into relief some crucial contours of the complex landscape of affectivity in medieval Christian theology and devotion. If there is an enduring obscurity in Bonaventure's account of synderesis, it is not due to the "untidiness" of Bonaventure's thought, but rather, I will argue, to the very intractability of affect, the limits of reducing it in an account, and the ways in which the distinction between the cognitive and the affective pushes, pulls, and twists (yet never fully breaks) Bonaventure's theological synthesis.

In this chapter, then, I will trace the distinctive moves by which Bonaventure realigns the commonplace arguments about the nature of synderesis with attention to the contexts of that realignment. First, I will examine some of the views of Bonaventure's immediate predecessors, in the context of which the novelty of Bonaventure's contribution appears more clearly. Then, I turn to another important context of his treatment of synderesis—his commentary on Peter Lombard's *Sentences*, Book Two, Distinction Thirty-Nine, in which his most extended exploration of the concept occurs. Bonaventure's introduction of synderesis into this context was not original; it was commonplace for lecturers on the *Sentences* to discuss conscience and synderesis at this point. The placement is nevertheless significant: For synderesis, as Bonaventure defines it, echoes and fulfills the main subject of the work that he outlines in his prologue—the original rectitude of human beings lost in the Fall—and thus reveals the crucial significance of synderesis for Bonaventure's larger themes in the commentary. Orienting Bonaventure's discussion of synderesis in this context, then, will in turn set the stage for analysis of how Bonaventure relates synderesis to conscience, and the limits of integration that he encounters in this project.

Background

By the time Bonaventure began lecturing on Lombard's *Sentences* in 1250 or 1251, the main lines of scholastic debate on synderesis and conscience had been drawn. A number of questions, derived from Jerome's commentary, were commonplace in these debates: If synderesis is unerring, is it then extinguished in grave sinners and the damned? What is its relationship to the sin that human beings perform? Insofar as it is good, does it confer merit to the soul? But perhaps the most fundamental question— and one about which no consensus emerged—had to do with its nature: Exactly *what* is synderesis in the soul and "where" does it reside? Writing in the first years of the thirteenth century, Alexander Neckam (d. 1217) surveyed the variety of opinions on this point: Some equate synderesis with Augustine's *ratio superior* (this was the opinion Alexander himself favored), or along similar lines refer to it as the "spark" of superior reason.[13] But others, Alexander observes, "say that synderesis is a natural affect by which the mind always desires the good and tends to that good whose image it carries in itself."[14] That is to say, for some, synderesis is a capacity that reveals or illuminates what should be done, while for others, it is the stimulus that motivates action toward the good. Roland of Cremona (d. 1259), first to hold the Dominican chair at Paris, argues that Ezekiel's vision identifies synderesis with the face of the eagle because its function is to *see* or to discern; thus he defines synderesis as an intellectual capacity.[15]

More influential, however, were those commentators who saw synderesis as pertaining, in some way, to both the cognitive and affective parts of the soul. In the first extended treatment of conscience and synderesis, Philip the Chancellor (named for the office he held at Notre Dame de Paris from 1217 until his death in 1236) staked out what might be called a moderate voluntarist position on synderesis. Philip defines synderesis as a *potentia habitualis*, a power perfected by a habit, i.e., a capacity of the soul that is naturally informed by a disposition for a particular end.[16] As such, it pertains both to "apprehension" and "desire," but more properly to desire.[17] Philip is also among the first to distinguish *conscientia* as a distinct phenomenon from synderesis. In earlier treatises, when *conscientia* was mentioned at all, it was used more or less interchangeably with synderesis. But with Philip the two concepts become distinct, even if only partially: Philip defines conscience as the conjunction of synderesis and free choice (*liberum arbitrium*).[18] Philip's definition of synderesis as a power informed by a habit appears in several subsequent treatments of the subject, as in the *Summa* of Bonaventure's teacher and predecessor, Alexander of Hales (d. 1245).[19] Alexander attributes synderesis to the cognitive aspect of reason. It is natural rather than deliberative, and belongs to practical reason — that is, reason concerned with moral action. But for Alexander, synderesis can also be called motive, owing to the overlap of the cognitive and motive powers.[20] Conscience, too, belongs both to the cognitive and the motive aspects of the soul, and is situated, as it were, below synderesis but above reason.[21] Thus, Alexander notes, it is not inappropriate simply to call synderesis the higher part of conscience.[22] In this way, Alexander's account proves to be ambiguous. But this ambiguity reflects a concern to avoid drawing the lines between faculties—especially between the cognitive and affective faculties—too sharply.

Like Alexander, Bonaventure's Franciscan teacher Odo of Rigaud (d. 1275) regards the cognitive and motive parts of the soul as two aspects of reason. Because synderesis belongs to natural reason, he concludes, the name synderesis could be applied, substantially speaking, to a cognitive habit as much as to a motive habit. But more strictly speaking, synderesis names a power of the natural *will* determined to the natural law. And, following Philip's account, Odo identifies *conscientia* as the conjunction of synderesis with free choice (*liberum arbitrium*). "Whence," Odo explains, "conscience is related to synderesis and to free choice, so that conscience in acting is, as it were, a medium between knowledge of universals and knowledge of particulars."[23] As for Alexander, the substantial unity of the cognitive and affective aspects of reason forbids any absolute distinction between conscience and synderesis. And more significantly, Odo's analogy indicates that synderesis, though properly called motive, still must function as knowledge (of an innate and general kind) in order for conscience to carry out its operation. For Odo, it seems, synderesis supplies the general principles that conscience applies to particular situations. The act of free choice is the result of all of these capacities working in concert. Or, as Odo puts it in another analogy, synderesis is the light that illuminates the vision of conscience.

Each of these authors deserves a more thorough treatment than I can give here. Yet even a brief examination is sufficient to demonstrate that Bonaventure was not the first medieval Christian thinker to suggest some interpenetration between the cognitive and affective components of moral action. Indeed, while he upholds the substantial unity of the intellect and will, Bonaventure, I argue, revises the tradition of Philip the Chancellor — and does so precisely in ways that sharpen rather than attenuate the distinction between the cognitive and judicatory functions of conscience on the one hand and the affective motion of synderesis on the other. This revision testifies not to a gradual ossification of the "faculties" in later thirteenth-century scholastic theology, but instead represents a specific and careful effort by Bonaventure to account for human beings' desire for the Good in ways that do not reduce that desire to a deliberative operation.

In the early years of the thirteenth century, a very different conception of synderesis was elaborated by Thomas Gallus, the Victorine scholar and Dionysian commentator discussed in the previous chapter. As noted by Declan Lawell, who has examined Gallus's use of the term "synderesis" in painstaking detail, "synderesis" appeared in Gallus's writing as early as his 1218 *Commentary on Isaiah*.[24] There Gallus describes synderesis as a power of the soul (*vis animae*) above the sensitive appetites and even above *ratio*. The power of synderesis reaches out for God's grace, which Gallus describes as a "fiery river" that flows into the *affectus* rather than the *intellectus*. In one of his final works, an extended commentary on the Dionysian corpus, Gallus describes the *principalis affectio* of the mind, which, he writes, "exceeds the intellect no less than the intellect exceeds reason, or reason exceeds the imagination." And this *affectio* is "the spark of synderesis which alone is capable of union with the divine spirit."[25]

Gallus's treatment of synderesis ignores many of the questions raised by Jerome's commentary that other masters discussed. But his association of synderesis with the soul's union with God, and his placing of synderesis above *ratio*, exercised a great influence on Bonaventure's discussion of the term, both in the *Itinerarium* and in the discussion of synderesis and *conscientia* in his *Sentences* commentary. Thus, in the case of Bonaventure, Lawell's caution that Thomas Gallus's unitive sense of synderesis must be "distinguished from the use it acquired in ethics to designate a kind of perception of moral truths or an inclination towards moral goodness" does not apply.[26] What is most distinctive about Bonaventure's account is his attempt to integrate Gallus's affective understanding of synderesis into previous debates about the term. For Bonaventure, synderesis as the capacity of the soul to be carried into union with God and synderesis as the infallible inclination towards goodness are one—and thus the latter sense, as I will argue, cannot be understood except with reference to the former. Indeed, the concept of synderesis serves as an index of the ways in which Bonaventure's understanding of natural law and moral action are rooted in a devotional program of affective union. Because the ascent to God is ultimately a passage beyond knowledge, the principle or agent of that ascent must itself exceed knowledge and stand apart from it.

Bonaventure on Conscience

All medieval discussions of synderesis were in some sense a gloss on Jerome's Ezekiel commentary. But for Bonaventure and many of his scholastic contemporaries and predecessors, the concept of synderesis helped to explain a problem posed in the second book of Peter Lombard's *Sentences*. The question Peter frames in the thirty-ninth distinction of that book is how the will, if it is a natural good inhering in the human soul, can ever be called wicked. As Ambrose affirmed in the fourth century, human beings, even while slaves to sin, always will the good by nature. Peter interrogates the sense of nature intended in this affirmation: "For some hold there to be two motions: one by which we will the good naturally. But why 'naturally'? And why is it called 'natural'? Because this was the motion belonging to human nature in its first condition, in which we were created without vice, and which is properly called nature. For humans were created with an upright will."[27] And human beings were also endowed with free choice by which they sin, "not by necessity, but by their own will." The will is called a sin, then, according to this view, insofar as it freely chooses an evil act. But as a natural gift it is only and necessarily good, and Peter identifies this aspect with the *scintilla* of Jerome's Ezekiel commentary: "Therefore it is said rightly that human beings naturally will the good, since they were created with a good and upright will. For the superior spark of reason, which, as Jerome said, could not be extinguished even in Cain, always wills the good and hates evil."[28] The will is thus called good because of its natural righteousness, which remains in the soul as the "spark of reason" and which, distinct from free choice, cannot be corrupted.

As Bonaventure glosses it, Peter's question concerns two issues: the "cause of corruption in the deliberative will" and "the rectitude of the human will as it is moved through the mode of nature."[29] Bonaventure is primarily concerned here with the latter issue—how are human beings created to desire the good naturally? The answer is twofold: through the "natural judge" of conscience and the "spark of reason or conscience" known as synderesis.[30] Yet in the three articles he devotes to the subject, conscience turns out to be more complex than simply a natural judge. Instead, he defines conscience as a cognitive habit perfecting the practical intellect. Each component of this definition requires elaboration.

The initial question on conscience is devoted primarily to clarifying the first aspect of the definition: whether conscience belongs to the intellect (*intellectus*, or *potentia cognitiva*), or to the affect (*affectus, potentia affectiva*, or, sometimes, *pars motiva*). Bonaventure—through the initial supporting arguments or *fundamenta*, and through his own conclusion and response— primarily establishes the cognitive nature of conscience by appeal to its function (*per actum*). Conscience judges, testifies, argues, rules, and directs, and these are clearly cognitive operations.[31] Further support for this position is found in Ecclesiastes 7, which attributes knowledge to conscience ("Scit conscientia tua, quia et tu crebro maledixisti aliis"). And it is self-evident, according to these initial arguments, that "all knowledge (*scientia*) is from the part of the intellect," and "all that belongs to conscience is knowledge (*omnis conscientia est scientia*)."[32] Thus the noetic nature of conscience is obvious (to a Latin reader) even from the form of the word.

The prefix, however, suggests an important inflection to the kind of knowledge that belongs to conscience. Conscience is not concerned with knowledge in general, but with knowledge directed to works. And so conscience belongs to the practical intellect, which Bonaventure defines as the intellect "as it is joined, in a certain way, to affection and operation."[33] Accordingly, the "con" of conscience signifies this conjunction, and this practical orientation. It is concerned not with speculative knowledge, such as geometrical principles, but with moral imperatives, such as the honor and obedience due to God and one's parents. Thus, conscience is distinguished from the affective power not by reason of its object (which is the good, or the performance of good works), but by its function. Still, we should note that Bonaventure's explanation of this conjunction reflects some concern about the interpenetration of cognition and affect (or intellect and will), insofar as he is at pains to reaffirm the distinction of the powers: "'For the speculative and practical intellect are the same power, differing only by extension,' as the Philosopher [i.e., Aristotle] says. Nor should it in any way be understood that the practical intellect is an appetite or will; even the Philosopher himself denies this."[34]

In this way, Bonaventure cites Aristotle in support of an un-Aristotelian scholastic distinction of powers. This ambivalent Aristotelianism is also evident in his characterization of conscience as a *habitus*. By naming conscience a habit, Bonaventure distinguishes it both from a determinate object of knowledge (in this case, the principles of the natural law) and from a power or potentiality of the soul, which is in itself undetermined toward a number of possible objects (and which, therefore, may resolve itself toward right or wrong).[35] As a habit, conscience is neither fully determinate nor fully indeterminate. Rather—and in an Aristotelian sense—it is an acquired disposition that informs or "perfects" the practical intellective power. That is, through the acquisition of good (or bad) conscience, the practical intellect acquires a particular character, a trained readiness to act in a certain way.[36] (Analogously, speculative knowledge is a habit that perfects the speculative intellect.) But habits, unlike the principles of the natural law, vary from person to person—a habit can dispose the practical intellect to good works or to sin.

Or at least this is the case insofar as the habit of conscience is acquired through repeated actions and experience (such actions and experience being the source of *habitus* in the Aristotelian sense). Bonaventure recognizes another sense in which conscience inheres as a habit of the intellect, one which he indicates by naming conscience the "natural judge" in the soul. In this sense, the habit of conscience is not acquired but innate and serves as a principle of acts. Thus, Bonaventure's conception of conscience holds together an Aristotelian understanding of *habitus* with a concept of "natural habit," which is oxymoronic in the Philosopher's terms. It is therefore ironic that, again, Bonaventure turns to Aristotle to explain and defend a distinction between the natural and the acquired habits of conscience. Bonaventure regards "the Platonic position [of *anamnesis*] which posits all habits of knowing to be simply innate" as too absurd to be worthy of serious consideration (and refuted both by Aristotle and Augustine).[37] He thus attempts to reconcile the notion of a "natural judge" of conscience with the Aristotelian axiom that the soul is created a "blank slate" (*tabulam nudam*). Accordingly, he is not content to conclude, as some have, that the universal principles of good works are known innately and the particular conclusions are acquired. Rather, particular conclusions are indeed the result of

acquisition, but, as Aristotle demonstrated, knowledge of universal principles is also acquired "through the senses, memory, and experience."[38]

Yet as Bonaventure explains, knowledge requires both a knowable object and a mediating light by which we judge that object.[39] It is this light
that is innate and is called a "natural judge." Thus, there are no innate
objects of knowledge, only an innate light, which allows those objects derived from sense and experience to be known. A distinction between universal principles and particular conclusions is still operative here, but it
does not correspond neatly to the distinction between innate and acquired
conscience. On the one hand, particular conclusions are acquired, for they
require some moral education and experience in order to be known. General principles, on the other hand, are both innate and acquired. The general principles (construed as universal tenets of moral action) include, for
example, the command to honor one's father and mother or to treat others
as one wishes to be treated. In a sense, these principles are innate to the
soul because the natural light of conscience is sufficient to recognize their
validity. Yet such principles are not known innately because they are only
meaningful if one knows the particular objects (in Bonaventure's words,
the "exterior species") to which they refer. Until I learn what a "father" or
"mother" is, I do not really *know* that I should honor them.[40] The acquisition of these exterior species occurs through sense perception and experience. Even innate moral knowledge (at least from the perspective of the
knowing subject), then, is embodied, temporal, and linguistic.[41]

More precisely, all knowledge is acquired to the extent that it becomes
present to the soul through conceptual and imaginal representations derived from sense perception (an "abstracted likeness"). But some things,
Bonaventure adds, are present to the soul through the soul's own essence,
thereby requiring no exterior species. Concepts like "parent" and "neighbor" depend on sense perception, and therefore the commandments regarding them are, in a way, acquired. God, on the other hand, "is not
known through a likeness received by the senses," but through a knowledge naturally and essentially present to the soul. Thus, we know to love
and to fear God (*Deum amare et Deum timere*) with a truly innate understanding because "human beings know what love and fear are not through
a likeness accepted exteriorly, but through essence. For in this way, affects
are in the soul essentially."[42] This kind of knowledge, then, is innate to the
soul for two reasons: because it pertains to God and because it is affective.
The knowledge of God to which Bonaventure refers here is not a discursive (much less exhaustive) understanding of God's attributes, but simple
infinitives—*to love* and *to fear* God.

The innate, affective disposition of the soul toward God demarcates a sphere of absolute interiority, of a strictly *essential* ineffability. In itself, free from the contingencies of sense perception to which all other knowledge is subject, this affective knowledge (if that word is still appropriate here) can only be represented or made known by a betrayal of that interiority into exterior species. The only knowledge that is entirely natural to the soul is not really knowledge at all but an immediate and interior affective relationship to God. With respect to these affective dispositions, Bonaventure concludes, conscience is a simply innate habit. Yet an innate affective orientation to God is *also* how Bonaventure characterizes synderesis.[43] One might be tempted to see here, then, nothing more than a blurring of the distinction between conscience and synderesis. But it is not simply a matter of imprecision: Bonaventure has, after all, drawn very clearly the line between the truly innate love of God and those modes of conscience characterized by knowledge obtained through external species. Rather, insofar as conscience names a truly and simply innate habit, it proves indistinguishable from synderesis. Synderesis, then, would be the interiority of conscience, or its secret, the absolute limit of its representability to itself.[44]

Bonaventure on Synderesis

If the soul's innate love of God is thus set apart in the soul, what practical effect can it have on concrete moral action? This is the problem to which Bonaventure turns in his discussion of synderesis—one that, I argue, he cannot fully resolve given the heterogeneity of the affective orientation toward God and the operations of the practical intellect. Bonaventure acknowledges the difficulty of determining the best way of distinguishing synderesis from the other powers.[45] Some have said that conscience is the habit that orients the power of synderesis toward the object of the natural law. Synderesis would then be the superior portion of reason directing the inferior powers in the performance of the law. Bonaventure sees no problem with this scheme *per se*, but it contradicts Jerome's claim that synderesis is not mixed up in the errors of the other powers. The proper way of speaking must, then, render synderesis more autonomous, or more aloof, with respect to the fallible power of cognition.

More to the point, Bonaventure surmises that if synderesis were simply a knowledge of the natural law (for example, a knowledge of the universal principles of the law), then one would still have to posit some further motivation to follow the law. As Douglas Langston rightly observes, in

Bonaventure's terms, a purely cognitive theory of moral action could provide no explanation for why human beings should follow, rather than disregard, the principles of the law. Only a motive cause could provide that explanation: "It is part of Bonaventure's achievement to see that the goal which justifies our following first principles must be found outside the rational order, viz., in the affective order."[46] On the face of it, however, this solution remains tautological (we are motivated to the good by our motivation to the good). To have any explanatory value, Bonaventure must account for the role this natural motivation plays in the discernment of and concrete action towards the good. And at the heart of this task lies a basic dilemma, of which Bonaventure was certainly aware: How can synderesis be utterly infallible if it is efficaciously involved in fallible human desire and action?

After considering several unsatisfactory opinions about the "place" of synderesis in the soul, Bonaventure then offers a definition of synderesis as the "weight of the will [*pondus voluntatis*], or the will with that weight, insofar as it inclines to the noble good [*bonum honestum*]."[47] In the next chapter, I explore the significance of Bonaventure's use of the term "weight" in this connection. But the explicit point to be made here is that Bonaventure's definition works to restrict the goal of synderesis to the noble good (*bonum honestum*). Corresponding to the distinction between speculative and practical knowledge in the intellect, the things that the affect desires are of two genera: the noble and the pleasing. Those things belonging to the latter type (*in genere commodi*) are not intrinsically and universally good, though they may represent a genuine good to the one desiring them (such as food and drink). Synderesis refers, by contrast, to the affective power insofar as it desires the noble good of the natural law—the obedience due to God and the respect due to one's neighbor. Further, synderesis may be distinguished from the desirous powers of the soul more generally by its movement. The rational, concupiscible, and irascible powers are either moved naturally or deliberatively, while "synderesis names the affective power as it is moved naturally and rightly."[48] In this way, Bonaventure sets the natural rectitude of synderesis in opposition to deliberative movement. To move deliberatively, for Bonaventure, means to act in accordance with free choice (*liberum arbitrium*), which involves the cognitive and affective powers working together.[49] If "free choice" names the deliberative (and fallible) movement of the will in conjunction with the intellect, then "synderesis" refers to the will's natural (and thus infallible) motion—that is, the affective power insofar as it can be considered distinct from the operations of the cognitive faculty. "And this is why synderesis," the eagle of Ezekiel's vision, "is said to soar above the others."[50]

Only in terms of movement, and not in essence, then, is synderesis distinguished from the rational, concupiscible, and irascible affective powers. Furthermore, it shares with these other powers its essential functions—and in this way, too, synderesis is to be distinguished from the cognitive functions of conscience. Corresponding to the concupiscible and irascible powers, the functions of synderesis are to desire (*appetit*) the noble good and to flee (*refugit*) evil (that is, to feel remorse over sin). Synderesis moves and inclines the soul; without it, the directives of conscience could never be translated into action. Moral action requires, then, some cooperation between synderesis and conscience, in the same way that action generally requires the interpenetration of cognitive and affective functions: "Just as reason is not able to move without the will mediating, so neither can conscience move without synderesis mediating."[51] This is why synderesis is called the "spark" or stimulus of conscience. Moral action requires the integration of synderesis and conscience. But this integration produces certain conceptual problems. If the conjunction of reason and will is deliberative action, in what sense can the motion of synderesis still be called natural when it is working in conjunction with conscience and is dependent on its cognitive judgments? And in what sense can it be called infallible if it is involved with the fallible actions of human beings?

Bonaventure considers these problems at length, according to the terms set by Jerome's commentary, by way of two questions. First, can synderesis be extinguished through sin? That is, can the soul be so corrupted that synderesis no longer has any effect? And second, can synderesis *itself* be corrupted (*depravari*) by sin or "lose its place," so that it desires evil instead of good? To the first question, Bonaventure responds that synderesis cannot be extinguished totally (as Jerome wrote, "not even in Cain"). Because synderesis is natural to human beings, its removal would constitute a change in human nature, which, as divinely instituted, sin can never effect.

Yet with respect to the act of synderesis, three vices can interfere: blindness, lasciviousness, and obstinacy. The last case refers to the damned, who, Bonaventure maintains, still possess synderesis but are so confirmed in their wickedness that it no longer inclines them to the good. In the damned, synderesis marks the site of a punitive and unredeeming sorrow over sin. The other two vices are found among the living. One's lust for carnal pleasure can be so powerful that it drowns out the murmuring and remorse of synderesis. The darkness of blindness, similarly, can impede synderesis from murmuring against evil, "because the evil is believed to be good."[52] Here, it appears, an error of *judgment* causes the function of synderesis to go awry. Though it continues to stimulate the soul toward the good, it cannot murmur against evil because that evil is misidentified as the good. Thus, it would seem, not only is synderesis impeded, but it is stimulating the pursuit of evil, insofar as it inclines toward an evil end which is wrongly identified as good.

The problem may seem abstract, but it raises serious practical and theoretical problems when one considers, as Bonaventure does, the case of heretics, "who, dying for the impiety of their errors, believe that they are dying for the piety of their faith. And therefore they feel no remorse, but in fact feel a false and vain joy."[53] Heretics, no doubt, are in error, but are they right to pursue the wrong good? According to Bonaventure's understanding of conscience, they are not. Such people are guilty of an "erroneous conscience," a culpable bad *habitus* developed through a long history of sinful actions, and thus are accountable for their bad consciences—and morally bound to correct them.[54] But what about synderesis? Is it right in inclining the soul even if, due to a cognitive error, its inclination is, in fact, directed toward evil? Heretics do not necessarily pose a threat to the understanding of synderesis as inextinguishable. After all, as Bonaventure notes, being wrong about one important thing does not preclude being right about many other smaller issues: Thus, synderesis in heretics "does not carry out the function of murmuring against the errors because of which they are killed. Yet it is not extinguished, because it murmurs against other evils . . ."

This show of fair-mindedness toward heretics on Bonaventure's part is primarily in service of a theoretical point—synderesis is not extinguished so long as *some* aspect of its operation is carried out, even if it is partially impeded from time to time. This seems sufficiently clear in itself, and it is therefore curious that Bonaventure presses the example of heretics further than would appear necessary to make his point. That is, he goes on to contend that synderesis is not extinguished in heretics, in spite of their confusion of good and evil, not only because it murmurs against other evils, but also because it murmurs "against that which the heretics believe to be evil."[55] With this clause, then, Bonaventure appears to affirm the dependence of the natural movement of synderesis on a deliberative judgment of reason.

On one level, this dependence would seem to be inevitable. How, after all, can synderesis move toward the good and flee evil unless the soul has some understanding (whether correct or incorrect) of what that good and evil are? If synderesis is an act of the affective part of the soul, then it must be preceded by cognition because, as Bonaventure affirms repeatedly, intellect precedes affect.[56] This axiom in itself does not jeopardize the infallibility of synderesis, which Bonaventure understands to follow the innate aspect of conscience as natural *lumen* of the practical intellect, prior to an act of deliberative reason.[57] Understood in this way, synderesis's dependence on conscience would precede the introduction of any possibility of error. That is, synderesis follows the natural light of conscience as it is truly innate, not as it is informed by the external species abstracted from sense perception. And thus, synderesis must not be dependent on actual knowledge. Yet the example of heretics is problematic from this standpoint. There a judgment regarding evil (undoubtedly deliberative because erroneous) directs or determines the course of synderesis. Synderesis, in turn, is in some way misled by reason, even if it is not held to be culpable for that error.

Note, however, that despite Bonaventure's frequent use of language of priority and precedence, it is clear that he is not offering a temporal account of the soul's operations. A concrete act is, after all, not the final outcome in a temporal chain, but the sum of all the soul's powers acting in concert. Yet especially in matters of rectitude and error, it is important for Bonaventure to distinguish the various operations of the soul—and in doing so he relies, even more than on temporal metaphors, on a topography of the soul, delineating spheres of operation within a hierarchy of the soul's powers. If this topographical language is not strictly literal, since the soul is not localized, it is nevertheless indispensable to the distinctions Bonaventure draws and, especially, to the account of synderesis that he gives.

To further clarify synderesis's relation to sin, Bonaventure distinguishes between synderesis itself, which is incorruptible, and its dominion in the soul, which can be compromised through the sins of the inferior powers. Repeating a common analogy for synderesis, Bonaventure compares it to "a knight who, in himself, always sits well on his horse, but when his horse falls, he is said to have fallen too."[58] Thus, reason (through cognitive error) and will (through obstinacy) can resist the promptings of synderesis. The distinction between the act of synderesis and the resistance of the other powers depends on a hierarchical scheme that protects the superior from the deficiencies of the inferior, while allowing for the interpenetration that makes a concrete action possible.

The hierarchical scheme, however, is simply one spatial logic that Bonaventure offers to explain the place of synderesis, and it stands in tension with other analogies he draws, such as the comparison of synderesis to

the bodily organ of sight. Just as the eye itself remains faultless when it is
used to take in an illicit sight, so too does synderesis remain free from sin
even when its inclinations are carried through to wicked ends.[59] Bonaventure hesitates over this analogy, however, because it implies that synderesis
is subject to the deliberative movement of free choice—that which synderesis is supposed to "soar above." As he affirms, "synderesis, since it is
a natural power and is moved naturally, is not subject to the rule of free
choice. And therefore it does not follow that free choice can misuse it."[60]
The analogy to the eye, then, is a hedging of analytical bets: "Moreover,
even if free choice is able to misuse synderesis, it does not follow that there
is sin in synderesis."[61] Just as the body is not morally accountable for the
sins of the soul, so synderesis is not corrupted by the depravations of free
choice. Thus even if synderesis can be moved in the service of a deliberative error (as seems to be the case with heretics who believe themselves to
be martyrs), still it is not, strictly speaking, the subject of that error.

What accounts for this persistent ambiguity in the relation between
synderesis and free choice—that is, between the natural and deliberative
motions of the will? One factor, perhaps, is that Bonaventure seems to
hold little esteem for the practical value of such speculative discussions.
He prefaces a discussion of the substantial unity of reason and will, for
example, with the caveat that the issue is more a matter of curiosity than
utility—one's moral and spiritual life simply does not depend on getting
it right.[62]

Additionally, the ambiguity regarding synderesis may be traced back to
a more fundamental ambiguity, one previously encountered in the discussion of the innate and acquired aspects of conscience. The fact that *all*
actual knowledge is acquired—that is, informed by the species of things
derived from sense—means, as Potts argues, that practically speaking,
Bonaventure provides no criterion with which to distinguish categorically
our knowledge of the universal principles of the law (which are certain)
from our particular conclusions (which can be erroneous). Bonaventure re-
curs to this uncertain distinction in responding to the objection that, since
conscience can be right or wrong, so too can synderesis, since it "follows
conscience as its natural judge."[63] He explains that "conscience, insofar
as it remains in the universal and is moved by a simple aspect, is always
right. But as it descends to particulars and connects them, it is able to be
mistaken, on account of the fact that it is mixed up with the act of deliberative reason."[64] It is thus only with respect to universals that synderesis
can be said to follow conscience because synderesis is "moved not against
this or that evil thing, but against evil in universals. Or, if synderesis is in

some way inclined to detest this or that evil thing, it is not insofar as it is a this or that, but insofar as it is evil."[65] Again, the ambiguity between the universal and the particular prevents a univocal determination as to the precise domain of synderesis. A further example provided by Bonaventure offers little clarification:

> Even the conscience of the Jews, by the original natural command, dictates that God is to be obeyed. And they assume still that God now commands circumcision and discretion in food. And from this their conscience is formed in particular to circumcise themselves and to abstain from food. The error does not come from the first principle, which was certainly true, but comes from an assumption which does not issue from conscience insofar as it is a natural judge, but rather from an error of reason.[66]

The command to obey God is truly innate to the soul, prior to any information by sense perception or language. But the attempt to define what it means to obey God requires the operation of reason and thus introduces the possibility of error. Thus synderesis cannot be held to "descend" with conscience to particulars. But does this mean that synderesis has no place in the carrying out of universal commands? Perhaps, or perhaps not: Synderesis may move toward good and detest evil not only in universals, but also insofar as those universals exist (universally) in particular beings and acts. What is certain, and apparently the crucial point to get right, is that "synderesis does not deviate (*obliquatur*) as conscience errs (*errat*)"[67]; rather, "synderesis is always right (*recta*), but conscience can be right or wrong."[68]

Despite Bonaventure's agnosticism on many aspects of synderesis and its relationship to the other powers, two points appear to be fundamental: Synderesis is always right, and synderesis is wholly affective. The conceptual difficulties that arise in maintaining the former proposition in relation to the deliberative action of the soul, I contend, help to explain the emphasis Bonaventure places on the latter. The distinction between universals and particulars, both in relation to conscience and to synderesis, proves to be too ambiguous and too porous to secure the place of rectitude in the soul, and to keep synderesis free, as it were, from the imputation of error. But synderesis is always right *only insofar as it is heterogeneous to the order of cognition*. Rectitude in synderesis means something very different from rectitude in conscience. The rectitude of synderesis is not a question of right belief or correct knowledge—its object is not truth but the good, and its operation is not the apprehension of the good but the simple movement toward it. Thus its rectitude consists not in knowledge but, like the rider on his horse, in its posture, its place, the straightness of its motion. However interdependent with conscience it may be in the functioning of the practical intellect, synderesis, in itself, remains set apart from cognition in the soul.

What, then, of the rectitude of conscience? Perhaps it is better to say that the crucial distinction between the natural and the deliberative is more fundamental than that between the cognitive and the affective. Indeed, Bonaventure makes a place for inerrancy in conscience insofar as it is innate. Yet the only truly innate aspects of conscience that Bonaventure mentions—to love and to fear God—are themselves affections, which, Bonaventure explains, are truly present to the soul prior to and apart from the intrusion of knowledge acquired exteriorly. The natural, the affective, and the infallible converge in his account at a point that can never be translated into concrete knowledge without breaking it apart—a pure interiority that, as such, never betrays its mute allegiance to the good.

In a gesture that appears to anticipate the analysis of Husserl's *Logical Investigations*, Bonaventure establishes synderesis as a (non)space of pure interiority as the exclusion of exterior species, prior to and uninterrupted by representation. And yet, in Bonaventure's attempts to represent this pure interiority, a strange reversal or torsion occurs—the innermost becomes ecstatic, a curiously alien force acting upon the soul. More intimate than knowledge and prior to language, synderesis is the "spirit which *intercedes* with ineffable sighs."[69] It is not a light but the "weight" and "heat" of the soul, carrying the soul inexorably to its end. The innate affective motion to God, more interior than the structures of discursive knowledge, is also ecstatic, standing outside those structures. As an interiority that exceeds and eludes the order of reason and the logic of cognition, synderesis conforms itself instead, perversely, to the dynamics of embodied movement. The goal of the next three chapters is to elucidate those embodied dynamics of the natural *affectus*, tracing at the same time this torsion of interiority and exteriority that manifests itself most spectacularly in the body of Francis, as it is shaped and inscribed in Bonaventure's account.

CHAPTER 3

Elemental Motion and the Force of Union

This chapter examines more closely the corporeal language with which Bonaventure describes synderesis, the soul's instinct for the good, according to the physical properties of fire. Rather than treating Bonaventure's extensive use of fire imagery as an illustrative metaphor, I argue that this pervasive imagery indicates something important about the cosmic significance of the soul's natural desire for God, and reveals the corporeal dynamic at the heart of spiritual ascent. The body is exemplary of the soul's most fundamental desire—not only the glorious and wretched body of Christ as refracted through the body of Francis, but even, more fundamentally, what ancient and medieval philosophers called the simple bodies—above all, the body of fire.

Bonaventure's divergence from previous scholastic discussions of synderesis is perhaps most evident in the imagery he evokes to define it. In arguing for the affective nature of synderesis, an analogy helps to clarify the stakes: "Just as the intellect needs a light for judging, so the *affectus* needs a certain spiritual heat and weight [*calor et pondus*] for loving rightly. Therefore just as in the cognitive part of the soul there is a certain natural judge, which is conscience, so in the affective part of the soul there will be a weight directing and inclining to the good, and this is synderesis."[1] In the same place, as discussed in the previous chapter, he defines synderesis as the "weight of the will [*pondus voluntatis*], or the will with that weight, insofar as it inclines to the noble good [*bonum honestum*]."[2] Bonaventure is not the first medieval theologian to ascribe a weight to the soul, as I will discuss shortly. But with the image of a "weight and heat for loving," he gives the concept of synderesis an entirely new cast.

By contrast, Alexander of Hales, commenting on the same section of Lombard's *Sentences*, asks, "And in the same way as there is a material light in the senses for seeing and in the intellect for understanding truth, why would there not be in the motive force a light to the good, always turning away from evil?" Elsewhere in the same text, he writes that synderesis "lights and burns [*lucet et ardet*], and is thus always opposed to darkness, and thus to sin."[3] Alexander sets up a correspondence between material light, intellectual light, and a motive or affective light. By positing an affective light to the good, Alexander seems to be suggesting that there is some cognitive component to the affect, an idea that is not at all unprecedented in ancient and medieval theories of the soul.[4] What is remarkable, by way of comparison, is how differently Bonaventure draws the lines. For Bonaventure, there is no "affective light"—such an image muddles the operations of the cognitive and affective parts of the soul, and confuses the affect's movement toward the Good with the practical intellect's illumination of that good.

Bonaventure's dispensing with the light metaphor for synderesis also represents a departure from his other teacher and predecessor Odo of Rigaud. In answering how synderesis can be free of error, Odo considers approvingly a slightly different optic metaphor: "Otherwise we could say that conscience and synderesis differ just as light and vision, so that synderesis is, as it were, light, but conscience is the vision enabled through that light. Whence it is able to see rightly and wrongly, without there being an error in the light."[5] Here Odo's analogy tightens the connection between synderesis and conscience, enlisting synderesis in the service of judgment, and binding both together in a comparison with vision.

By shifting the register of synderesis from "light" to "heat," Bonaventure divorces the natural motion of the will from the dynamics of intellectual vision in which conscience, as natural "light," participates. Yet insofar as light and heat refer to two properties of a single substance, fire, Bonaventure's imagery also works to draw an even tighter connection between conscience and synderesis. In fact, the attributions of *calor* and *pondus* both refer to the analogy to fire. In 2 *Sent.* 14 he identifies three formal properties (*proprietates*) of fire: *luminositas, caliditas*, and *levitas*, "through which it is moved through an upward motion" (*per quam movetur motu, qui est sursum*).[6] In fact, the comparison with fire makes for a fairly precise comparison. Synderesis and conscience are not distinct substances, but as properties or powers they are properly distinguished.[7] If the light, heat, and weight of fire are found together in a single substance, they are not dependent upon one another. The contrast between light, heat, and weight expresses a very different relationship than that between light and vision: The properties may be concurrent without one being subordinate to another.

If synderesis does not pertain to the properties of light and the dynamics of intellectual vision, what function does it serve in the soul? Just as *levitas* is that by which the fire is moved upward, so, too, does the weight of synderesis refer to a particular way that the soul is moved. As Bonaventure clarifies later, synderesis is not essentially distinct from the concupiscible, irascible, and rational powers (the triad named in the Cistercian, pseudo-Augustinian treatise *On the Spirit and the Soul*),[8] but differs in its mode of movement (*modus movendi*), which, invoking Jerome's gloss, is to fly over the other powers, high above their errant motions. By identifying synderesis as a weight, Bonaventure reinforces the point that it belongs to the motive, or affective, part of the soul.

But the metaphorical investment of synderesis with the language of weight and motion yields a return. The linking of synderesis with weight not only illustrates the motive and affective nature of synderesis, but helps to clarify in turn what belongs to *affectus*. Bonaventure's shifting of synderesis from the image of light to that of weight is significant not only for his understanding of synderesis, but also for the nature and constitution of *affectus*—of which synderesis is a crucial aspect. How, exactly, does affect move? Why does Bonaventure describe synderesis, the soul's spark and infallible inclination to God, in the seemingly crudely physical terms of weight and heat (crude, at least, in comparison to the subtle and spiritual image of light)? And what does Bonaventure's understanding of affective motion reveal about the role of desire in the soul's ascent towards God? In this chapter, I argue that the association of synderesis with *pondus* is not an isolated use of an illustrative metaphor, but an instance of a crucial theme that structures Bonaventure's understanding of *affectus* throughout later writings.

According to Bonaventure in his *Sentences* commentary (and in conjunction with his treatment of synderesis), natural *affectus* is a particular kind of motion within and beyond the soul. As I will highlight in what follows, thinking that motion in relation to the other kinds of action that the soul is capable of proves difficult, presenting ambiguities that Bonaventure does not attempt to solve. To put these ambiguities in a clearer light, I will then look briefly at some aspects of Aristotelian motion that resonate with Bonaventure's account of the soul's natural motion, and consider two earlier Christian thinkers who draw broadly on Aristotelian physics in order to describe love as a weight of the soul moving it toward God: Augustine and the Cistercian William of St-Thierry. As I will ultimately argue in an analysis of the *Breviloquium*, Bonaventure employs this philosophical and spiritual motif as a conceptual linchpin in his understanding of both the soul's ascent and the consummation of the cosmos. The language of weight and motion are not for Bonaventure physical metaphors for an incorporeal reality, but rather describe a dynamic that is more fundamental than the distinction between soul and body and that governs them both alike. This common dynamic is more evident in the simple bodies than in the confounded and distorted human soul, so that the former become exemplary for the latter. In this way, the natural order is a means of meditating human beings' spiritual progress: The soul's ascent to God is an *imitatio* of the simple and inexorable motion of fire.

The Soul in Motion

For Bonaventure, synderesis is distinguished among the powers of the soul not as a separate faculty but as a particular capacity for motion, a capacity that he describes as the soul's "weight" (*pondus*). The existence of sin, however, demonstrates that the soul is all too capable of being moved otherwise than toward the good. To understand how the soul can be moved always to the good and yet still sin, Bonaventure relies on John of Damascus's distinction between the natural and deliberative motions of the soul. This distinction raises its own problems, however—for example, how can these two motions coexist in the soul?—and thus presses the question of what it means to say that the soul has motion at all.

As discussed in the previous chapter, the context of Bonaventure's treatment of synderesis is a commentary on a distinction in Peter Lombard's *Sentences* about the goodness and corruption of the will. The problem that Peter's text poses is how the will, as a natural good inherent in the soul, can ever be made wicked by sin.[9] What is the relationship between the will's innate goodness and its proclivity to evil? Peter also raises a question about the will in relation to the intellect. Why is it that it is not a sin for the intellect to think some evil thing, but it is always a sin for the will to will something evil?

Because this distinction concerns the innate goodness of the will, it was routine for thirteenth-century commentators to discuss synderesis in relation to this passage (though Peter's text does not mention the concept by name). Yet though synderesis helped theologians conceptualize the will's natural goodness, the idea that synderesis moves infallibly only heightened the problem framed in the *Sentences*: What is the relation between the natural movement to the good and the deliberative movement to sin? Bonaventure considers the objection that "it is impossible, at one and the same time, for the will to be moved by contrary motions, or even disparate motions."[10] In response, he acknowledges the difficulty and admits that the authorities have understood the relationship between these movements of the will in different ways. Some hold the motion of the natural and deliberative will to be indistinct, and say that a morally wicked act is simply a deformed act of willing a natural good. That is, a wicked act is a deformed and morally culpable attempt to attain the natural good of happiness.

But Bonaventure finally rejects this interpretation, wishing to uphold the moral integrity of the natural will to the good, "since, when Ambrose says that human beings naturally will the good, he does not mean only the natural good, which is indeed an act of will, but even the moral good. For human beings desire justice and hate injustice by their natural will."[11] The alternative, which Bonaventure endorses, is to admit two motions of the will, one "by which the will naturally desires the good, and the other by which the will deliberately desires evil."[12]

But even here opinions are divided as to whether the two motions can exist simultaneously. Some say the act of the deliberative will does not exclude the act of the natural will. Others say that, if the power of the will is simple, it cannot be moved by different or contrary motions at the same time. Those who hold this position, Bonaventure argues, claim that synderesis is "always" acting in the sense of a *habit*, rather than literally acting at all times. Thus, they can claim without contradiction that the natural will is always acting (because it is always capable of acting), and that the will moves to sin from time to time, and that there is only one motion in the will at a time. Bonaventure agrees that the natural will is not in fact continually acting: "And therefore the text should be understood thus: that the word 'always' means the continuity of the habit of willing, not the act."[13] The substantial operation cannot be taken away, but the consequent operation can be impeded; in other words, the movement of the natural will toward the good is constant, but its realization in a concerted act of the soul is not. Nevertheless, Bonaventure explicitly leaves unresolved the more perplexing question: whether the deliberative *motus* to sin and the natural *motus* to the good can act simultaneously. Can there be two contrary motions in the soul at the same time?

What is clear is that the natural and deliberative motions of the will *should* act together, in whatever way that might be possible. Bonaventure understands moral progress to involve the entire will, natural and deliberative. In 2 *Sent.* 39, he clarifies that the natural desire for the good does not make the will good as such. Here he takes up obliquely a question that earlier commentators on synderesis frequently discussed—whether the movement of synderesis is meritorious. Bonaventure responds: "It must be said that the goodness of the will is inchoate in the natural appetite and consummated in deliberative virtue. Nor is the will wholly (*simpliciter*) good and upright unless it is upright insofar as it is moved both deliberatively and naturally."[14]

Bonaventure also considers explicitly the other dilemma posed in Peter's text: Why is the will more corrupted in its act than any other power? Why is it a sin to will evil, but it is not necessarily a sin to understand evil? Given that an act's value depends on its object, the evil of an object of intellect should, it seems, confer evil upon the act of understanding that object. The objection recognizes a distinction between the act of willing and the act of understanding: The former involves a motion from the will to its object, whereas the latter is accomplished by the motion of the object toward the intellect. Therefore, it seems, the wicked object should pollute the intellect more than the will.

Bonaventure endorses the premise of the objection in his response: Willing does indeed involve a motion toward the object, whereas understanding involves a motion of the object toward the intellect.[15] The will is that which is said properly to have motion, while the intellect remains at rest in its act. Yet for Bonaventure, this difference in orientation to objects proves that the will is more corrupted in its act than is the intellect, for to move toward the object *transforms* the will into its object, while the intellect is merely *conformed* to its object. To will an evil object is to be transformed by and into that evil. The difference between intellect and will is not, however, simply the direction of force involved in the act, but also its intensity: "This is so on account of the greater force of union which consists in love itself, just as Dionysius said: 'We call love [*amor*] the unitive force'; moreover it is said in 1 Corinthians 6: 'Whoever adheres to God is made one spirit.'"[16] The claim that Bonaventure makes elsewhere that responsibility—the capacity for merit and blame—is based in the capacity for free choice is tied to a conception of the will as a susceptibility to an intense force, one that binds the soul to its object for better and for worse.[17] The affective part of the soul's greater capacity for corruption also accounts for its greater force of union with and transformation into God. The force of union is the force of the object acting on the soul, drawing the soul to itself; the affective part of the soul is its capacity to be *affected* by a good (or perceived good) beyond itself.

This interpretation of affective movement is reinforced in Bonaventure's discussion of *amor* in the first volume of the commentary, where he discusses the relationship between the terms *amor*, *dilectio*, and *caritas*. Though Bonaventure acknowledges shades of meaning in the different terms, he does not offer a disjunctive picture of affect as a whole. He defines *amor* as "the adhesion of an affection with respect to the one loved."[18] But with this general definition of love, Bonaventure rejects the opinion that *amor* names a "libidinous affection," while *dilectio* signifies an act of a well-ordered will (*ex voluntate ordinata*). And he cites Dionysius in *Divine Names* 4 in support of this conclusion: "Theologians seem to me to signify the same thing by the words *amor* and *dilectio*," with *amor* translating the Greek *eros* and *dilectio* translating *agape*.

Nevertheless, Bonaventure does draw a distinction between the terms: To the basic definition of *amor*, the term *dilectio* adds (*addit*) the sense of election (*electio*). That is, *dilectio* is the adhesion of affection with respect to the loved object *chosen* out of a number of possible objects. This is the love spoken of in *Song of Songs* 5: "My beloved [*dilectus*], chosen out of a thousand." Finally, *caritas*, from *carus* or dear, adds to the sense of *dilectio* an appreciation for the great value of the beloved object.

This passage alerts the reader to the importance of attending to the nuance of affective terms in Bonaventure's writings. Yet it would be too simple to expect to find in the passage a legend for decoding every discussion of love in Bonaventure's corpus, or to simply equate *amor* with the will's natural motion and *dilectio* with deliberation. However, the passage demonstrates Bonaventure's concern to uphold the basic understanding of *amor* that he derives from the Dionysian authority: Love, in every case, is an affective adhesion of lover and loved, a unitive and transformative force. The definition leaves unresolved, then, the ambiguity evident both in the concept of *dilectio* and in the operation of the deliberative will: The soul's capacity for choice is simply one mode of the force by which the soul is attracted by and transformed into the object of its desire.

Aristotle and Elemental Motion

The ambiguity that I am suggesting is constitutive of Bonaventure's understanding of *affectus* is not unique to him, and can be found in a number of his philosophical and theological sources. But here I am particularly interested in exploring the way in which Bonaventure's theory of affect depends on a theory of motion. And while it would be misleading to call Bonaventure's understanding of affective motion "Aristotelian," Aristotle's theory of natural motion and its relation to the soul's movement forms part of the framework for Bonaventure's reflection on affect. It may therefore provide a helpful point of reference for thinking through aspects of Bonaventure's conception of affective motion, while also further illuminating the intractability of the ambiguity that characterizes the motion of *affectus* in its relation to the intellect and to its object of desire.

Bonaventure uses the term *motus* both of conscience and synderesis. In the discussion of whether synderesis can sin, Bonaventure says that conscience is "not moved by a simple motion alone, but by a collative one."[19] Yet elsewhere he suggests that *motus* applies only analogically to the cognitive part of the soul: "Conscience is the habit perfecting our intellect insofar as it is practical, or insofar as it directs in works. And thus the intellect has in a certain way a motive cause, not because it effects movement, but because it dictates and inclines to movement."[20] He is even clearer on this point when, in arguing that synderesis is affective, he writes, "Therefore just as reason is not able to move without the will mediating, so neither can conscience move without synderesis mediating."[21] In attributing motion to the practical intellect and, to a greater extent, to affect, Bonaventure follows the outlines of Aristotle's account of animal motion in *De anima* III.10. Accordingly, he reads Aristotle's discussions of the acts of the soul through the thirteenth-century language of faculties and powers.

Aristotle had argued that both desire and practical intellect together are necessary for motion, but, strictly speaking, it is desire alone—or desire in conjunction with the object of desire—that effects motion.[22] Bonaventure, like other medieval theorists of the soul, equates the motive part of the soul with the *affectus* (and the natural mode of the motive part with synderesis). But perhaps reflecting either the ambiguity in Aristotle's text or simply the conjunction of the practical intellect to affect, he also attributes motion, in a less proper sense, to *conscientia* in the cognitive part of the soul. In his discussion of synderesis and conscience, however, Bonaventure leaves unexamined the question of the agent of motion—whether the object of the *affectus* (the *bonum honestum*) is properly considered the cause of motion, or whether the cause is internal to the soul itself. Nevertheless, the question—and its attendant difficulties—may still be discerned in Bonaventure's texts. Here close attention must be paid to the analogies and the images he uses to describe the soul's natural tendency to motion—as a weight or *pondus* of the soul by which it ascends, just as fire ascends to its natural place.

Though Bonaventure does not cite Aristotle as the source for his account of elemental motion, Aristotle's comments on this point, as found in *Physica* and *De caelo*, influenced medieval cosmological and physical theories through a number of late ancient channels. The geocentric cosmology that underwrites this theory of motion is by no means unique to Aristotle, nor is the presence of such a cosmic scheme in a later author necessarily evidence of Aristotelian "influence." The philosopher's accounts of elemental motion within a geocentric cosmos, however, bring into relief a number of conceptual ambiguities that attend any such theory, and so Aristotle, though not an absolute beginning for ancient and medieval physics, is nevertheless a helpful place to start.

The equivocation in *De anima*, which appears to explain motion *both* as a function of a desire internal to the soul and as a function of the external object of desire, points to a major difficulty in Aristotle's theories of animal self-motion.[23] In an influential essay, David Furley argues that Aristotle needs both explanations of motion to be true in order to maintain a distinction between the motion of animals and the motions of inanimate beings, including the elements, which, rising or falling inexorably to their natural places, may seem to contain some inherent principle of motion themselves.[24] Aristotle considers this problem at greatest length in *Physics* and *On the Heavens* (*De caelo*). In the first, he states that the natural movements of animals come from themselves and that, in fact, all self-movement is natural.[25] This is obvious enough because in Book Two Aristotle had already defined a *physis* of a thing as a "certain principle and cause of change and stability in the thing."[26] Natural movement would be that movement that is due to a nature—that is, an inhering cause of motion. The soul of the animal is, by virtue of its embodiment, also susceptible to unnatural, external movements. An important link is established between interiority and self-motion, on the one hand, and exterior motion and corporeality, on the other.

More difficult is the case of simple bodies—fire, air, water, and earth—and inanimate things composed of them. The simple bodies are natural, and they have their own natural movements: Fire moves upward or toward the extremity; earth moves downward or toward the center. But they cannot be self-movers, both because self-motion belongs only to living things, and because, if they moved themselves, they would also have the ability to stop moving. But, though lacking the ability to cause movement, the simple bodies do contain a source of movement: "it is a source which enables them to be affected."[27] The problem of the natural movements of simple bodies is solved (though only partially) by positing a potentiality to particular kinds of motion in those simple bodies. So, for example, air has the natural capacity to be moved upward—to actualize its potential for rising—if a hindrance is removed.

In *De caelo*, Aristotle provides greater detail about the nature of elemental motion. Book Four presents an inquiry into the meanings of the terms "heavy" and "light," which constitute "a proper part of the theory of movement, since we call things heavy and light because they have the power of being moved naturally in a certain way."[28] He considers two previous theories of this natural motion. The first, which he identifies as coming from the *Timaeus*, holds that heaviness is a function of the quantity of identical parts of which a body is composed. If quantity were the determinant of heaviness and lightness, Aristotle counters, then a larger quantity of fire should rise more slowly than a smaller one. But the opposite is in fact the case. He then considers a second theory, which deems lightness a result of the void that is trapped in bodies, and raises a number of objections to this theory before advancing to his own.

In offering his own account, Aristotle provisionally accepts "the common statement of older writers that 'like moves to like,'" because, he says, "the movement of each body to its own place is motion toward its own form."[29] Elemental motion would then be a continual process of cosmic sorting, all bodies moving to their own kind. But this principle in itself is not sufficient to explain the determinant motions of elements to fixed positions. To advance the explanation further, Aristotle hypothesizes, "If one were to remove the earth to where the moon now is, the various fragments of earth would each move not towards it but to the place in which it now is."[30] The reason for this surprising conclusion, Aristotle continues, is consistent with the principle that like seeks like, for what bodies move toward when they move toward their like is a common *form*. Thus for the earth to abandon its natural place would be to abandon its form. A thing's natural "place" is the boundary that contains it, and this boundary is simply the thing's form—and so, "it is to its like that a body moves when it moves to its own place."[31] The natural place of a simple body *is* its form; its tendency to movement toward that place is its potential for its own form; its attainment of that place is its actualization. The change that is natural motion, then, is explicable as a species of alteration in general: "Thus to ask why fire moves upward and earth downward is the same as to ask why the healable, when moved and changed *qua* healable, attains health and not whiteness."[32] The difference with elemental motion—and what makes the elements seem to have some internal source of their motion (even though in fact they are moved by their natural place)—is that they are "closest to matter." That is, the simple bodies appear to have some internal agent of motion because they are observed to move so determinately, so inexorably, to their place (and because there is no visible external agent of change acting upon them). Whereas according to *De anima* III.10, the soul moves itself through a complicated interplay of desired object, the faculty of desire, and the practical intellect, by contrast, the simple bodies are moved immediately by the form (that is, their place), which is external to them. The trajectory of external motion is so certain that it appears to be internally driven.

Bonaventure's discussion of synderesis and conscience explicitly refers to Aristotle's theory of animal motion. But his description of natural motion as a weight by which the will is drawn more closely resembles the Aristotelian explanation of bodily, elemental motion.[33] What are for Aristotle two different kinds of motion proper to two different kinds of beings—the self-motion of the soul and the external motion of bodies—are for Bonaventure two kinds of motion (natural and deliberative) *both* belonging to, though not simply internal to, the soul.

Augustine and the pondus amoris

A number of Christian theologians before Bonaventure saw in the movement of elements a fitting description of the soul's tendency to the good. Perhaps the deepest reflection in early Christian literature of the theme of the "weight" of the soul is in the final book of Augustine's *Confessions*. Here Augustine expands the scope of his inquiry to the whole created order:

> A body inclines by its own weight towards its own place (*Corpus pondere suo nititur ad locum suum*). Weight does not always tend towards the lowest place, but to its own proper place. Fire tends upward, stones tend downward: they are both led by their weight, seeking their place (*ponderibus suis aguntur, loca sua petunt*). Oil poured into water, rises again above the water, but water poured over oil will sink beneath the oil: they are both led by their weight, seeking their place (*ponderibus suis aguntur, loca sua petunt*). When things are out of order, they are not

at rest; coming to order, they find rest. My love is my weight (*Pondus meum amor meus*). By it I am carried wherever I am carried. By your gift we are inflamed and carried upwards; we are enkindled and we set off (*imus*). In our hearts we rise as we sing a song of ascent. By your fire, your good fire, we are inflamed and we rise (*imus*) . . .[34]

Augustine puts the movement of bodies in the passive voice: By weight all things are led (*aguntur*) to their place. *Pondus* is the capacity for being moved in a certain way, whether in the physical bodies or in the human soul. As Augustine writes just before the cited passage, "Our place is where we come to rest. Love carries us there."[35] The passage hesitates between the active and passive, locating in love the point at which activity and passivity meet, where the distinction is confounded because the love felt by the soul for God is never truly its own. This is far from Aristotle's account of motion. And yet there is an echo of the Aristotelian hesitation in *De anima* III, between desire and the object of desire, *orexis* and *orektikon*, as the agent of affective movement.

For Augustine, if *pondus* is the capacity to be moved, it is also that by which all things *loca sua petunt*—seek or strive for their place. Aristotle's own writings about the elements in motion, though denying an internal source of change, suggest some kind of desire or longing for place. With the term *peto*, Augustine also attributes a kind of desire to material bodies. He expands on this theme in *De civitate Dei* 11: "If we were stones or waves or wind or fire, or something like these, without any sense or life, we would nevertheless not be without a certain appetite [*appetitus*] for our own place and order. For the movement produced by weight is, as it were, the body's love [*amor*], whether it bears downward by heaviness or upward by lightness. Just as a body is carried by its weight, so is the soul carried wherever it is carried by its love."[36] On one level, this passage works precisely to distinguish human beings from stones or waves because love in the human soul seeks the Creator and not simply place, or fruitfulness, or sensual goods. But what grounds the comparison of human beings to inanimate bodies is a common term, *appetitus*, which all things have in common and which functions in an analogous way in both bodies and rational souls. The force of the comparison is that the love of God is as natural to the soul as downward or upward motion is to stones and flames.

One of the most striking differences between Augustine's description of *pondus* in the *Confessions* and Aristotle's *baros* is Augustine's claim that weight does not always tend toward the lowest place, that is, toward the element of earth. In *De caelo*, Aristotle argues at some length that weight is the principle of downward motion (or—what amounts to the same in a geocentric cosmos—motion toward the center). While even air has some weight, Aristotle maintains that pure fire is absolutely light—that is, absolutely without weight. But for Augustine, *pondus* signifies a natural appointment to a proper level or place within the physical order and has no contrary.[37] Augustine discusses *pondus* most frequently as the last term in a triad of properties of all created things—measure, number, and weight—following Wisdom 11:21, "God ordained all things in measure, number, and weight."[38] In the fourth book of *De Genesi ad litteram*, he examines the role of this triad in God's creation: "Measure set a mode on everything, number bestows form, and weight draws everything to rest and stability. And God is all three of these things originally, truly, and uniquely, who limits all, and forms all, and orders all."[39] As the means by which God ordained his creation, *mensura*, *numerus*, and *pondus* are not only properties of bodies:

> Measure, number, and weight can be observed and understood not only in stones and wood and such corporeal things with mass and quantity, whether terrestrial or celestial. There is also the measure of something to be done, lest it run out of control and out of bounds; and there is the number of the affections and virtues of the soul, by which the soul is drawn away from the deformity of foolishness and drawn towards the form and splendor of wisdom; and there is the weight of the will and of love, in which appears the value of what is to be desired [*appetendo*], what is to be avoided [*fugiendo*], and what is to be given priority.[40]

The weight of the soul is not a quantity or a function of mass as it is in bodies, but like the *pondus* of the body, the *pondus* of the will or love is a principle of movement—that by which the soul seeks what is good and flees what is not. In the case of both bodies and the soul, as Augustine writes, *pondus* is that which "draws each thing to repose and stability."[41] By contrast, Augustine identifies a further sense of measure, number, and weight to which the others are subordinated: "And there is a measure without measure, to which must be reckoned all that is from it, though it is not from anything else; there is a number without number, by which all things are formed, though it itself is not formed; and there is a weight without weight, to which those whose rest is pure joy find that rest, though it is still not drawn to any other."[42] In one sense, God can be said to have *mensura*, *numerus*, and *pondus* insofar as God is the source and destination of all created beings; but in himself, he is without measure, without number, and without weight. God is not subject to limit, to form, or to being moved.

Pondus in creatures, then, would seem to refer simply to the passivity to movement. But there is an ambiguity to Augustine's notion of weight in the soul. On analogy with the weights of material bodies, Augustine suggests that the soul has a particular weight by which it moves to its appointed place. But elsewhere, *pondus* in the soul appears less determined. If every body has a specific weight drawing it to its proper place, the weight of the soul may be a means of ascent or descent. As the passage from the *Confessions* cited previously states, by love I am carried *wherever* I am carried. If the soul can be carried aloft by the love of the Spirit, it can also descend by the *pondus cupiditatis* into the depths of sin—the depths being not a local, physical place, but the inordinate passions "which drag us downward to love of worldly concerns."[43] In *De libero arbitrio*, Augustine compares the will's movement to the movement of a falling stone. While both the will's movements and the stone's are proper to them, the movements are dissimilar in that "a stone lacks the power to restrain the motion by which it is carried downward, but the soul is not moved to abandon higher things for inferior things only so long as it does not will it. Therefore the stone's motion is natural, but the soul's is voluntary."[44] It would be beyond absurd, he continues, to attribute moral culpability to the stone for falling given that it is naturally moved downward. But when the soul descends to the depths, this is a voluntary movement in that it results from an abandonment of the love that bears the soul aloft and is a gift of the Holy Spirit.

The soul, then, is capable of a downward movement, which is to be distinguished from elemental movement by the presence of volition. Augustine is also careful to distinguish the interior downward movement of the soul from the motion of bodies. In *Confessions* 13.7, he reflects on the difficulty of speaking about the motions of the soul. The depths to which we sink are not places, he admits, but states of the soul—affections, loves, and impure spirits—and yet they are not entirely unlike places. *Quid similius, et quid disimilius?* Augustine does not answer his own question, leaving the analogy—and its attendant ambiguities—for later medieval theologians to parse.

The Place of the Soul: William of St. Thierry's
De natura et dignitate amoris

In the twelfth century, the Cistercian abbot William of St.-Thierry was also concerned with the applicability of *locus* to the soul and to God. His caution against the theory that the soul is localized in the body does not inhibit him from fully embracing the theme of the soul's movement to its natural place. In the prologue to his treatise on the growth of love in the religious novice, *De natura et dignitate amoris*, William identifies love as "a force (*vis*) of the soul, carrying (*ferens*) it by a certain natural weight (*naturali quodam pondere*) to its place or destination (*locum vel finem suum*)."[45] Here the Augustinian theme of love as the weight by which the soul ascends is reprised, only with a greater emphasis on the proper *place* of the soul: "Every creature, whether spiritual or corporeal, has a fixed place [*certum locum*] to which it is naturally carried, and a certain natural weight by which it is carried. For weight, as a certain philosopher correctly teaches, does not always move downwards. Fire rises, water descends, and so on."[46] Whatever William may understand incorporeal place to be (a question that I will revisit shortly), his statement here must be read as more than a simple metaphor: Bodies do not possess weight or a place in a truer sense than do spiritual creatures. All creatures—corporeal or spiritual—are alike in possessing *pondus* and having a proper place. Nevertheless, determining the weight and place of the elements such as fire and water, as William well observes, is a simpler thing than explaining precisely what is proper to spiritual place. And when it is a question of human beings, composed of bodies and souls, the situation becomes even more complicated:

> Human beings are also moved by their weight, which carries the spirit upward, and the body downward, both toward their place or destination. What is the place of the body? Scripture replies: "You are earth and to earth you shall return." Yet it says in the *Book of Wisdom* concerning the spirit, "and the spirit returns to God who created it." Look at humans in their disintegration, how completely they are carried along by their own weight to their place. When things go well and according to order, the spirit returns to God who created it, and the body to earth, not only to earth but into the elements from which it was composed and formed. When earth, fire, water, and air reclaim for themselves something of it, when there is a natural disintegration of a natural composite, each part returns by its own weight to its own element. The disintegration is complete when all of them are restored to their proper place.[47]

It is a poignant description of the human being, a fragile composite whose members are all out of place. The physical elements that compose the body find, without deviation, their proper place upon the corruption of the body. Here the likeness of spiritual weight to corporeal weight also breaks down: "While not one of the elements deviates from its natural course, only the miserable soul and degenerate spirit, corrupted by the vice of sin, although by itself naturally tending to its place, does not know or learns with difficulty how to return to its origin."[48] Why, if love is a natural force within the soul, must it be learned by the soul, when the physical elements move immediately to their places?

In the prologue, William explains that love is implanted in the soul by the "Creator of nature," so that, barring love's destruction by "adulterous affections," it teaches the soul from within how to love properly. In the rest of the treatise, William describes the process of preparing oneself to receive that teaching within the structure of a monastic community. He describes the will as the *affectus* of the rational soul—that is, the soul's capacity to be filled with good (by grace) and with evil (by its own failings). Love is kindled when, by grace, the will fixes itself to the Holy Spirit, for love is "nothing other than the will vehemently attached to something good."[49] In the beginning stages of this love, the religious novice engages in the hard labor of self-discipline at the hand of an external authority, until, under the direction of his own reason, the external regulations he has been following impress themselves on him interiorly.

As the novice grows into spiritual maturity, his love is illumined (*illuminari*) by God. At this stage, the love that was previously guided by reason and inculcated in the performance of exterior commands begins to "pass over [*transire*] into the *affectus*."[50] *Affectus* is an intricate and multivalent term in William's writings.[51] In the most general sense, he uses the term as the capacity of the soul to be moved, with an emphasis on the passivity of the soul to the object of its desire. Here, however, in describing the passing over of love into the *affectus*, William seems to be using the term in a more exalted sense as *charitas*. As he defines it a bit later on, "The *affectus* is that which seizes the mind by a kind of general force and perpetual virtue, firm and stable and maintained through grace."[52] He contrasts this with the various *affectiones* (referred to elsewhere in the work as *affectus* in the plural), which vary with time and circumstance. To be gripped by the enlightened *affectus* is to be held steady from the attacks of the *affectiones*. The enlightened *affectus*, or *charitas*, awakens the five spiritual senses in the soul, and, with its two eyes of *amor* and *ratio*, is able to see God: Reason sees God through what He is not, while love abandons itself (*deficere*) in what He is.

Upon this self-abandonment, the soul takes rest from its labors and finds repose in wisdom and the enjoyment of God. But only upon the death of the body does the spirit truly return to its place: "When all things proceed well and according to order, just as we said at the beginning, the weight of each thing bears it to its place: the body to the earth from which it was taken, to be raised up and glorified in its time, and the spirit to God who created it."[55] The return of the spirit to its origin in God is in accordance with nature, but it is not inevitable like the return of the physical elements to their places. Neither, however, is it a result of an effort of loving. By calling the *affectus* a natural *pondus* of the soul, William makes clear that the love of God is not an act that the soul performs. Its effort is aimed at removing the hindrances to that motion.

Bonaventure: Pondus *as* Ordinativa Inclinatio

As is clear, then, Bonaventure by no means invented the trope of *pondus* as the means by which the soul rises to God. What he did do, however, was elevate it from a trope to a key dynamic in his theology of creation and return. This dynamic is perhaps most evident in his *Breviloquium*, or *Brief Discourse*, written as Master of Theology around 1257. Covering the basic articles of faith, from the Triune God to the Last Things, the *Breviloquium* serves as a kind of short summa, or, to use Bonaventure's own imagery, a map through a dense and difficult forest. It provides, by the work's stated intention, a synoptic view from which to observe connections and patterns across different areas of Christian teaching, and the theological concepts through which those connections are forged.

The concept of *pondus* plays a surprisingly far-reaching role in these connections for Bonaventure, especially as a force accounting for the Neoplatonic hydraulics of procession and return that structure the *Breviloquium* (and which can be discerned everywhere in Bonaventure's writing). In the *Breviloquium*, *pondus* signifies a created, intrinsic property by which all creatures, corporeal and incorporeal, are moved to their end. Bonaventure writes that "the whole structure of the world [*universitas machinae mundialis*] was brought to being in time and out of nothingness by one first, single, and highest principle, whose power, though without measure, disposed all things in a certain weight, number, and measure [*in certo pondere, numero et mensura*]."[54] As he explains, the attribution of measure, number, and weight to all creatures is a statement about their threefold cause:

> The phrase "in a certain weight, number, and measure" indicates that creation is the effect of the Trinity creating through a threefold kind of causality: as efficient cause, by which there is unity, mode, and measure in creatures; as exemplary cause, by which there is truth, species, and

number in creatures; and as final cause, by which there is goodness, order, and weight in creatures. These vestiges of the Creator are found in all creatures, whether corporeal, or spiritual, or composites of both.[55]

In *De Genesi ad litteram*, Augustine, too, correlates *mensura*, *numerus*, and *pondus* with *modus*, *species*, and *ordo*.[56] Bonaventure explains the relation between creator and creature by means of a threefold causality derived from the fourfold Aristotelian scheme. The properties of creatures are expressions of their relationship to God as their maker, exemplar, and end.

Later in the same chapter of the *Breviloquium*, Bonaventure repeats, almost to the word, the same formulation, but this time, instead of *numerus* he uses the term *discreta* ("distinction") and he appends a gloss to *pondus*— "for *pondus* is an ordering inclination" (*ordinativa inclinatio*).[57] It is clear, then, that *pondus* is not primarily a physical quantity that is analogously, or metaphorically, applied to incorporeal things. Rather, in its most literal application, *pondus* is an ordering tendency directing creatures toward God as their final cause. This is true of the weight of bodies as well as the weight of souls.

Thus, the *pondus* of human beings, as body-soul composites, is complex. First of all, Bonaventure says explicitly that all creatures have measure, number and weight, whether those creatures are spiritual, material, or composite, as is human nature. Whereas for William, the weight of the human soul was to be distinguished from the weight of the human body, each going its own way upon disintegration, Bonaventure does not make this distinction. Perhaps, then, he has in mind a tighter integration of soul and body in the human being, ordained to one *pondus* or ordering inclination. Yet Bonaventure elsewhere seems to suggest that the weight of the human person is multiple, or, rather, variable. In fact, in Part 5 he suggests that the proper weight of the soul is something that must be achieved through the ordering of the soul, which occurs through grace.[58] These statements point to the complexity entailed in Bonaventure's conception of the *pondus* of human beings in light of his statements about human dependence on grace.

This complexity is apparent throughout Part 5 of the *Breviloquium*, which treats the grace of the Holy Spirit. Grace, Bonaventure begins, is a gift infused by God, by which the soul is "perfected and made the bride of Christ, daughter of the eternal Father, and temple of the Holy Spirit."[59] It is a gift that cleanses, enlightens, and lifts up the soul. And the lifting up of the soul is at the same time the condescension of God, not through his essence but through "an outpouring emanating from him."[60] What is this movement of ascent that is at the same time a descent? It is not that "the spirit is elevated above itself in place [*per situm localem*]," but rather, it takes on the form of God (*per habitum deiformem*). And this elevation, so understood, is not effected "through a habit naturally inserted, but only through an infused gift divinely given."[61] In one movement, the soul ascends to God when God condescends in grace to the soul.

In the subsequent chapters of Part 5, Bonaventure traces the operations of grace in relation to sin, virtue, and meritorious acts. Grace has three senses. In its most general sense, grace is a gift to all creatures enabling them to continue to exist. Because creatures are created from nothing, they would revert to nothing without the continual support of their Principle. Bonaventure's term for this contingency is *vanitas*, itself a kind of weight whose motion God hinders through his presence in all things. He draws the comparison to someone holding a heavy object (*corpus ponderosum*) in mid-air. If the object is released, it will fall down.[62] Though he does not call *vanitas* the weight of creatures, his simile makes it clear that the *pondus* of creatures, properly speaking, is itself the presence of grace, God's action in sustaining all creatures from reverting to nothingness.[63]

This general grace is a gift to all creatures, from stones to human beings. The other two senses of grace pertain only to the rational spirit: Grace in its special sense (sometimes called actual grace) prepares the rational spirit for receiving the third grace. This sanctifying grace makes the soul capable of attaining merit and advancing to salvation. This is the grace of which Augustine wrote, it "prevenes in the will, so that it wills, and follows the act, so that it does not want in vain."[64] Bonaventure then examines the workings of sanctifying grace as a remedy for sin in the virtues, the gifts of the Spirit, the five spiritual senses, and other aspects of sanctification. Then he turns to examine the workings of grace in meritorious acts: belief in the articles of faith, the ordering of the affections, the performance of the divine law, and petitioning God in prayer.

It is in the context of the ordering of affections that Bonaventure discusses the *pondus* of the soul. Four things must be loved with *caritas*— God, ourselves, our neighbor, and our body. The ultimate end of loving is the ordering of oneself to the Good in which human beings find rest and enjoyment. Because of this, charity is due, first, to God, who is that Good, and secondarily to ourselves and our neighbors, who will be made capable of enjoying the Good, and finally to our bodies, which will be beatified with the spirit and will share in this enjoyment. To love these things properly, however, the soul's affections must be brought to order, *against* their own reflexive tendency: "Love [*amor*], the weight of the soul [*mens*], and the origin of every spiritual affection [*omnis affectionis mentalis*], is brought back toward the self with ease, extends to the neighbor with difficulty, and is raised up to God with greater difficulty."[65] Because the soul in loving tends toward itself and its body, it needs ordering by two commandments—to love God and to love one's neighbor.

In addition to the commandments, God has given another grace for ordering the affections: "Charity is the root, form, and end of virtue, at the same time joining everything to its final end and binding all things together in order. Thus charity is the weight of ordered inclination and the bond of perfect union."[66] By using the term *pondus* both for the reflexive love of the soul and for the ordering grace of charity, Bonaventure casts the ordering of the affections and the sanctification of the affect as a kind of play of forces. The weight of the soul is transformed by the pull of a greater weight, which draws up the affections of the soul and binds them to God and to neighbor, and, in an extended sense, to everything in creation. For as charity orders and hierarchizes, it at the same time unifies.[67] Charity should not be understood simply as a gift to the soul or an aid in moral progress, but as the telos of creation. As Bonaventure writes in concluding this section: "With this union consummated through the bond of charity, God will be all in all in true eternity and perfect peace. Through love all things will be ordered to communion and bound in an indissoluble connection."[68] When he asserts that all things will be in "perfect peace," this, he later explains, is to be understood not simply as a psychological state of the human being, but rather as a perpetual state of cosmic quiescence— one in which the heavenly motions that mark time and the simple elements now in flux will all come to rest.[69]

But though the final state is one of repose, the events leading up to it are anything but peaceful. At the final judgment, a fire will devour the face of the earth—though not completely:

> It is said that "the form [*figura*] of this world will pass away," not in
> the sense of the complete destruction of this sensible world, but that
> through the action of that fire inflaming all elemental things, plants
> and animals will be consumed, and the elements will be purified and
> made new, especially air and earth, and the just will be purified and the
> wicked will be consumed in flame. With these things accomplished, the
> motion of the heavens will cease, so that, with the number of the elect
> fulfilled, the bodies of the world will in a certain way be made new and
> rewarded.[70]

Just as the association of the affective movement of the soul with fire evokes the ancient Stoic conception of fiery *pneuma* as the motive and animating substance of the body and of the cosmos, so too the influence of the ancient Stoic vision of a periodic conflagration that renews the cosmos is evident in Bonaventure's depiction of the final renewal of heaven and earth through fire.[71] Bonaventure's account, like the Stoic doctrine of conflagration, describes a balancing of elemental forces. At the beginning of humankind, a flood of water devoured and cleansed the earth, and so its contrary, fire, will devour and purify the earth at its end. Moreover, fire is the necessary antidote to the "cooling of charity" (*refrigerium caritatis*) that has befallen the world in its old age.

Because this cleansing is eternal, no creature could bring it about on its own, and thus a higher power must initiate the conflagration. Nevertheless, Bonaventure explains, the effect is produced by means of the natural powers of fire: "inflaming" (*inflammare*), "purging" (*purgare*), "rarefying" (*rarefacere*), and "subtilizing" (*subtiliare*). All things will be subject to this "concourse of fires"—the just will be purged by the fires of purgatory, the wicked tormented by the fires of hell, the elements refined, and the animals and plants consumed by elemental fire. The heavenly bodies will burn with an intense brightness and come to rest.

It may be tempting to parse here an analogy between the spiritual "fire," which purges the just, and the real fire, which refines and consumes the bodies of earth. However, Bonaventure explains with terrible clarity the nature of the fires of purgatory and hell. It must be held, he insists, that the fire of purgatory is a corporeal fire (*ignis corporalis*) that burns the spirit of the sins it carries and causes it to suffer.[72] Because the soul sinned by sinking to the body, it is fitting to divine justice that the punishments of purgatory come from the body and affect the soul. Thus the spirit is burned by a material fire (*ab igne materiali*) in purgatory. The fires of hell are also corporeal, Bonaventure writes, tormenting both the bodies and souls of the damned "in a corporeal place down below" (*in loco corporali deorsum*), and the "smoke of their torments will ascend forever and ever."[73]

These statements leave no refuge for the wicked in metaphor. For the just, however, the effect of corporeal fire on the spirit is, ultimately, good news. The soul is punished for its faults and "relieved of the burden of its guilt" (*reatuum onere alleviatam*). This occurs, Bonaventure explains, either on the basis of some God-given power in the fire, or, more likely, through the interior working of grace with the external fires assisting. He sees, however, the difficulty introduced by claiming that corporeal fire directly affects the incorporeal spirit—and yet does not wish to deny that the corporeal fire itself, in whatever way effected by grace, has a role to play in the cleansing punishment. When the purgation is complete, immediately the purified spirits, "whom the fire of charity lifts up, and who have no impurity of the soul or any guilt to hold them back (*retardans*), necessarily fly away."[74] The purification of the soul is, here again, understood as a contest of forces, the removal of a weight (*impuritas* or *onus reatuum*) that acted as a hindrance to another, greater weight (*caritas*). And this action occurs through (at least the assistance of) corporeal fire, which will envelop the earth and inflame, subtilize, and rarefy all things—that is, will transform all things into itself. Thus the conflagration of the earth appears to achieve the goal of the ordering weight of charity: all things are set in upward motion, bound together, and ultimately brought to rest.

The connection between the affective heat of the soul and the cleansing fire of the cosmos recalls the Stoic identification of the warm *pneuma* that produces changes in bodies with the "craftsmanlike fire" that creates and recreates the cosmos.[75] The resonance here with the Stoic teaching stresses the deep continuity between the movement of souls and the movements of bodies. And just as, for the Stoic philosophers, this fire is both natural and divine, for Bonaventure, too, the affective movement of the all things to God is at the same time natural and gratuitous.[76] But Bonaventure's vision of the final conflagration is at the same time the devastating eschatological realization of Dionysius's erotic cosmos: "We call love the unitive force."[77]

This love, as Bonaventure makes clear, has fully cosmic dimensions, and extends to every aspect of creation. Nevertheless, the rational soul, being immortal and possessed of the image of God in memory, intellect, and will, receives this love in a distinctive and greater mode than other creatures. Bonaventure affirms the Aristotelian distinction between the motion of the soul and the motion of bodies when he argues that, in all cases of corporeal motion, there must be distinguished an agent and patient of motion, but in the case of the will, true self-motion is possible. That is, the will is both the mover and moved, whereas in cases of bodily motion, there is an external agent (whether *place*, or some efficient cause) and the thing that is moved.[78]

Rather than obviating the force of Bonaventure's corporeal analogies for the ascent of the soul toward God, this distinction between self-motion and external motion renders the analogies all the more remarkable. For though the deliberative motion of the soul is unlike the motion of bodies, the highest motion that human beings are capable of (the ascent toward and union with God) most closely resembles the most basic kind of motion in the universe—that of the elements moving toward their natural places. Bonaventure is clear that the will is not subject to coercion: "Since attaining beatitude is not glorious unless it is through merit, and there is no merit in something unless it is done voluntarily and freely, it is fitting that freedom of choice [*libertatem arbitrii*] be given to the rational soul, through the removal of all coercion, for it is of the nature of the will that it in no way can be forced."[79] But while Bonaventure maintains that even the attainment of beatitude is not the result of any coercion of the will, he does, as we have seen, embrace the language of "necessity" in describing the ascent of purified souls to God by the fire of charity—that is, when the agent of motion in the soul is the weight of charity, a gift of the Holy Spirit. It is the sanctifying grace of the Holy Spirit that troubles the basis of the distinction between spiritual motion and bodily motion. The deliberative motion of the will to any number of determinate ends is properly understood as self-motion, in which the agent of motion is the will itself (though this is without doubt dependent on grace in a general sense). When it is a matter of the infused grace of charity bearing the soul upwards, certainly the freedom of the will is not destroyed. Yet in this case the most fitting comparison for this motion is the movement of the elementary bodies toward their natural places. The motion of grace in the soul is, like the inexorable motion of fire to its sphere, both a divine and a natural motion.

CHAPTER 4

Hierarchy and Excess in the
Itinerarium mentis in Deum

This chapter and the next examine Bonaventure's development of the theme of love as unifying fire not only as a vision for the consummation of creation, but also as a medium and goal of Christian devotion in contemplation, prayer, and the practice of charity. In this chapter, I analyze the excessive order of creation and of the soul in *Itinerarium mentis in Deum*, Bonaventure's treatise on the stages of the soul's ascent modeled on the Seraph of Francis's vision at La Verna. In the next chapter, I turn to the relation of the will's self-motion and the movement of affect in Bonaventure's *Life of St. Francis*, and the affective movement that the presentation of Francis's life effects in the reader. Together, I suggest, these two works (albeit, in different ways) lead the reader into a practice of devotion whose goal is the transformation of the affect and the ecstatic erasure of the boundary between nature and grace, interior and exterior, action and passion.

On Mount La Verna

In the crucial, curious prologue to the *Itinerarium mentis in deum* (The Soul's Journey Into God), Bonaventure's enchiridion of Franciscan spiri tual pilgrimage, the author describes the displacement that served as the impetus for the work. He composed the *Itinerarium* in 1259, thirty-three years after Francis of Assisi's death (*transitus*) and just two years after Bonaventure was appointed to "the place of this most blessed father" (*loco ipsius patris beatissimi*) as Minister General of the Friars Minor.[1] Feeling the pressures of his new role as Francis's lieutenant, he was moved by a divine inclination to seek retreat in "a place of rest" (*ad locum quietum*). This was the place in which Francis, too, had sought rest—Mount La Verna, where Francis saw a Seraph, its six wings blazing and affixed to a cross, and received the wounds of Christ's passion. Writing in the first person, Bonaventure reflects on that vision: "In considering this, it appeared to me at once [*statim*] that this vision pointed not only to the uplifting of our father himself in contemplation, but also to the path by which it is reached."[2] A second vision thus occurs in the very place of the first. The exemplary nature of Francis's vision—that is, the path it describes for the reader— appears to Bonaventure *statim*, "on the spot"; the peak of La Verna serves rhetorically as a single point condensing the time of the two visions and the space of the spiritual journey that follows.

Conveniently for historians, this passage provides plausible evidence for the dating of the work and for Bonaventure's appointment as minister general.[3] Yet the passage is just as valuable for the interpretive clues it offers to the theological vision outlined in the work as a whole. By locating the inspiration for the work at Mount La Verna, Bonaventure frames the *Itinerarium* as a spiritual geography and itinerary that describes at once 1) the ecstatic order of the cosmos as the unfolding of God's being in likeness, image, and vestige, and 2) the order of the soul as a hierarchy of powers by which God is revealed and loved. The account of successive illuminations that it traces can be read, in light of this framing, as an account of how the soul is elevated through this order and brought into union with God.

By the year 1259, Francis's Seraphic vision and stigmata were a commonplace legend, one whose theological and scriptural significance Bonaventure would further exploit in his biography of Francis.[4] The body of the Seraph defines the hierarchized and ecstatic space of the *Itinerarium*. The six wings divide the work into six chapters, describing six successive "illuminations" by which the mind is elevated through the contemplation of created things until it reaches its *transitus*—the soul's final "passing over" or "death" in which the acts of the intellect are abandoned, illumination is replaced by darkness, and the soul is immolated with the ardent love witnessed in and made possible by the life and death of Francis.[5] For Bonaventure, the figure of the Seraph is significant not only for the enumerative possibilities of its six wings, but also for its Dionysian position of greatest intimacy to God within the angelic hierarchy and its identification with burning love, as I discussed in Chapter 1. Bonaventure exploits these associations in his description of the soul's *transitus* in a seventh and final chapter of the *Itinerarium*, adumbrated in the Prologue when he identifies the way as "nothing other than through the most ardent love of the Crucified one."[6]

That same love is, not by chance, also the destination of the ascent, a coincidence that renders dynamic—and problematic—the relation between the elevating contemplations of the first six chapters and the consuming affective ecstasy of the seventh. The *Itinerarium* proceeds less as an ordered progression toward a goal than as a series of displacements, culminating not in a fixed destination that can be charted in advance, but in the soul's *excessus* (exceeding) of itself and *ecstasis* (standing outside) of the intelligible in a transformation of its affective power.[7] The desire that draws the soul toward the summit through contemplation of the interior and cosmic hierarchies ends with the silencing of the mind's contemplations and the transformation of the affective part of the soul into God.

The nature of this journey's goal surely indicates something about the path that leads to it. Yet even scholars who have taken seriously the apophasis of knowledge described in the *Itinerarium*'s seventh chapter have often read it as a kind of coda to the spiritual progression of the first six chapters. Responding to a recent article by Gregory LaNave on the structure of the *Itinerarium*, Jay Hammond suggests the importance of the framing of the work.[8] Hammond asks, "How can one accurately understand a text if its introduction and conclusion are ignored?" He offers an illuminating reading of the work in light of the structuring devices that Bonaventure introduces in the prologue that suggest a six-part structure. There are good reasons for this reading, both internal and external to the text. First, the figure of the six-winged Seraph suggests, literally, a six-part body to the text. Moreover, the *Itinerarium*'s six body chapters can be seen as a doubling of a three-part structure that Bonaventure repeats throughout the work. And in its historical context, the six-part progression corresponds to the structure of several similar twelfth- and thirteenth-century guides to prayer, including, most proximately, Richard of St. Victor's *Beniamin Maior*, which undoubtedly informed Bonaventure's own work.[9]

Considering each of these factors in turn, I hope here to build on LaNave and Hammond's work, and take Hammond's suggestion further by asking what difference it makes to the whole that Bonaventure posits a state beyond the sixth contemplation. If, as I suggest, the *transitus* described in

the seventh chapter stands as a distinct stage or state beyond the six contemplations, its purpose is not to add one more stage to a six-fold ascent,
but rather to recast the movement of the whole in terms of the *ecstasis* to
which it leads. Treating this final chapter as the interpretive key to the entire text, I argue, in turn necessitates a re-evaluation of the structure of the
work—and not only that, but indeed a re-evaluation of the very concept
of structure in Bonaventure's spiritual cosmology. To this end, I will first
examine the order that Bonaventure posits within the soul and the role
of desire in its becoming hierarchical. I will then turn to Bonaventure's
elaboration of the hierarchical arrangement of the cosmos as vestige, image, and likeness. Already contained within these discussions of hierarchy,
I will ultimately suggest, is the affective *transitus*, which he outlines in the
seventh chapter of the *Itinerarium*.

   In this way, I contend, Bonaventure's very understanding of hierarchy
—both the hierarchy of the soul's powers and the cosmic hierarchy of vestige, image, and likeness—depends upon a theology of ontological and
spiritual *ecstasis*. The affective *transitus* that Bonaventure describes in the
seventh chapter, then, is not a coda to the *Itinerarium* or even the final
stage. It is rather, along with the prologue, an indication that the *itinerarium* is not the soul's movement through a static hierarchy, but its participation in the ecstatic, self-negating time and space of the Christocentric
cosmos, which is at the same time participation in the passion of Christ
enacted through Francis's wounding vision. As Michelle Karnes rightly
notes, "When it comes to the *Itinerarium*, the line between mysticism and
philosophy is hard to draw."[10] This is true not just because Bonaventure
has melded genres, but because a single conception of hierarchy underlies
Bonaventure's philosophical speculation and his devotional program. The
instant in which Francis's vision occurs on Mount La Verna to Bonaventure *statim* is itself *ecstasis*, where the *transitus*—both passage and death—is
always already taking place.

Ordering Desire

The relation between desire and excess is established early in the *Itinerarium*. In the prologue, Bonaventure locates the starting point of the journey
(*itinerarium*) in the "groans of prayer," by which desire is enkindled in the
soul.[11] Then again at the beginning of Chapter 1, he writes that "prayer is
the mother and the origin of upward movement [*sursum-actionis*]."[12] Here
he explains, with recourse to a citation of Dionysius's *Mystical Theology*,
that ascent must start with prayer because the ascent of the soul is a matter

of the soul exceeding itself, rising above itself, "not by a bodily ascent, but by an ascent of the heart." Yet the soul cannot exceed itself *by itself*: "We cannot be elevated above ourselves unless a superior power lifts us up. No matter how our interior stages may be ordered, nothing will happen if divine aid does not help us. But divine aid comes to those who pray from their heart humbly and devoutly."[13] Ascent begins in affective prayer not as the soul's first act, but as the initial giving over of oneself to the divine agency that enables the soul's movement. Moreover, the fact that ascent cannot occur without divine aid (because ascent entails self-surpassing) means that *ecstasis*, the state of the soul as above or outside itself, is not reserved for the final stage of the *itinerarium*. That is, Bonaventure does not present a series of steps that the soul takes to bring itself to order, at the end of which that order is exceeded. Rather, the entire journey into God is an *ecstasis*, or, better, a series of them. If the six wings of the Seraph entail an ordering of the soul's illuminations from vestige to image, and from image to likeness, Bonaventure is emphatic from the beginning that the entire Seraphic order is set on fire and affixed to the cross.

As Hammond argues, the goal of the *Itinerarium* is peace, understood as "right order,"[14] but it is clear that this is an ecstatic order from beginning to end, an order of movements. The threefold ordering scheme (which Bonaventure then doubles to arrive at six stages) is presented not as a three-step, vertically oriented ladder, but as a movement from without, to within, and finally to above or beyond. The order described and traversed in the *Itinerarium* is oriented around the human soul. And since it is the soul (*mens*)[15] itself that is the wayfarer on this journey, the movement is ecstatic in each of its stages.[16] The soul is never simply "in itself": even (and perhaps especially) its turn inward is ecstatic, since in the inward movement of the journey one discovers the image of God and is thus taken beyond oneself. Outside itself, the wayfaring soul moves through the *vestigia* of God, within itself as an *imago* of God, and finally beyond itself, to the eternal and *spiritualissimum*.

In the progression through this order, desire (*desiderium*) plays an overarching role—as initiator, vehicle, and consummation of the ascent. In the prologue Bonaventure writes that "no one is disposed at all for divine contemplations which lead to mental ecstasies without being, like Daniel, a man of desires [*vir desideriorum*]."[17] And in the final chapter, he explains that the mystery of the *excessus mentis* can be revealed only to those who desire it, "and no one desires it but one who is inflamed to the marrow with the fire of the Holy Spirit whom Christ has sent into the world."[18]

At the same time as it frames the entire journey, desire also has a precise psychological valence for Bonaventure, and in a sense has a specific place among the soul's powers. Early in the *Itinerarium*, Bonaventure lists six powers of the soul: *sensus, imaginatio, ratio, intellectus, intelligentia,* and *apex mentis* or *synderesis scintilla*.[19] This sixfold list is only one of many ways that he enumerates and distinguishes the soul's powers, and this one works here, clearly, to reinforce the Seraphic structure of the work: The six powers may be understood to correspond to the six illuminations of the journey. In this scheme, *desiderium* takes its place in the third power, *ratio*, which corresponds to the contemplation of the rational image of God.

For Bonaventure, this *imago* follows the familiar Augustinian triad of memory, understanding, and will *(memoria, intelligentia, voluntas)*.[20] Because the subject at hand remains the ascent of the soul, Bonaventure explains these powers in terms of their ability to lead the soul back through itself to the eternal Art, the supreme Truth, and the highest Good. Memory holds all things in the soul—past, present, and future; it is not only a depository of things derived from sense, but also a kind of "inner reason" (quoting Augustine) that is able to assent immediately to the first principles of the sciences, "as though it recognizes them as innate and familiar *(tanquam sibi innata et familiaria recognoscat)*."[21] The intellective power *(virtus intellectiva)*—Bonaventure's precise term here for Augustinian *intelligentia*—is the ability to understand terms, propositions, and inferences. Bonaventure describes this power as the process of reducing specific definitions and propositions to more general ones until the intellect arrives at the exemplars of knowable things in the eternal Art. The third power—what Bonaventure calls the "elective power" *(virtus electiva)*—involves three aspects: *consilium, iudicium,* and *desiderium*.[22]

The first of these, *consilium* (commonly translated "deliberation") is the determination of better and worse. This is, Bonaventure explains, in fact a determination about a thing's proximity to what is best, and requires some notion of a highest good *(summum bonum)*. *Iudicium* (judgment) makes a determination about the rightness of something with respect to some higher law. When the soul judges itself, it requires some law higher than itself, and thus depends on a divine law for its operation. The first two aspects of the elective power, then, involve both deliberation and a notion of the highest good. The third aspect is desire *(desiderium)*: "Desire is principally concerned with that which moves it the most. And that which moves it the most is that which is loved the most. And that which is loved the most is to be happy. But happiness is attained only by reaching the best and ultimate end. Therefore, human desire wants nothing but the supreme Good, or that which leads to it or in some way reflects that Good."[23] Desire is that which is always moved by and to the *summum bonum*,[24] a goal that lies well beyond what the soul can reach with its own powers. Bonaventure's discussion of the soul's powers, then, and especially his account of desire in the third chapter, serves less to highlight the role these powers play in ascent than to chart more precisely how human beings are created with the capacity for a grace that exceeds them.

And it is not only human beings who are so created. The cosmic hierarchy also has an essentially ecstatic structure. The fourth stage of ascent—the transformation of the *imago* of God in the mind's powers to the *similitudo* of God in the hierarchized soul—depends on this structure. In the fourth stage, Bonaventure writes, the soul is like someone fallen who lies waiting for the help of another to get up again. In the soul's case, this help comes from the three theological virtues—faith, hope, and love. Bonaventure details the several effects of the clothing of the virtues on the image of the soul. Most significantly, the virtues purify, illumine, and perfect the soul—that is, they make the soul hierarchical according to Dionysius's triple operation. The remainder of the chapter describes this threefold operation. The soul's becoming hierarchical involves the awakening of the five spiritual senses and three ecstasies. Invoking the *Song of Songs*, Bonaventure argues that this awakening is brought about by the lover's desire for her beloved. Here the interlocking analogies make clear that "becoming hierarchical" is both inward and ecstatic, experiential and affective.

The spiritual senses have everything to do with the soul's love for Christ because, as Bonaventure explains, they are capacities for receiving and experiencing Christ the beloved. By faith, the soul recovers the spiritual senses of sight and hearing by which the soul perceives the light and the words of Christ. Hope enkindles the soul's sense of smell (which, according to the analogy, is linked to the capacity of breath) as it yearns to be filled with the inspired Word. In love the soul embraces the Bridegroom and, "receiving delight from him and passing over [*transiens*] to him in ecstatic love [*ecstaticum amorem*], it recovers its taste and touch."[25] In the hierarchy of the corporeal senses common to the thirteenth-century schools, taste and touch are the basest of the senses, the perceptual modes in which bodies (of the perceiver and the perceived) are most implicated. As Bonaventure explains earlier in the *Itinerarium*, what is sublime and luminous enters through sight, while what is solid and earthly enters through touch.[26] Yet here, in describing the spiritual senses, taste and touch are the very senses that love awakens.[27]

Why would something as exalted as the soul's love for the Bridegroom be described through the mode of these most bodily and earthly senses? The embrace of the Bridegroom is above all a matter of taste and touch because these senses involve the closest contact (a contact that can only be conceived, even if analogically, as corporeal) between perceiver and perceived.[28] Thomas Gallus makes a similar point in his Commentary on the *Song* when he writes that the external senses are "models of love because love meets its objects by touching, smelling, and tasting."[29] Yet the spiritual senses of taste and touch signify more than just intimacy for Bonaventure here.[30] Thomas Aquinas explains in the *Summa Theologiae* that touch and taste (the latter being a species of the former) are the most material senses insofar as they are modes in which the body is affected naturally by the object according to its proper quality.[31] For example, a hand becomes hot by touching a hot object. In this way, then, the bodily senses of touch and taste are modes in which external objects act upon the perceiver naturally and materially; that is, they are modes of natural affect.[32] In the embrace of the Lover and the Bridegroom, touch is not only the most intimate apprehension of the soul's object, but the most vulnerable opening of the soul to being affected by and transformed into her Beloved.

With its spiritual senses restored, and the soul able to feel her Beloved, she now assumes the voice of the Solomonic lover. In fact, Bonaventure says, the *Song of Songs* was written for and about this fourth level of ascent, which "no one grasps [*capit*] except one who receives it, for it is more a matter of affective experience [*experientia affectuali*] than of rational considerations."[33] It is at this stage that the soul becomes prepared for three spiritual ecstasies (*mentales excessus*), as performed in the *Song*. The awakening of the spiritual senses leads directly to these ecstasies, in that the fivefold spiritual sensory experience of Christ causes the soul to overflow itself in three ways: through devotion, admiration, and exultation. Bonaventure describes these three ecstasies with the language of the *Song*. In the first ecstasy, the soul is filled with an abundance of devotion, so that it becomes like "a pillar of smoke with the aromas of myrrh and frankincense."[34] In the second, the soul is filled to overflowing with admiration, through which the soul becomes like "the dawn, the moon, and the sun." These three lights correspond to the three illuminations that lift the soul in wonder at the Bridegroom. The third ecstasy occurs through an overabundance of joy or exultation. In this ecstasy, the soul is "filled with delight" and "leans [*innixa*] completely on her Beloved."[35]

The description of these three ecstasies echo Richard of St. Victor's much lengthier discussion of the three alienations of the mind in the

Beniamin Maior—through greatness of devotion, greatness of admiration, and greatness of joy, each of which is described by the same passages of the *Song* that Bonaventure cites here.[36] However, here as so often in the *Itinerarium*, Bonaventure does not borrow without casting his material in a very different light. Richard's text describes three different ways that the mind is lifted above itself and acknowledges that the mind is raised in different ways in different people. "For in order that the author of all goods might commend the gifts of His grace in us, He shows diverse effects from the same thing at diverse times and in diverse persons."[37] Even if Richard suggests at times that the third alienation is higher (or at least more dependent on divine grace) than the others, there is still no sense that the three alienations form an ordered progression of a single soul. Bonaventure, by contrast, describes the three ecstasies as a kind of triple operation, analogous to the other threefold transformations that occur at this stage: the infusion of three theological virtues, the opening of the three senses of scriptural meaning, and, the triad discussed most extensively, the three "hierarchizing" operations of the virtues—purification, illumination, and perfection.[38] Purification corresponds to the ecstasy of devotion, as indicated by the purifying "pillar of smoke." Illumination occurs in the overflowing of wonder, by which the soul becomes like "the dawn, the moon, and the sun." And the ecstasy of joy perfects the soul's delight in Christ, so that she "leans totally on her beloved." In a real sense, then, the ecstasies of the soul are what make the soul hierarchical: "With these [ecstasies] accomplished, our spirit is made hierarchical in order to ascend on high in accordance with that heavenly Jerusalem. No one enters that city unless, through grace, that city has first descended into the heart, as John sees in his *Apocalypse*."[39]

This becoming-hierarchical of the soul is at the same time the reformation of the image into a similitude of God. The opening of Chapter 4 makes this connection through an allusion to the parable of the Good Samaritan from Luke 10, by way of Bonaventure's own commentary on this passage. In his Commentary on Luke, Bonaventure interprets the human race as the man who

> went down from Jerusalem to Jericho, that is to say, from paradise into the world, and fell among robbers; namely, into the power of demons who robbed him of the gifts of grace and wounded him in his natural powers. They left him half-dead in that after the similitude had been taken away only the image remained. . . . That image, nevertheless, was despoiled because of a turning away and wounded because of a turning around.[40]

This is the soul at the beginning of the fourth stage. Like the wounded man, the soul lies waiting on external help to lift it up. In the fourth contemplation, the soul receives faith, hope, and charity from above. These virtues awaken the spiritual senses, through which the soul receives such delights that it overflows itself, lifting it up to the heavenly place which has already established itself in the soul.

More precisely, the soul is established as a heavenly place through the reformation of the *imago*: "The image of our mind therefore should be clothed with the three theological virtues by which the soul is purified, illumined, and perfected. In this way the image is reformed and made to conform with the heavenly Jerusalem and is made a part of the church militant which is the offspring of the heavenly Jerusalem, according to the apostle."[41] Note that in Chapter 3, Bonaventure recalled the Augustinian triad of memory, intellect, and will, which is the created image *through which* the soul contemplates the Trinity. Now here, at the fourth stage, the soul, reformed by faith, hope, and charity, is made into an *imago* of the whole heavenly retinue *in which* God dwells and is contemplated. By the lover's ecstasy the soul is stretched to encompass the heavens, and thus to become "a house of God," a "temple of the Holy Spirit."[42]

Hierarchy and Ascent: Vestige, Image, and Likeness

The "hierarchization" of the soul is thus both a *gradus* of ascent and a radicalization or a reversal of ascent's logic—for the journey of the soul into God shows itself to be the movement of God (and of the cosmic hierarchy) into the soul.[43] This reversal, however, is consistent with the character of incarnational grace. Christ descends in order that the soul might ascend. The movement underscores the passivity of the soul in its own reformation and the role of grace—specifically, the grace of the theological virtues of faith, hope, and charity—through which the soul becomes a dwelling place for the Spirit. The connection between the dwelling place of God and the theological virtues recalls a triad of distinctions that appears throughout Bonaventure's earlier writings as *magister*, though not with complete consistency. Vestige (or trace), image, and likeness (or similitude) are three grades or aspects by which creatures represent God. The second book of the *Breviloquium* contains the most extended account of this triad:

> The created world is like a book in which its maker, the Trinity, is reflected, represented, and read according to three grades of expression, namely, through the modes of vestige, image, and likeness. The aspect

of vestige is found in all creatures, that of the image is found only in intellectual or rational spirits, and the aspect of the likeness is only found in those which are conformed to God [*deiformibus*]. The human intellect is created to ascend these stages, like the steps of a ladder, to the highest principle which is God. This should be understood to mean that all creatures regard and depend on their Creator, and are likened to him in three ways. They may be likened to him as to a creative principle, as to a motive object, or as to an indwelling gift. In the first way all his creatures [*effectus*] are likened to him, in the second way all intellectual creatures [*intellectus*], and in the third way all righteous spirits accepted by God [*acceptus*]. All effects, insofar as they have *being*, have God as their principle. All intellects, insofar as they have illumination, are naturally created to grasp God through knowledge and love, and all righteous and holy spirits are infused with the gift of the Holy Spirit.[44]

Trace, image, and likeness are not only different ways that God is represented in creation; they also constitute the created order and provide a means of ascent or return (*reductio*) to God. According to Bonaventure's summary in Chapter 7, the *Itinerarium* is an elaboration of that order. Just before the final transformation of the *affectus*, Bonaventure writes, "our mind has contemplated [*contuita*] God outside itself through and in the vestiges; within itself through and in the image; and above itself through the similitude of divine light shining down upon us, and in that light insofar as that is possible in our wayfaring state and by the exercise of our mind."[45] This summary indicates that the contemplations of Chapters 1 and 2 occur, respectively, through and in the vestiges of God in creation, those of Chapters 3 and 4 through and in the image of God in the soul, and those of Chapters 5 and 6 through and in the likeness of divine light.

This structuring principle has been well observed by scholars.[46] Yet the unfolding of the triad in the *itinerarium* is not as neat as the summaries made by scholars or by Bonaventure himself. At the fourth stage, Bonaventure describes the point at which the soul is made a hierarchical, God-conformed dwelling of the Spirit infused with the theological virtues. Because this description conforms unmistakably to his description of the *similitudo* in the *Breviloquium* (and in several other places), it would seem that the structuring principle laid out in Chapter 7 is inaccurate. Chapter 4 contains a description of the similitude of God when the summary would lead us to expect a discussion of the image. In fact, Chapter 4 does not mention the similitude as distinct from the image. Has the terminology shifted from the *Breviloquium* to the *Itinerarium*? Or does Bonaventure's own summary misrepresent the contents of the work? While both possibilities must be admitted, the problem deserves further exploration for the light it may shed on Bonaventure's understanding of this triad and of the nature of hierarchy in general.

The conception of the created world as a scale of reflections of God's presence appears throughout Bonaventure's writings. In several of the works dated to his period as *baccalarius* at Paris and regent master of the Franciscan school there, he discusses this scale in terms of the difference between the *vestigium* and *imago* of God in creation. Here, *similitudo* sometimes completes the triad.[47] In all of these writings, it is easy enough to understand how these distinctions structure Bonaventure's descriptions of creation and the soul's ascent to God. What is more difficult to determine is precisely what these distinctions *are*. Or, more to the point, to what do these distinctions *refer*?

Most simply, "shadow," "vestige," and "image" all refer to God and can be understood as different ways of referring to God. In this sense, although they underlie the order of creation, the distinctions of shadow, vestige, image are not degrees of creatures. And although they determine what creatures are, they are not properties of creatures.[48] Bonaventure explains this in the third distinction of the first book in his *Sentences* commentary, and assumes it in later writings. The distinction between *vestigium* and *imago* arises first in the question of whether God is knowable (*cognoscibilis*) through creatures.[49] The fourth argument for the affirmative introduces the principle that "like is known through like." If God is known through creatures, then creatures must be like God (*similis Deo*), and there are different ways that a creature can be like God: as vestige and as image.

In his responses to the objections, Bonaventure considers the ways in which others have (inadequately) explained the distinction between vestige and image. Some, he notes, simply refer the distinction between vestige and image to the distinction between sensible and spiritual creatures.[50] But "vestige" concerns the ways in which the unity, truth, and goodness of God is evident in creatures. And spiritual creatures, certainly no less than sensible ones, evince these perfections; thus spiritual and sensible creatures alike are vestiges of God. Corporeality is therefore not the basis for the degrees of likeness to God. Moreover, every created thing, spiritual and corporeal alike, represents God vestigially in exactly the same degree. Others, Bonaventure continues, understand the distinction between vestige and image as a matter of degree of completeness: A vestige would be a partial representation of God, and an image would represent God as a whole. This is mistaken, he contends, on two counts: Because God is simple, there is no "part" of God to represent. And because God is infinite, no created thing, not even the universe itself, could represent the "whole" of God. Whatever the distinction between the ways of representing God, it is inadmissible to distinguish them based on greater or lesser degrees of completeness.

If an image, then, is not more spiritual than a vestige, and if it is not more complete than a vestige, in what sense does this distinction structure a hierarchy? Bonaventure offers several ways in which the image exceeds the vestige. A vestige refers the creature to God according to the threefold principle of causality (efficient, final, and formal), whereas the image refers the creature to God not only as cause but also as *object* of knowledge and love through the three powers of memory, intelligence, and will. This distinction, however, is based on a prior, and more obvious (*notior*) one: the mode of representing proper to each of these gradations, or what we might, in light of the pervasive spatial language, call Bonaventure's geography of God. Both the vestige and image represent God distinctly, but the vestige represents God from a distance or remove (*in elongatio*); the image represents God *in proximity to God* (*in propinquitate*). Bonaventure situates this discussion of *vestigium* and *imago* immediately after a response to the objection that, because the creature is separated from God by an infinite distance, no progression of steps will ever reach God. He therefore affirms that if by reaching God one means attaining equality with God, then it is true that no creature will ever arrive. But ascent can also refer to beholding the presence of God (*ad aspectum praesentiae*), and in this sense ascent is always already accomplished insofar as everything, by its very creation, leads to God (*quaelibet creatura nata est ducere in Deum*).

The spatial language, therefore, that is so integral to Bonaventure's understanding of the created order helps to clarify the proper referents of the terms "vestige" and "image." These distinctions are nothing *in* creatures any more than they are *in* the human intellect that cognizes them. Rather, they are different ways in which creatures, the human mind, and God are all related to one another, and at the same time they are degrees of proximity between creatures and God. That is to say, they describe relations and not properties or entities. Etienne Gilson's elaboration of these distinctions and the role they play in Bonaventure's thought remains indispensable: The distinctions constitute what Gilson called Bonaventure's doctrine of universal analogy (a term Bonaventure uses in 1 *Sent.* d. 3 for the likeness between Creator and creature).[51] But it may be better to call it a theory of universal anagogy. For the ontological resemblances that ground analogy are themselves grounded in the *reductio* toward which all creation is ordered.

Subsequent discussions of the triad of *vestigium, imago,* and *similitudo* in Bonaventure's writings only make this anagogical dynamic clearer. In the passage from the *Breviloquium* cited previously, Bonaventure compares the distinctions to "rungs of a ladder," upon which "the human mind is designed to ascend step-by-step" to God. The Augustinian distinction between *imago* and *similitudo,* furnished with thirteenth-century distinctions concerning grace, further emphasizes the role of creation in the soul's ascent or *reductio* to God. He explains the rungs of the ladder as degrees of conformity to God, each distinguished by its own triad reflecting the Trinity:

> For a creature cannot have God as its Principle unless it is conformed to Him in unity, truth, and goodness. Nor can it have God as its object unless it grasps Him through memory, intelligence, and will. And it cannot have God as an infused Gift unless it is conformed to Him through faith, hope, and love, the threefold gift. And the first conformity is distant, the second close, and the third most proximate. That is why the first is called a vestige of the Trinity, the second an image, and the third a likeness.[52]

The most intimate conformity—that of the image transformed into a likeness—comes about, as Bonaventure also explains in the *Itinerarium,* through the infused gift of the theological virtues. Yet even in the *Itinerarium,* Bonaventure does not consistently refer to the triad of vestige, image, and likeness.[53] Similarly, in both the *Quaestiones disputatae mysterio trinitatis* and *De reductione artium ad theologiam,* he refers only to vestige and image. Amidst the fluctuations in terms, these passages advance a consistent view that all things have God as their creative principle and reflect God's unity, truth, and goodness; that among creatures, rational beings have God as their object as well as their cause; and as such, they have the capacity to be drawn into God and conformed to God's likeness through infused grace.

Chapter 3 of the *Itinerarium* discusses the image of God in the natural powers of the soul, and Chapter 4 addresses the likeness of God in the reformed powers. Similarly, Bonaventure writes in the *Sentences* commentary that the image concerns the natural and the likeness concerns the gratuitous.[54] Yet the distinction serves only to draw a closer connection between what belongs to nature and what belongs to grace, for it is just such a dichotomy that the dynamic of vestige, image, and likeness forcefully resists. Nature and grace, image and likeness, belong to a single order and movement.[55] Creation is so ordered as to lead the mind, through the operations of its own powers, toward the excess and overcoming of itself. The transformation of the image into the likeness (*similitudo*) through the infusion of the virtues, the *mentales excessus* of the lover, and the hierarchical operations, means that the rational creature is created with a natural desire for intimacy with God that it cannot realize with its own God-given powers. This is what it means to say that the created order is itself an ecstatic order. The triad of vestige, image, and likeness in creation orders the human mind to excess.

The dynamic and ecstatic nature of this created order is reflected in the structure of the *Itinerarium* itself. Bonaventure's summary divides the work into three parts: In the first two stages, the mind contemplates the vestiges of God in creation, in the second two the image of God in itself, and in the final two the likeness of the divine brightness. This threefold structure is evident in the content of the chapters, but the division is not as simple as this summary suggests, and itself reflects the temporal and spatial disordering essential to hierarchy. Just as Chapter 4 (whose heading identifies its subject as the image of God in the soul) describes the infusion of the virtues into the soul, Chapters 2 and 6 also anticipate the stage immediately following. In Chapter 2, contemplation on the vestiges of God in sensible things develops naturally into an exploration of the capacities of the soul to apprehend, take pleasure in, and judge all sensible things. In this way, the inward turn of Chapter 3 is already begun at the previous level. Similarly, in the sixth contemplation, the intellect begins to fail at the consideration of the Trinity: "When in the sixth stage, the mind will have reached the point in which it sees in the first and highest Principle and in the mediator of God and humanity, Jesus Christ. No likeness [*similia*] whatsoever of these things is found among creatures, and they exceed every grasp of the human intellect."[56] Like the delineation of the powers of the soul in Cistercian treatises such as Isaac of Stella's (d. 1169), the stages of contemplation not only touch each other, but even overlap. For Bonaventure, this contiguity becomes the means by which the *transitus* takes place—the lower stages leading, as if inevitably, to the higher, such that excess is entailed in the created order. The staged reflections of God's light which structure the successive illuminations of the soul, then, contain within them the darkness to which they ultimately lead.

Transitus

Adopting Richard of St. Victor's symbolism for the highest stages of contemplation, Bonaventure illustrates the fifth and sixth stages of the *itinera-*

rium with the facing Cherubim seated on the Ark of the Covenant. Here, however, the Ark symbolism is placed within the motif of the tabernacle, with the fifth and sixth stages found at the innermost part of the temple, the Holy of Holies.[57] The two Cherubim are two modes or grades of contemplating the *invisibilia* of God—namely the two names of God, Being and Good. In the first case, the mind contemplates the divine essence; in the second, the persons of the Trinity. Though each may be contemplated individually, only in contemplating together the essence and the persons, the unity and the trinity, the being and the goodness of God, is the mind suspended in the highest wonder (*in admirationem altissimam suspendaris*) and lifted up to the perfection of the mind's illuminations.[58] Contemplating the unity and trinity together, the mind beholds mysteries surpassing the discerning powers (*perspicacitas*) of the intellect. The consummation of the mind's contemplations, in a sense, already entails its own surpassing, and so brings about the *excessus mentis* in which the intellect rests entirely.

The summary of the six contemplations at the beginning of Chapter 7 recalls, especially, the language used to describe the fourth stage: "We have explained now these six considerations, like the six steps to the true throne of Solomon, by which peace is attained. Here the true person of peace [*verus pacificus*] rests in a peaceful soul [*in mente pacifica*] as in an interior Jerusalem."[59] The summary also echoes on several notes the opening invocation of the prologue, in which Bonaventure prays for the peace of Francis, who "was like a citizen of that Jerusalem about which that man of peace . . . says: Pray for those things which are for the peace of Jerusalem. For he knew that there was no throne of Solomon except in peace, since it is written: His place was in peace, and his dwelling in Sion."[60] In the prologue, Bonaventure describes his journey to La Verna, a place of quiet, to find peace. Now nearing the end of the work, Bonaventure's summary reveals how many layers of allegory are condensed into this "place"—the place of Francis's vision, which was at the same time the throne of Solomon in the heavenly Jerusalem. This heavenly Jerusalem, in the course of the soul's ecstatic journey to it, takes place within the soul so that the soul finds this peace within itself and, at the same time, above itself. The celestial hierarchy is imaged in the interior hierarchy, established through the hierarchical operations (purgation, illumination, and perfection) which are ecstasies of the soul in love with Christ. Raised above itself, the soul contemplates God through and in the similitude of divine light.

This is the end of the *itinerarium*, for there is nowhere else for the soul, raised to the height of contemplation, to go. After this point, only death remains, but it is not the journey's destination. For if the consummation of contemplation brings rest, death sets the soul in motion in a different manner. As Bonaventure explains, "Having contemplated all these things, it remains for the soul to transcend and pass over [*transcendat et transeat*] not only the sensible world, but the soul itself."[61] This movement, the *excessus mentis*, is not a stage of contemplation, like the *mentales excessus* of the fourth stage. There, the lover's ecstasies were outside the soul and simultaneously interior to it. Here, by contrast, the phrase *excessus mentis* emphasizes the soul's going out from itself, especially given that the phrase is used interchangeably with the term *transitus*. There is no indication, however, that the difference holds great significance for Bonaventure; his use of the terms is fluid. The Chapter 7 heading identifies the topic as *de excessu mentali et mystico*.

Moreover, Bonaventure discusses the going out or passing over of the soul, which is the subject of Chapter 7, throughout the *Itinerarium*. In the prologue, his first gloss on the Seraph of Francis's vision identifies the six wings as six *illuminationum suspensiones*. Bonaventure writes that the cruciform Seraph of Francis's vision indicated the *suspensio* of the father in contemplation (*ipsius patris suspensionem in contemplando*).[62] The father is Francis lifted up in ecstasy, but Francis's *suspensio* is itself conformed to Christ suspended on the cross—just as Paul, carried off (*raptum*) to the third heaven, could say that he was nailed to the cross with Christ.[63] By identifying the six stages as six *suspensiones*, the prologue declares the entire ascent—from the contemplation of corporeal natures to the final passing over—to be the *via crucis*. The lexical connection is completed in the seventh chapter, when the soul in ascent repeats the words of Job: "My soul (*anima*) chooses hanging (*suspendium*), and my bones death."[64] *Suspensio* leads to *suspendium*; the groans of prayer that initiate the ascent of the soul anticipate its consummation on the cross.

The layered scriptural and Christological allusions in the seventh chapter perform the *excessus* depicted there. In ecstasy, nothing is simply what it is; every image empties out into another. The soul, like the language used to describe it, is beside itself. The movement of ascent, the *transitus*, is the rapture of Paul, which is the passing through the Red Sea, which is the Passover, which is the *pascha*, the sacrifice of Christ on the cross, which is— in a word whose shock is undiminished by the density of allusion—simply death.[65] *Moriamur*, exhorts Bonaventure: "Let us die, then, and enter into this darkness."[66] The darkness of death is the end of the illuminations and the consuming heat of desire: "not light, but the fire that inflames totally and carries one [*transferentem*] into God through excessive fervor and the most burning affections."[67] In his *Sentences* commentary, Bonaventure distinguishes the cognitive and affective parts of the soul with reference to the light and heat of fire, respectively.[68] He recognizes an analytical distinction between the heating and illuminating properties of fire, even if those properties are always naturally concurrent in act. Here those same properties appear again, this time in the uncanny image of a fire that gives heat without light. At the end of the soul's journey into God, the properties of light and heat, of intellectual knowledge and affective desire, are separable— and in fact must be so if the soul's ascent is to be consummated: "In this passing over, if it is to be perfect, all intellectual operations [*intellectuales operationes*] must be abandoned, and our *apex affectus* must be entirely carried into [*transferetur*] and transformed into God."[69]

As I discussed in Chapter 1, "intellectual operations" is a quotation from the opening of Dionysius's *Mystical Theology*, which Bonaventure goes on to cite at length: "Abandon sense and intellectual operations [*intellectuales operationes*], sensible and invisible things, and all nonbeing and being, and, insofar as possible, be restored, unknowing [*inscius*], to unity with the one who is above all essence and knowledge [*scientiam*]."[70] Bonaventure's statement that intellectual operations must be abandoned and the *apex affectus* transferred into God functions then as a gloss on the Dionysian passage. The Dionysian reference makes clear that the *excessus mentis* is truly a state of unknowing. Affect is introduced not to reinstate the knowledge that Dionysius so emphatically excludes from union, or to locate union in another power of the soul, but to give an account of the dynamics of union beyond knowing—a union that, in Bonaventure's reading of Dionysius, is thoroughly Christological. This union beyond knowing is the soul's participation in Christ's passion. In fact, given the importance and the extent of Bonaventure's citation of Dionysius (the *Itinerarium* is, after all, bookended with quotations of the *Mystical Theology*), Bonaventure's work may be understood as a kind of extended exegesis of Dionysius as much as it is an exegesis of Francis's vision. Or, better, the *Itinerarium* is Bonaventure's interpretation of the *Mystical Theology* by way of Francis's Seraphic vision— which is, at the same time, a vision and enactment of Christ's passion. The excess that marks each stage of the *Itinerarium* and prefigures the final passing over shows that, for Bonaventure, the Dionysian union beyond knowledge is entailed in and enabled by the ecstatic nature of hierarchy.

Bonaventure has long been counted, largely on the basis of this passage, in the tradition of "affective" readings of Dionysius, facilitated by the traditional association of the Seraphim (whom Dionysius associates only with fire) and ardent love.[71] To the extent that this manner of reading constitutes a tradition, Bonaventure indisputably belongs to it. And yet, as I have suggested, for Bonaventure the characterization of the *excessus mentis* as affective reflects not merely a priority for love over knowledge, but represents an attempt to work out the dynamics of Dionysian hierarchy in the cosmos and in the soul. For Bonaventure, desire is the agent of both the soul's movement into God and its own transformation. Yet precisely through the image of fire by which this desire is depicted, Bonaventure insists that such desire is no possession or activity of the soul. *Qui quidem ignis Deus est*: "It is God who is this fire." Fire is the most active element, and the one most responsible for motion. Thus to identify God with fire here is to name God as the agency that inhabits and moves the soul, as well as the desire that consumes it.[72] This divine desire is cruciform: "It is Christ who starts the fire with the intense heat of his burning passion."[73] In his final exhortations, Bonaventure invites the pilgrim soul to silence all its wants—using the word *concupiscentiis* rather than *desideriis*. For desire is not a having, like *conscientia*, or an operation of the soul, like contemplation; it is the grace of Christ's passion *taking place* in the soul.[74] This desire can be enlarged and perfected *in excessus mentis* only because, from the very beginning of ascent, it always already exceeds the soul.

In Bonaventure's account, the same desire that finally overwhelms the soul has been, in fact, innate to the soul all along. When all the powers of the soul are silenced or abandoned in the "pacified soul" (*in mente pacifica*), desire remains because it is not a power of the soul. It is, both at the beginning and end of ascent, the capacity of the soul to be moved above and outside itself, not by its own movement but by the drawing of its beloved. The transfer of the affect into God means the surrender of all the soul's higher operations—a ceasing of activity that is granted to the soul as its long-desired death. The soul's powers are ordered toward their own death, just as the gradations of God's presence in creation are ordered toward their own excess. This desire for death is the ecstatic force of the soul's journey, and the principle that establishes the structure of the *Itinerarium* as an ecstatic order, that is, a hierarchy.

CHAPTER 5

The Exemplary Bodies of the *Legenda Maior*

With the language of death in the final passage of the *Itinerarium*, Bonaventure insists that the *excessus mentis* is not simply a matter of abandoning intellectual operations in favor of affective operations. The *transitus* into God involves, after all, a *transformation* of the highest part of the *affectus*, and the drawing of that transformed affect into God. What does this transformation entail if it is not simply the death of the intellect? What must occur within the affect for the journey to reach its end? The answer to this question (insofar as an explanation is possible for what Bonaventure describes as "mystical and most secret") gets at the heart of the ecstatic death that the *Itinerarium* depicts. It involves, I suggest, not only the abandonment of the intellect, but also, and more radically, the abandonment of what Bonaventure properly calls the will (*voluntas*).

Though the seventh chapter of the *Itinerarium* contains no detailed discussion of the nature of affect, Bonaventure's writings on the various aspects of the soul's affective part lay the groundwork for—and are consistent with—the transformation by fire that occurs there. Making that case will require a look at Bonaventure's understanding of the will (*voluntas*) and how it relates to the affective part of the soul (*pars affectiva*, or simply *affectus*) on the one hand, and his understanding of free choice (*liberum arbitrium*) on the other.[1] The first part of this chapter examines Bonaventure's theory of the *voluntas* and how it relates to the higher part of the *affectus*. The second part examines a very different kind of account of affective transformation—but one, I argue, that is consistent with and helps to elaborate the vision of affective abandonment witnessed in the *Itinerarium*. The *Legenda Maior*, Bonaventure's longer *vita* of Francis of Assisi, depicts in the person of Francis the abandonment of the will for which the affective part of the soul is created. It culminates in the inflaming and death of Francis's soul, transforming him into an exemplar of affective fervor that is witnessed in his wounded and dying body.

Nature and Necessity in the Affective Part of the Soul

In order for the distinction between *liberum arbitrium*, the *voluntas*, and the *affectus* even to be legible in English, the misleading translation of *liberum arbitrium* as "free will" must first be abandoned.[2] This translation, among its other faults, obscures the painstaking distinctions by which medieval theologians sought to understand the rational capacities and limits of human beings—both intellectual and voluntary—to deliberate, judge, decide, and act.[3] The translations of *liberum arbitrium* as "free choice" or "free decision" avoid the confusion that the term "will" introduces and better capture the sense of *arbitrium* as an activity or capacity to act, rather than as a distinct power.

Augustine had declared that free choice refers to the soul as a whole. For Bonaventure this means that free choice spans the most basic division of the soul's powers, the cognitive and the affective.[4] As Bonaventure writes in the *Breviloquium*, "Freedom from compulsion is nothing else than a faculty of will and reason, which are the principal powers of the soul."[5] The name itself implies this: *libertas* belongs properly to the will (*voluntas*), wherein lies the capacity for self-motion and command (*imperium*) of all the other powers; whereas *arbitrium*, which is synonymous with judgment (*iudicium*), belongs to the cognitive part, whereby the soul is able to reflect upon its own act and discern right from wrong.[6] To simplify a long and complex discussion, Bonaventure defines free choice as a habit or faculty belonging to reason and will (distinguished from each in some way, but without constituting an entirely separate power). By it the soul acts deliberately and free from external coercion. Free choice is begun in reason and completed in the will, and for this reason is properly said to be in the will more than it is in reason.

Even though free choice spans the entire soul, it does not, Bonaventure clarifies, encompass the whole of reason or will. After concluding that free choice comprehends the reason and will, he deals with two arguments that reason and will are each more than that which properly pertains to free choice. Bonaventure concedes the point and offers a clarification:

> To the objection that free choice does not comprehend the whole
> of reason nor the whole of the will, it must be said that this is true.
> Rather, free choice comprehends the cognitive power only insofar as it
> is joined to the affective, and it comprehends the affective insofar as it
> is joined to the cognitive. Thus it can be called a "deliberative affect,"
> or a "voluntary deliberation." And therefore, since "reason" refers to
> the cognitive power as it is ordered to the affective, and "will" refers to
> the affective power as it is regulated and made rational by the cognitive,
> thus it is better to say that free choice is a faculty of the will and reason
> than a faculty of the intellect and the affect.[7]

Free choice, then, is simply the name for what happens when the soul's powers act in concert. But the response reveals a significant aspect of Bonaventure's understanding of the division of the soul: the will is not coextensive with affect, just as reason is not coextensive with intellect. Bonaventure acknowledges some affective capacity that is not *voluntas*—that is, a way of looking at affect in itself and not joined to intellect. What does this encompass? The objection that occasioned the reply gives an indication: "Our will is unchangeable [*impermutabilis*] with respect to some things; but whatever our free choice desires, it desires changeably [*permutabiliter*]."[8]

As Bonaventure explains at length in the twenty-fourth distinction of the same book of his commentary, the affective part of the soul can be divided, in a sense, into two aspects or activities—one in which the soul necessarily and unchangeably desires the Good or beatitude; and one in which the will, in conjunction with reason, deliberates and chooses among different proximate goods.

> It must be conceded that the natural will and the deliberative will are
> a single power, which is called natural or deliberative according to its
> mode of moving. The power by which I desire beatitude is the same
> as that by which I desire a virtue for doing this or that good thing
> ordained to beatitude. In desiring beatitude, it is called natural, since its
> desire is unchangeably inclined to beatitude. But as it desires to do this
> or that good, it is called deliberative, and according to the judgment of
> reason it is able to incline to the contrary.[9]

The idea that reason is capable of contraries was a common scholastic assumption derived from Aristotle.[10] For medieval theologians, "contrary" is used broadly to mean contingent existents: the soul is free to choose among things that could be otherwise. For Bonaventure here, the emphasis is on possible acts that the soul may elect to perform. By contrast, the soul is not free to choose beatitude as the object of its desire—not because it is constrained to do so, but because the Good in which beatitude consists has no contrary, evil being only a privation of the Good.[11] Thus the distinction of the affective part on the basis of different modes of moving is itself based on a difference in the objects of desire. The Good is not one among a number of desirable objects but the source and end of every desire.[12]

This same distinction appears in Bonaventure's explanation of synderesis discussed in Chapter 1. Here, however, the question concerns whether the natural and deliberative wills are essentially distinct powers. And in arguing the negative position, Bonaventure encounters the difficulty of demonstrating how the will can be rational and yet incapable of contraries in its natural movement. The arguments for the affirmative state explicitly the theological risk that lurks in all of Bonaventure's discussions of synderesis and the natural will: How is this innate and immutable desire for the good—the spark by which an otherwise fallen human nature remains upright—distinguishable from nonhuman varieties of desire, either simple natural attraction or brute animal instinct? If there is in the affective part of the soul both an immutable and an indeterminate will, then there must be two wills, the first irrational, the second capable of rational deliberation. The division, as the argument goes, would safeguard the rational nature of the deliberative will against the apparent irrationality of natural instinct, and, by extension, the uniquely human character of human desire: "The power that we have in common with brute animals cannot be the same as the power by which we differ from them. But we are like brute animals with regard to natural appetite, and we differ with regard to our rational appetite. For just as brute animals naturally desire the preservation of their being, so do we too desire this."[13]

Though it is not named here, the question invokes something like the Stoic conception of *oikeiosis*, the natural and nonrational desire for self-preservation found in human infants and animals alike.[14] In response, Bonaventure distinguishes two senses of "natural." On the one hand, there is a way of distinguishing natural and deliberative desires on the basis of different objects, "such as when one is desirable only by a rational substance, and another object is desired by an animal substance."[15] But on the other hand, when it is a matter of a common object that is desired naturally or deliberatively, the two desires are essentially one, and differ only in their mode of desiring. In this sense, "we say that synderesis is a natural will which naturally inclines and incites us toward the honest good and murmurs against evil. And we call the deliberative appetite the will by which, after deliberation, we cling sometimes to a good, sometimes to evil."[16] Thus, the natural will (which humans share in common with nonrational animals) constitutes a natural appetite directed toward a good that is desirable to a creature with or without reason.[17]

The mention of synderesis indicates that there is another way that desire can be natural, while also remaining essentially rational. A certain logic opposes this, too, as evidenced by the second objection: As Aristotle says, the rational powers are capable of contraries, that is, of choosing this or that object of intellection or desire. But to be moved naturally to an object is to be moved singly (*uniformiter*) and to be moved rationally is to be moved changeably (*vertibiliter*). In this way, the argument implies, a naturally moved desire is by definition not a rationally moved desire.

The force of Bonaventure's refutation to this objection is difficult to register, but it helps to clarify the stakes of the question:

> The rational will is ordained to *something* such that it in no way desires
> its contrary, as is clear in the ordination of our will to beatitude and
> felicity. And although it is determinately inclined to beatitude, this
> very same power of the will is nevertheless indeterminate with regard
> to many kinds of desirable objects, so that it is made to be moved to
> opposites. And for this reason the power is natural, while not ceasing
> to be rational and deliberative.[18]

The response clarifies the definition of "rational," which means, for the present purposes, to be determined toward beatitude and free to deliberate on everything else. It is clear now that the will must be essentially one— for if it were truly divided into a natural and deliberative power, then there would be an irrationality at the center of human desire. The end for which human beings were created as rational beings would be itself irrational, the object of an irrational appetite.

This is, as Bonaventure insists, not the case: The will is wholly rational because it is capable of contraries, even if not in every case. A purely natural power is one that cannot be otherwise. Fire, to use Bonaventure's example here, heats and illumines.[19] It cannot do otherwise. The will is rational because it is capable of contraries in most cases. But the surprising fact remains that the rationality of human beings' desire comes into question precisely where the ultimate and highest end of human rationality is concerned. If humans were to desire this ultimate end in such a way that they could not deliberate as to proximate ends—if the natural will were distinct from the deliberative will—then human desire for beatitude would be akin to the physical properties of the simple bodies.

Yet though the natural and deliberative wills are not, in fact, two powers, they are two diverse motions. The natural will is moved immutably and necessarily—rationally, yet without the deliberative and cognitive operations of reason. If *liberum arbitrium* is the operation of the will insofar as it is joined to cognition, then, it would seem to follow that the natural movement toward beatitude is not, strictly speaking, an operation of *liberum arbitrium*. The will is not coerced into desiring beatitude. But neither is the soul free to deliberate concerning the natural desire for the Good that is the end of all human activity, however much it may deliberate as to whether or not to assent to this desire.[20] Yet as Bonaventure insists in the *Breviloquium*, free choice and beatitude have everything to do with each other: "Attaining beatitude is not glorious unless it is through merit, and there is no merit in something unless it is done voluntarily and freely."[21]

How can beatitude be the sole object about which the soul does not deliberate, and at the same time be the end and glory of the soul's power of free choice? And what kind of moral pedagogy does such a seemingly paradoxical end require? When Bonaventure takes up these questions in the following distinction, he turns again to animals.

Free Choice and the Interiority of Desire

It is telling that the first question that Bonaventure treats on the subject of *liberum arbitrium* is whether the faculty is found in non-rational animals. Augustine's declaration that "When we speak of free choice, we are speaking not of a part of the soul, but of the whole" (a key *auctoritas* for scholastic reflection on the subject) positions free choice as the very definition of spiritual substance, in which humans and the higher intelligences participate by virtue of their rationality. So the question of free choice in brute animals is not an oblique opening. Rather, it gets to the heart of what free choice is and what it does theologically. And Bonaventure's resolution of the question is unequivocal: "It must be said that free choice is without a doubt found in rational substances alone."[22]

In his conclusion, Bonaventure explains that to affirm *liberum arbitrium* in rational creatures is to affirm two things: their special liberty and their distinctive capacity for judgment or choice. On the first count, to be "free" means, on the one hand, to be unconstrained in desiring and in fleeing an object of the concupiscible or irascible appetite. Anything that can be desired or fled can be so on account of three types of desiderata: the delectable or pleasurable, the agreeable or convenient, and the Good itself, that is, the *bonum honestum*. While irrational animals can desire or flee an object on account of its delectability or agreeability, only rational substances are capable of desiring the Good itself—that is, the intrinsic and highest good that is the object of synderesis. The rational substance is the only one that can be said to be truly free, since it is unconstrained with respect to all three genera of desiderata. Thus, in an apparent paradox, what makes rational substances free is their necessary and natural inclination to the Good. It is not actually a paradox in Bonaventure's account, however, because the necessity of desiring the good is no restriction on the soul's liberty; it is, in fact (and following Augustine), the very condition of liberty.

At the same time, to be free means to be totally unconstrained not only with respect to the object of desire, but also with respect to the act of desire. While animals may be able (or can be trained) to restrain themselves from acting on their appetites, they cannot, Bonaventure assumes, restrain the interior act of desire itself; "And so if they love (*amant*) something, they are unable *not* to love it." What appears as self-restraint in irrational animals will always turn out to be a constraint of some feared outcome (punishment, for example): "And this is why John of Damascus says that 'they are more acted upon than acting (*magis aguntur quam agant*),' because the agent of restraint in animals is always external to them."[23] Rational beings, by contrast, can restrain not only the exterior act of desire, but even the interior desire. The rational will can choose to stop loving something it previously loved, without any external stimulus or threat provoking the change. That is to say, the rational will can truly restrain *itself*, and this capacity for self-reversion is crucial to the distinction between rational and irrational appetite. Bonaventure cites Anselm to the effect that the rational will is "a self-moving instrument," and maintains that even though animals seem to move from some intrinsic cause, the interior appetite arises in every case from an exterior object rather than true self-motion.[24]

Accordingly, both with respect to objects and acts of the appetite, a certain notion of interiority defines true voluntary liberty. With respect to the object of desire, only the rational and thus truly free creature is able to desire the intrinsic good of something, as opposed to its goodness "for me" as a source of pleasure or advantage. With respect to the act of desire, the rational will has control over its own interior impulses; no outside force need act upon the will for its movement. A similar interiority and the capacity for self-reversion also characterize the second of the two words in free choice (*liberum arbitrium*), which, Bonaventure argues, belongs properly to rational substances alone.

> Arbitration [*arbitrium*] is the same as judgment [*iudicium*], at whose command [*nutum*] the other virtues are moved and obey. And "to judge" with a complete accounting [*secundum rationem completam*] is proper to that which discerns between the just and the unjust, and between what is proper to oneself and what is proper to another. And no power knows (*novit*) what is just and unjust except the one which participates in reason and which is made to recognize (*cognoscere*) the Highest Justice, from which comes the rule of every law.[25]

The power that participates in reason is the mind, which is the image of God, and which alone is able to know itself and its own act: "And no power that is bound to matter ever knows itself, nor is turned back upon itself."[26] Because the rational substance alone among the powers of the soul is not bound to matter, then only reason is capable of self-reversion, and is thus capable of judging what is proper to oneself and what is *alienus*.

The Quaracchi editors attribute this assertion to the *Liber de Causis*, a digest and paraphrase of Proclus's *Elements of Theology* that was read under the authority of Aristotle in the medieval schools.[27] This indirect invocation of the Proclean understanding of *nous* as the self-reverting principle indicates that interiority, as a capacity for self-reversion through self-knowledge and self-motion, is central to the conception of rationality and of the *voluntas* as the rational appetite. In this sense, a natural motion of the will is not contrary to reason, insofar as the inclination to the good, while not itself subject to deliberation or error, is innate to the soul, fully intrinsic to the will that desires it. The self-determining character of the will is thus reconciled to the necessary movement toward the good, insofar as the object of desire is not external to the soul itself.

This "Neoplatonic" or "Augustinian" gesture is not a departure from Aristotle. Even leaving aside the question of Proclus's own "Aristotelianism," as well as the Aristotelian attribution under which Proclus's words circulated, Bonaventure is careful to uphold the Aristotelian dictum that rationality is capable of contraries. The second argument for attributing free choice to animals observes that "a free power is one that is capable of opposites, and in brute animals there is a power to do opposing things, since sometimes they show kindness, sometimes ferocity; sometimes they are willful, and sometimes they respond and come."[28] To this Bonaventure responds that animals clearly are not able to be moved to all opposites, "but only those which are below the dignity of free choice." Free choice properly respects the *bonum honestum*, the same good that is also the proper object of synderesis.

However, although they have the same object, free choice and synderesis (or the natural will to the good) are not identical. The natural and the deliberative wills, after all, are not distinguished according to their objects, but by their mode of moving toward that object. This is how the honest Good can here be classed as an *oppositum*. It is not that the Good itself has a contrary, but rather that the free soul may choose whether or not to pursue a particular act toward that Good. The desire for this Good is always present, yet the merit of attaining beatitude consists in choosing the acts and the objects that will lead the soul to the Good it seeks. The will wills rightly when it consents to its own most fundamental desire.

The paradox, the point at which opposites coincide, is this desire—as desire for God's presence is never, as the *Itinerarium* makes clear, simply one's own. The will's self-consent (so to speak)—the fulfillment of the soul's capacity for free choice and reversion of the rational will to itself—is a state of being moved wholly by the soul's natural desire for the Good.[29] And to desire the Good, as the whole of the *Itinerarium* attests, is a movement within and ultimately above oneself, an ascent of the mind toward its own *excessus*. In this ecstasy, deliberations cease. Thus, the will's self-control comes to resemble nothing so much as the complete abandonment of that self-control to the Good, the object of the soul's most intimate and most excessive longing.[30]

If the distinction between rational will and irrational appetite is measured in the distance from an interior impulse to an external attraction, then the ecstatic character of the soul's desire—a desire which is both internal to the soul and which lifts the soul out of itself—cannot be understood in any straightforward way as rational. Animal affections are "more acted upon than acting." Divine desire, at the same time complete interiority and complete exteriority, would seem for Bonaventure to be a state in which being acted upon and acting are the same movement.[31]

Carried by Desire: Francis and the Legenda Maior

In the previous chapter, I suggested that because of the analogical structure of creation and the ecstatic character of desire, the transformation of affect that occurs in the *excessus mentis* is always already underway from the very beginning of ascent. That is, the soul, insofar as it is constituted by the desire for the good into which it is ultimately consumed, exceeds itself even as it remains possessed of its powers. If so, then according to the Seraphic movement of the *Itinerarium*, the transformation of the *affectus* that occurs in ecstatic union is already begun *in statu viatoris*. And the will's self-motion, ordained naturally and determinately to beatitude, is always also a kind of being moved. Given the prevalence of this theme in Bonaventure's exposition of Francis's Seraphic vision in the *Itinerarium*, it is not surprising that this dynamic also appears in his account of Francis's life, the *Legenda Maior*.

The remainder of this chapter examines Bonaventure's depiction of Francis in the *Legenda*. Generically, Bonaventure's hagiography is far removed from his early scholastic speculations on free choice and the will. But I examine these two disparate sources together in order to demonstrate their affinities on a theological level. In both accounts, what Bonaventure reveals is the paradoxical coincidence of activity and passivity, the surprising but not inexplicable torsion of inner and outer effected by the divine origin and goal of human beings' natural capacities. Nature, in Bonaventure's metaphysics, is after all divine, and the identity of these two poles keeps in motion the hierarchies that the distinction between nature and grace underwrites. As I suggested earlier, in Bonaventure's accounts of free choice and the will, the ecstatic nature of desire upsets the distinction between interior self-motion and external, corporeal motion, such that the consummation of self-motion is its becoming external motion. If this is so, then the progressive perfecting of the soul should manifest itself in some way, should become, in other words, external. This is precisely what takes place, I will argue, in Bonaventure's depiction of Francis's life—his effusive compassion, his attachment to nonrational animals, and his long, spectacular death, his ardent desire literally transforming him into a corpse, a martyr whose lifeless form witnesses the progressive perfection and manifestation—the embodiment—of his love.

By the end of Bonaventure's *Legenda*, it is clear that he has positioned the work as a kind of companion or hagiographical counterpart to the *Itinerarium*, echoing its seven-stage structure, whereby "through six stages you were led to the seventh in which at last you have rest."[32] Though the stages described in Francis's life do not correspond one-to-one to the stages of the soul's ascent in the *Itinerarium*, the seventh stage in which the affections are inflamed and transformed finds a clear resonance with Francis's seventh stage. This is the ecstatic Seraphic vision that leaves his body marked with the death he undergoes in taking on Christ's passion.[33] Both the parallels in Bonaventure's own text and the exemplary nature of Francis's life and spiritual death invite the reader to examine how the desire that transforms the soul is manifested in Francis's disposition and

actions. In other words, Bonaventure frames the *Legenda Maior* as a model
of what a soul carried along by desire toward God looks like.

For this reason, the *Legenda* deserves attention alongside Bonaventure's other works outlining the dynamics of the soul's natural affection for
God.[34] The *Legenda*, however, is more complicated as a source for Bonaventure's thought. Bonaventure was the third biographer of Francis, after
the two *vitae* of Thomas of Celano and the *vita* of Julian of Speyer. And
Bonaventure relied heavily on these previous accounts for his own, in many
cases simply reproducing entire passages. Thus the question of Bonaventure's authorial voice in the *Legenda* is a complicated one[35]—and rendered
all the more complicated by the circumstances surrounding Bonaventure's
compilation of the work (which included heightening divisions within the
order regarding Francis's intentions for the friars minor).[36] These authorial questions, however, do not discount the *Legenda* as a source for Bonaventure's thought, but rather make particularly visible the imbricated and
situational nature of authority in all medieval theological works. Generic
conventions, institutional exigencies, and the presence of other authorial
voices in the text are constitutive of all of Bonaventure's writings. Reading
them well is not a matter of discerning his authentic voice behind these
circumstances, nor it is simply a task of explaining every assertion as a
function of those authorial voices.

Rather than searching for the authentically Bonaventurean thought in
his compilation of Francis's life, I suggest that the text as a whole be read for
the ways in which it complicates and amplifies the ideas I have been tracing in Bonaventure's other works thus far. This involves, then, an exploration of how Francis's desire for God and his will to the good appear in the
text. In this view, the generic differences between the *Legenda* on the one
hand and the *Itinerarium* and Bonaventure's university texts on the other
are paramount. In the *vita*, the pedagogical medium is neither the scholastic *quaestio* nor the mnemonic six-winged figure of the Seraph, but the
embodied actions and appearance of a holy man. This is not a claim for the
text's greater realism or relative lack of allegorization, but rather for a different form of theological expression. Because the subject is the person of
Francis, desire in the *vita* can only appear in and through the human body.
Perhaps one of the most remarkable aspects of the *Legenda* is its exploration
of the ways in which the body *bears* the affections of desire and compassion.
Francis's body is not only the sign of his ecstatic love—in the form of the
stigmata of Christ's passion—but the site upon which it is enacted.

In the prologue, Bonaventure gestures to the end of Francis's life, in
which he was "given an angelic office, and was totally inflamed with a

Seraphic fire. Like a hierarchic man, he was carried up [*sursum vectus*] in a fiery chariot."[37] Through the invocation of the Seraph and the description of Francis as a *vir hierarchicus* (a man whose soul has been made hierarchical through the threefold operation of purgation, illumination, and perfection), Bonaventure frames Francis's life in terms of the Dionysian ascent in the celestial hierarchy. In this way, he immediately establishes a link to the threefold Dionysian framework of his other writings, including not only the *Itinerarum*, but also *De Triplici Via* and the later *Collationes in Hexaemeron*.

Francis's angelic nature is not realized only at his stigmatization and death, however.[38] As the prologue goes on to explain, "while living among human beings he imitated angelic purity, by which he was made an example for perfect followers of Christ."[39] And though the story Bonaventure relates of Francis's life is one of progressive transformation, he establishes at the beginning of the narrative that the qualities that ordained Francis to an angelic office toward the end of his life were present from an early age.

In the first chapter, Bonaventure writes that even as a young man, Francis's heart was filled with a "generous compassion [*miseratio liberalis*] for the poor," such that when, on one occasion, after ignoring a beggar, he realized what he had done and ran to the man. Francis then resolved never to refuse a beggar again, and especially if that beggar appealed to divine love. He kept this promise and "merited a great increase of love and grace in God."[40] Here the interplay between Francis's inborn affective disposition and his great merit in doing good is established early in his life, and at the very beginning of Bonaventure's account. This disposition is moved not only by the sight of poverty but also at the sound of God's name: "Later, when he had perfectly put on Christ, he would say that even while remaining in his worldly habit, he was almost never able to hear someone mention divine love without being changed in his heart [*sine cordis immutatione*]."

As described here, Francis's compassion for the poor and his special affection for the love of God are rooted in a single inborn disposition. In striking terms Bonaventure states that this disposition was natural to Francis, present in him before his perfection by grace: "He possessed an inborn sympathy, which was doubled by the infused holiness of Christ. Therefore his soul melted [*liquescebat*] for the poor and infirm, and he extended his affection [*affectum*] even for those to whom he was not able to extend his hand."[41] Here Bonaventure clearly distinguishes a natural affective tendency from the superadded (*superinfusa*) love, which intensifies and perfects Francis's innate compassion, extending the reach of his affection.

That Francis's life bears witness to the unity of love of God and compassion for God's creation is a hallmark of devotion to Francis, both medieval and modern. But reading the *Legenda* alongside Bonaventure's other writings about the *affectus*, it becomes clear just how deep that connection runs in Bonaventure's understanding of creation and the nature of the soul. As he writes, "True holiness, which according to the Apostle is good for all things, so filled Francis's heart and penetrated his flesh [*viscera*] that it seemed to have claimed [*vindicasse*] the man of God totally to its rule. This is what drew [*agebat*] him to God through devotion, transformed him into Christ through compassion, inclined [*inclinabat*] him to his neighbor through lowering himself, and refashioned him to a state of innocence through the universal reconciliation of every creature."[42] The same spirit that carried Francis to God and inclined him to his neighbor also restored in him the original rectitude of creation. All of the language here is reminiscent of Bonaventure's descriptions of the movement of synderesis—a movement that lifts the soul to God and inclines it to every Good as such (the *bonum honestum*), and is that by which human beings remain upright as they were before sin. Bonaventure presents Francis as one whose natural affect was so strong, or whose will was so bent back upon his inborn love for God, that he seemed to be driven entirely by this natural affective spark. Not incidentally, it is this same Francis who is depicted earlier as praying incessantly with the "unutterable groanings" of the spirit—groans which Bonaventure in his *Sentences* commentary attributes to synderesis.

For all of the displays of virtue and good works that appear in the *Legenda*, the picture that emerges of Francis is of one who "is more acted upon than acting," with passive verb forms repeatedly used to underscore the ease with which Francis is moved by his desire for God and for the poor. As I suggested in the beginning of this chapter, free choice, a capacity whose hallmark is the uniquely rational ability to restrain interior impulses, is paradoxically perfected in the inability to restrain the soul's most deeply rooted affective impulse. In the *Legenda*, likewise, the question of Francis's restraint is raised on several occasions. In the first chapter Francis is praying alone when Jesus appears to him on the cross. At the sight (*conspectum*) of this, Francis's soul melts, and "the memory of Christ's passion was so impressed into the marrow of the flesh of his heart (*visceribus cordis medullitus*), that from that moment whenever Christ on the cross came to mind, he could scarcely (*vix*) restrain his outward tears and sighs."[43] The interior affections, spurred by the sight of Christ crucified before his mind, are so overwhelming that he is almost—though not quite—completely overtaken by them to the point of tears. Tears are a common sight for those in the presence of Francis, so much so that they eventually cause a disease in his eyes. When his doctor warns him to hold back his tears in order to preserve his vision, Francis replies that celestial vision is to be pre-ferred over "the light which we have in common with flies."[44] In this way, Bonaventure explains, Francis prefers to go blind from tears, "by which the interior eye is purified so that it may see God," than to impede the spirit by repressing his fervor.[45] Here it appears that Francis is to be revered for his decision not to restrain his affect as it manifests itself in excessive tears. Could he? In this instance, Francis chooses to give free rein to the impulses of desire that threaten to overwhelm him. His exercise of choice—and thus his virtue—lies in surrendering to an affective devotion in both its inward and outward manifestations.

This is not the first instance of Francis's body being afflicted with devo-tion. While he is still involved with the affairs of his father's business and has "not yet learned to contemplate heavenly things and had not acquired a taste for divine things," God afflicts his body with a long illness, in order to prepare his soul for being anointed by the Holy Spirit.[46] The bodily illness wears off eventually, but the interior change it effects is terminal. Upon recovering his strength, he sees a poor and ragged knight in the street. Moved (the word is *affectu*) to compassion over the man's poverty, Francis immediately removes his clothes and gives them to the man.[47] This fore-shadows Francis's more dramatic disrobing in the presence of his father later on. But the episode on its own also dramatically illustrates the way in which God's compassion is conducted, in a sense, through and in the body of Francis. The compassion of God first appears as physical illness, then moves to effect an interior awakening of compassion. Finally, when Francis is moved by the sight of suffering, it manifests itself again outwardly in the nakedness of Francis's body.

The *Legenda*'s concern for visibility is surely in part a function of the forensic demands that such a text must satisfy. This is true, of course, of hagiographical writing in general. But it is especially the case in Fran-cis's *vita*, which, Bonaventure writes, he was commissioned to produce by the General Chapter of Norbonne in 1260 (only a year after the date he gives for the inspiration of the *Itinerarium*, indicating that the two texts are very closely contemporary). Bonaventure's *vita* was to be the authori-tative account of Francis's life, a unifying document meant to set to rest the divisions within the order about the true nature of Francis's life and the community of his followers. As Bonaventure writes in the prologue, "In order to establish with greater clarity and certainty the true facts of his life to hand down to posterity, I have visited his place of birth, the places in which he lived, and the site of the death [*transitus*] of this blessed man and have had thorough conversations with those still living who were close to him, and especially with those who were most familiar with his holiness and were its closest followers."[48] As in the visit to La Verna, which Bonaventure relates in his prologue to the *Itinerarium*, Bonaventure again puts himself in Francis's place—as the locus of true authority about Francis's life and death and also as witness to Francis's holiness in Bonaventure's own body. He relates that when he was a child, he "was saved from the jaws of death through the invocation of Francis and his merits."[49] Thus, in gratitude he seeks to gather the true accounts of Francis's life, for, he writes, "I recognize that I have experienced his power in my very self."[50] Francis's spiritual power inhabits Bonaventure, and Bonaventure inhabits the text that follows, either as eyewitness to the site or as recipient of the report of Francis's holiness, compassion, and spiritual fervor.

The physicality of Francis's concourse with God is stressed even in the absence of witnesses, as in the pivotal vision in the Church of San Damiano.[51] Francis is praying with his head inclined toward a crucifix, his eyes characteristically filled with tears, when he hears "with his bodily ears" a voice coming from the cross, telling him to restore the Lord's house. He eventually sets about restoring the church building, only later realizing the spiritual meaning of Christ's command. But immediately upon hearing that voice—and before he acts—he begins to tremble. Receiving the power of divine speech in his heart, he is "carried out of himself in an ecstasy of mind [*mentis alienatur excessu*]."[52] The entire scene is structured on the dialectic of body and spirit. Francis is made to tremble as the words that strike his ears are commuted to divine power in his heart, so that he loses his bodily senses. And from mental ecstasy he returns to act, first building a physical structure that itself signifies the spiritual renewal to come.

The authenticity of this story derives not from an external witness to the event, but from Francis's own report to his followers later in life. Had there been a witness, how would Francis's ecstasy have appeared? Bonaventure affirms that there is a sensible effect of the *excessus mentis* when he describes Francis's follower Giles of Assisi as being frequently "rapt in God in ecstasies, as I myself have truly observed as an eyewitness [*ego ipse oculata fide conspexi*]."[53] Only later episodes from Francis's life give an indication of what it was like to see him in the full ecstasy of love. His body weakened by age and the rigors of his devotion, Bonaventure reports that "he was often suspended in such an excess of contemplation that, rapt above himself and feeling [*sentiens*] something beyond human understanding [*ultra humanum*

sensum], he was unaware of what was going on around him."[54] On one occasion, as he was riding on a donkey through the busy town of Borgo Santo
Sepolcro, he was thronged by devoted followers: "He was pulled and held
back by them, and pushed here and there and touched many times, but he
seemed unaware of all of it, and paid attention to nothing, just as if he were
a dead corpse."[55] And in an unusually cinematic scene, Bonaventure depicts
Francis praying alone at night in the woods, beating his chest, groaning,
and "watering the place with his tears."[56] Onlookers glimpse him "with
his hands extended in the shape of a cross, his entire body raised up from
the ground and a cloud shining around him."[57] The outward light exhibits
the illumination of his soul, but his posture is that of a man crucified. As
in the scene at Santo Sepolcro, the physical presence of Francis in ecstasy
of mind is a body of death—insensate and inanimate.

The figure of death gestures forward to the climactic episode on Mount
La Verna, in which Francis's vision of the cruciform Seraph leaves him
branded with the wounds of Christ's passion. Around two years before his
death, Bonaventure writes, Francis asked a friend to open the book of the
Gospels three times. Each time, the book opened to reveal the account of
the crucifixion. Francis then became filled with a desire for martyrdom,
as "the unquenchable fire of his love for the good Jesus had risen up in
him into such a torch of flames that many waters could not quench such
a strong love."[58] This love, described in language from the *Song of Songs*,
will be the instrument of Francis's spiritual martyrdom, the flame that consumes his soul. But the vision of the Seraph itself elicits more than simple
caritas in Francis: "By the Seraphic ardor of his desires he was being raised
above [*ageretur*] into God, and by sweet compassion he was being transformed into him who chose to be crucified on account of his excessive love
[*ex caritate nimia*]."[59] The vision of the Seraph is glorious, but the vision of
the crucifix is pitiable: "Seeing it, he was powerfully overcome, and a mix
of joy and grief flooded his heart. He rejoiced in the gracious expression
with which Christ, in the form of the Seraph, looked at him, but that he
was affixed to a cross pierced Francis's soul with a sword of compassionate
sorrow."[60] Affective death *in excessus mentis* is at once greatest joy and greatest pain, a violent overthrow of human understanding and an elevation to
the place of Christ himself.[61]

The sublime ambivalence that consumes Francis's soul and leaves his
heart ablaze at the same time pierces and tears his body as well. The wounds
left by his vision are referred to as "stigmata," but they are more than sig-
nifying marks. The wounds he sustains transform his body, rendering him
a living corpse: A wound in his side bleeds continuously, with blood real

enough to wet and stain his clothes. On his hands and feet are not only wounds but miraculous nails protruding from his flesh so that he can no longer walk for himself. Thus, in the last years of his life, in the glory of his martyrdom, Francis's dying body (*corpus emortuum*) must be carried by his friends through the streets, exhibited like a corpse while still living.

In this way, Francis's body is a martyr to his inflamed soul.[62] But to what perfection does his dying, nearly immobile body witness? Francis himself provides an interpretation of this sign earlier in the *Legenda* in a discussion of obedience. Here, the *exanime corpus* with which I opened this book appears, foreshadowing Francis's own later martyrdom:

> Once when he was asked who should be judged truly obedient, he gave as an example [*pro exemplo*] the image of a dead body. "Take a corpse, [*exanime corpus*]" he said, "and place it where you like! You will see that it puts up no resistance to motion (*non repugnare motum*), nor does it grumble about its position, or complain when it is put aside. If it is propped up on a throne, it does not raise its head up, but rather looks down. If it is clothed in purple, it will look twice as pale. This," Francis said, "is the truly obedient one, who does not judge [*diiudicat*] why he is moved, and does not care where he is placed. He does not demand to be transferred. If he is appointed to an office, he retains his usual humility. The more he is honored, the more he counts himself unworthy."[63]

There are many reasons to wonder at this passage. Most simply, the example is a graphic illustration of the virtue of humility. At the same time, the darkly comic image of a corpse slumped on a throne, neck slack and draped in purple, mocks the pretensions of worldly glory. Yet the power of the image itself is heightened by the rhetorical context in which it appears. Francis presents this image in response to a group of his followers seeking an example, a model of perfect obedience to be imitated. And in this way, as the exemplar of true obedience, he offers an example of obedience that reflects a pale light back onto himself. His life is a movement toward perfection in death, a gradual transformation into the macabre image he presents here. At the same time, the corpse offers a proleptic glimpse of Francis's own living yet martyred body—a body that is always also the appearance of Christ's crucified body. Francis is offering himself as the example of perfect obedience, while at the same time offering a lens through which to understand his virtue.

In what does this virtue consist? The lifeless body, or, literally, the body without a soul (*exanime corpus*), not only does not judge (*diiudicat*) where it is moved, but even has no will of its own with which to move itself.

The body as *speculum* and *exemplum* reflects Francis as one who has surrendered the will entirely, or, in view of Francis's ecstatic "conflagration," one whose will has been wholly consumed by desire. Francis's dying body makes visible the consummation of love. No less than three times in the ninth chapter (which recounts the saint's fervent love for Christ), Francis is described as being "carried" (*ferebatur*)—by *affectus*, by *devotio caritatis*, and by *desiderio*.[64] His soul puts up no resistance. It is moved like a body, an example of perfect obedience and consummate desire.[65]

To Take Place: Francis Among the Animals

Bonaventure's account of Francis does more than simply render desire visible. In the *Itinerarium*, Bonaventure writes that Francis's *transitus* made him the example of perfect contemplation—such that all spiritual persons are invited not simply to imitate Francis's *transitus*, but to pass over themselves *through* Francis. The soul passes *with* and *through* Francis into spiritual ecstasy and the conflagration of the soul. Francis is the example of this passing over; and for Bonaventure, an exemplar is much more than a didactic convenience for the cultivation of virtue. As he writes in the prologue to the *Breviloquium* (describing scripture's *modus tractandi*), "the affect is moved to examples more than to arguments, to promised rewards more than to ratiocination, and through devotion more than through definitions."[66] An *exemplum* is not simply that which instructs the soul in how to act, but is also that which moves and draws the soul affectively to itself. Francis's desire makes him the exemplary subject of the soul's desire for God, and in turn transforms him into its object as well. In his trip through Borgo Santo Sepolcro, when Francis is perched like an inanimate body on his donkey, lost in ecstasy and pushed and pulled by the townspeople, he is not the only figure in the scene drawn by love: "The crowds rushed toward him out of devotion," the account reads.[67] But the multiple vectors of love ultimately miss each other in this scene. The crowds are drawn toward Francis even as he is drawn up in love and contemplation to God—the present and absent object of their devotion, unaware of his surroundings and yet entirely acquiescent to their physical demands: a body abandoned to the desires of the crowd.

Francis's powers of attraction are nowhere more evident than in the celebrated stories of his interactions with animals, both in the *vitae* and the *fioretti*.[68] They present Francis as a figure of exceptional compassion and gentleness. In Bonaventure's renditions, the stories of Francis ministering to animals reflect also Francis's understanding of the structure of vestige, image, and likeness whereby all creation testifies to God as its cause: "When he considered the primal origin of all things, he was filled with even greater piety, calling all creatures, however small, 'brother' and 'sister,' for he knew that they had the same principle as he himself did."[69] In addition, Bonaventure adds another interpretive gloss on these stories, supplementing his source material with two additional anecdotes concerning lambs, because "he embraced more warmly [*viscerosius*] and sweetly those creatures that present a natural likeness of Christ's gentle mercy and represent him in scriptural signification."[70] The animal in question is not a mere brute beast, but an allegorical stand-in for Christ.

In addition, the story of a falcon waking Francis for divine office signifies, in Bonaventure's account, the saint's eventual elevation in contemplation and Seraphic vision. But even so, Bonaventure includes more in these stories than an affirmation of God's universal causality and Francis's allegorical imagination. The falcon, for example, remains with Francis because he is attached to him in friendship (*magno se illi amicitiae foedere copulavit*). Birds, hares, and even a fish are drawn powerfully to Francis's presence. He is also given a pheasant who "clung to him with such affection that it would in no way suffer to be separated from him."[71] Whenever the pheasant was placed outside, it returned immediately to Francis. And when it was given away, it refused food until it was returned to Francis, upon which it recovered its joy and its appetite.

These miracle stories illustrate Francis's extraordinary holiness and compassion, rather than the extraordinary virtue of the animals. The animals do not cling to Francis by a resolve of their will, but by a natural filial attraction to his love. And so in their response to Francis's affective fervor, they also reflect it back upon him, just as the pliable corpse reflects Francis's obedience and humility. They are more acted upon than acting. But in the devotion of the birds and hares and fish, the purity of Francis's own affection for Christ is manifest, and the animals themselves, through Francis's exemplary love, become examples of devotion. Francis becomes the figure and presence of Christ among the lower creatures. In a dynamic that could rightly be called analogical, Francis takes the place of Christ in these stories, as the animals take the place of Francis.

As I discussed in the previous chapter, for Bonaventure, analogy is a dynamic relationship that draws each stage of creation to its own excess. Thus, Francis does not simply represent Christ; he takes the place of, or *becomes* Christ through the force of his love. And the reader, for whom Francis appears as the desirous and desirable object of the *Legenda Maior*, is moved and transformed into Francis. Analogy is not simply a representational

strategy, but a devotional technique ordered by affect. As the motive principle of the rational and irrational soul alike, the affect moves the soul to
that which it loves. As the unitive principle, affect is that by which the lover
and the beloved are joined as one, and that which transforms the lover into
its beloved. The movement of exemplarity is the affective movement to the
place of the exemplar.

In the displacement that occurs, subject becomes object, lover becomes
beloved, the moved becomes the mover. For Francis to follow the example
of Christ means to take the place of Christ by being drawn into and transformed into him through affection—and as exemplar Francis functions
in the same role for "all spiritual persons." For Bonaventure, exemplarism
names both the metaphysical relationship of all things to their source, and
the devotional technique by which the reader is transformed through love.
The animals only gesture toward the outer limits of exemplarity's reach.
The love that draws Francis to Christ and the love that draws the animals
to Francis is not irrational any more than it is an act of human reason. All
things are drawn back to their source by the moving and unifying force
of desire—exemplified in and transferred through the body of Francis—
powerful as fire and inexorable as death. Ascent to God by way of Francis
is the becoming-body of the soul.

A Corpus, in Sum

> A question of reading or hearing. In any case, negative
> theology would be nothing, very simply nothing, if this
> excess or this surplus (with regard to language) did not
> imprint some mark on some singular events of language and
> did not leave some remains on the body of a tongue . . .
>
> A corpus, in sum.
>
> —JACQUES DERRIDA, "Sauf le nom (Post-Scriptum)"[1]

Throughout this book, I have attempted to trace a coincidence of opposites in Bonaventure's devotional program, in which the innermost affective disposition of the soul—what Bonaventure calls the natural instinct
for the good or synderesis—coincides with the brute, inanimate body.
The soul's natural instinct for the Good is its innate capacity to exceed its
own faculties and operations. This capacity is at once constitutive of those
deliberative, volitional faculties and irreducible to them. In a way that is
similarly paradigmatic for much of late medieval affective devotional practice and reflection, a site of excess, affect names for Bonaventure a place of
immanent otherness that is finally inassimilable to the operations of intellect. This place is *unknown* to the soul and yet as intimate to the soul as the
body to which it is joined. At once secret and manifest, then, the affective
conforms to the paradoxical logic of mystical theology.

For Bonaventure, this logic is also exemplified by Francis's body. In
the *Legenda Maior*, the drama of secrecy and disclosure unfolds immediately upon Francis's wounding Seraphic vision: "Christ's servant, seeing
that the stigmata impressed so vividly in his flesh could not be concealed
from his close companions, was nevertheless afraid to expose the secret

[*sacramentum*] of the Lord."[2] Illuminato, however, warns Francis not to hide the divine secret from the benefit of others: "The holy man was moved by these words, even though at other times he used to say, 'My secret is mine [*secretum meum mihi*].'"[3] Thus Francis recounts his vision to his companions, though not fully: "He added that the one who appeared to him said some things that he would never disclose (*aperiret*) to anyone as long as he lived."[4] There are secrets that Francis will take to his death, even as his dying body betrays him: "Though he tried with great diligence to hide the treasure he found in the field, still he could not keep others from seeing the stigmata in his hands and feet."[5] The "Lord's secret" can neither be disclosed nor hidden. The secret (or mystery, or sacrament: *sacramentum*) unleashes a play of hiding and revealing, and yet it is not a matter of one or the other. Francis's secret is as open as the bleeding wound at his side. And like his wounds, it is not contained within the boundary of interiority, but produces a radical, ecstatic reconciliation of inner and outer. The secret is not something that Francis can hide, because there is nothing to hide, and so nothing to disclose.[6] The spiritual depth of Francis's compassion is at the same time the porous and protruding surface of his body. Marked with the signs of Christ's passion, Francis's body is a text, indicating the reconciliation of spirit and flesh, inner and outer.

At the opening of the final chapter of Francis's life, Bonaventure announces that Francis was now "nailed to the cross as much in his flesh as in his spirit" as he depicts Francis's dying body (*corpus emortuum*) being carried through the streets.[7] The near-dead body is the obedient body, the body that does not resist the prompting of desire. Thus the glorified and stigmatized body contrasts with the body that Francis used to address as Brother Ass: the body in its stubborn resistance to the promptings of Francis's love of God.[8] The miraculous Seraphic vision transforms Francis's body not only by the signs of Christ's passion but also by the weakening of its resistance—not to the soul's promptings but to a different motion. Francis's body becomes Christ's body in that it no longer moves itself but is fixed to the cross, carried simply by its passion. The body comes to be moved in accordance with the movement of the spirit. And the spirit moves inexorably toward God, like a simple body, by its weight.

Nevertheless, the paths of soul and body diverge in death. At Francis's death, his followers witness the ascent of his soul in the form of a star rising on a cloud to heaven.[9] Yet for all the radiance of this vision, it is Francis's corpse that becomes the locus of wonder and desire. Abandoned to death, the miraculous nails in his hands and feet are not only plainly visible but tangible. The body of Francis "confirmed the faith and incited the love" of the many citizens of Assisi who came to experience the presence of the saint's body, and news of the glorious body "excited the desire" of all who heard of it.[10] Bonaventure reports that Francis's formerly dark flesh became dazzlingly bright, contrasting brilliantly with the iron black protrusions from his hands and feet. The natural contraction of the flesh after death shrank the holy man's side wound into a perfect round rose. And at the same time, in an unnatural reversal of *rigor mortis*, his limbs became soft and easily movable (*mollia et tractabilia*).[11]

It would be clear, then, even if Bonaventure did not point it out explicitly, that Francis's corpse has been transformed, miraculously, into a resurrection body (*illius secundae stolae pulchritudinem praetendebat*).[12] More specifically, Francis's body has become the resurrected body of Christ, with a doubting knight by the name of Jerome playing the part of Thomas.[13] Touching the wounds with his own hands, and moving the nails around Francis's hands and feet, the knight is cured of his doubt. Yet where Jesus appeared in his glorified body to his disciples walking and speaking, Francis's resurrection body remains inanimate. Just as was done before his death, Francis's body is now carried into the streets of Assisi. His corpse is transformed into a radiant example of perfect obedience, beautifully wounded, entirely unresistant to being moved, and bereft of both intellect and will. Francis's sanctity, which began with an inborn affective ardor, reaches consummation finally in his inanimate body, obedience perfected in death, virtue materialized in flesh. His body is at once silent and eloquent. It heals the wounds of doubt and yet stupefies the intellect.[14] The body keeps its secret in the exhibition of the body and the certainty of death.

If Francis's death is the enactment of Christ's passion, then the soul's *excessus* in union with God is itself an enactment of this death. The soul's journey into God and the Dionysian abandonment of intellect that takes place at the journey's consummation is a prefiguration, a living into, the glorified corpse that Francis's body miraculously exhibits on earth prior to resurrection. The soul's ascent to God is its becoming-body, its natural desire for God is its groaning to become body, to be consumed and moved wholly and simply by God. Both the *Itinerarium* and the Franciscan spirituality for which it serves as blueprint are often described as a journey from the appreciation of the corporeal traces of God to God's incorporeal being and goodness. Yet the enduring presence of Christ's suffering body at the culmination of the journey suggests that the stages of ascent chart, paradoxically, not only an ascent from the corporeal to the spiritual but also a transformation, effected by love, of soul into body—that is, into the body of Christ and the body of Francis. And that, as Bonaventure writes in

the seventh chapter of the *Itinerarium*, is "mystical and most secret." Like
the Seraphic revelation to Francis, the secret is not *scientia*, something that
could be revealed to the intellect, but something that can only be "known"
in the darkness devoid of intellect. The secret remains hidden from intellect essentially; it can only be experienced as the ecstatic body that the
soul becomes *in excessus mentis*: the body of Francis *in excess of* the soul in
its deliberative faculties. The *itinerarium* is the journey of the soul out of
itself and into the body of Christ. What remains hidden from intellect, the
secret that cannot be *known* because it is heterogeneous to knowledge as
such, is the embodiment of the soul that is fulfilled and redeemed in union
with God.

Not only for Francis, but for his followers, the practice of ardent devotion to Christ's suffering is similarly oriented toward this ecstatic
becoming-body of affect. As I suggested in the Introduction, the climactic
episode of Francis's vision of the crucified Seraph is itself an exemplary
scene of Passion devotion, an icon and model of the practice of vivid and
highly wrought meditation on Christ's crucifixion that Bonaventure com-
mends to his brothers and sisters in the Franciscan orders. As an example
of Passion meditation, Francis's vision at LaVerna establishes the endpoint
and purpose of meditating on Jesus's human suffering: The lover takes the
place of Francis taking the place of Christ on the cross, in a double displacement of the self in desire. Passion meditation is an ecstatic practice
leading to Dionysian union.

As Karnes rightly observes, Bonaventure's treatises on Passion meditation—most notably the *Lignum vitae* and *On the Perfection of Life Addressed
to the Sisters*, engage the reader's imagination, memory, and conscience; neither their purpose nor their methods can accurately be described as wholly
affective.[15] Meditation on the scenes of Christ's passion is effortful, Bonaventure indicates. The practice requires the mind's focused attention. But
in drawing a devotional template that begins in purgative self-examination
and ends in the meditant standing outside herself and—through the fulfillment of the proper affections of fear, love, and compassion—becoming so
intimate to Christ that his lifeless body becomes hers, Bonaventure depicts
the practice of Passion meditation as a Dionysian ascent into a crucifying
and ecstatic union in which love is the binding and transforming force.

In Bonaventure's most extensive treatment of the practice of Passion
meditation, the *Lignum vitae*, the reader finds herself in the text from the
opening words: "With Christ I am nailed to the cross."[16] While narrating
and interpreting the meaning of Jesus's crucifixion, Bonaventure weaves

the first person through the text, placing the reader in the scene, until Paul's identification with Christ with which Bonaventure opens the work becomes the reader's identification with Christ—even and especially unto death. Accordingly, "the true worshipper of God and disciple of Christ" should strive to carry Christ's cross "in both his soul and his flesh [*tam mente quam carne*] . . . until he can truly feel [*sentire*] in himself what the Apostle said above."[17] Such an effort engages the memory, intellect, and the will, and indeed the form of the *Lignum vitae* appeals explicitly to the imagination as an aid to understanding.[18] But to be nailed with Christ to the cross, to take Christ's place in that moment, is, Bonaventure writes, an affection (*affectum*) and a feeling (*sensum*). Compassion for Christ's suffering is finally ecstatic, lifting the meditant outside herself and bringing about a total identification with and transformation into Christ. This is no less the case when Bonaventure addresses the *sponsae Christi*, a group of Poor Clares for whom he composed *On the Perfection of Life Addressed to the Sisters*, probably during the period just after his election as Minister General.[19] While the treatise *On Perfection* is focused on practical instruction in the pursuit of devotion, its organization is less a step-by-step outline of perfection than a primer in the virtues and habits proper to the religious life. Like the *Lignum vitae*, *On Perfection* details the practice of exercising the imagination in order to witness the graphic details of Jesus's human suffering and scripts the appropriate interpretations and affective responses to that suffering.

In Sarah McNamer's opinion, *On Perfection* presents a more emotionally immediate program of meditation than the *Lignum vitae*, in which the immediacy of affective response is mitigated by a heavily allegorical framework.[20] McNamer attributes this difference to the fact that in the former work, Bonaventure is addressing religious women and encouraging them in a practice in which they are already engaged. However, while Bonaventure highlights certain devotional topoi as particularly suited to women (he is particularly scandalized at the prospect of garrulous nuns who neglect their commitment to silence), and while Jesus is frequently referred to as "your spouse," the text gives no indication that meditation on Christ's passion, or the affections proper to that practice, are inflected by sex, or that compassionate meditation on Jesus's sufferings is the special province of women. Instead, the text presents Passion meditation as one of a repertoire of devotional practices (including examination of one's faults, fear for future punishment, focused attention on God, and gratitude for one's vocation) proper to a mendicant life aimed at cultivating and sustaining an ardent, consuming love.

In this way, the devotional program addressed to the sisters is consistent with the itinerary toward union with God that Bonaventure develops in other devotional works such as the *Itinerarium* and *Triplex via*.[21] The leit-motif of *On Perfection* is not nuptial fidelity but self-immolating affection. Lamenting the resistance to poverty among members of his own order, Bonaventure blames the cooling of desire, which leaves the heart frozen and in need of clothing and shelter to cover it. In an oblique allusion to Francis's life, Bonaventure notes that those who burn with the heat of love seek nakedness, casting off their garments. Remembrance of the Passion is offered as a means of tending the fires of love. One must feed the altar of the heart daily with the wood of the cross.[22]

In a chapter on perfect prayer, Bonaventure explains the goal of this ardent devotion in terms that recall the final chapter of the *Itinerarium* and the culmination of the *Legenda*. Citing Augustine's definition of prayer as "the turning of the mind in to God [*conversio mentis in Deum*]," Bonaventure explains:

> When in prayer, you should recollect your whole self and enter, with your Beloved, into the little chamber of the heart, and remain there alone with him. Forget all exterior things [*omnium exteriorium*], and with your whole heart, your whole mind, your whole affect, your de-sire, your whole devotion, raise yourself above yourself. Do not slacken your spirit from prayer, but keep ascending upwards through the ardor of devotion, until you enter into the place of the wonderful tabernacle, even to the house of God. There, when you have in some manner seen your beloved with the eye of your soul, and tasted how sweet is the Lord, and how great the multitude of his delights, fall into his em-brace, and kiss him with the lips of intimate devotion. Then you will be wholly alienated from yourself, wholly rapt into heaven, and wholly transformed into Christ.[23]

This passage, in the context of the treatise's emphasis on gospel meditation, corroborates Karnes's observation that medieval meditation on Christ's passion had a mystical purpose. Passion meditation charted a progression from visualizing Jesus's human sufferings to beholding the glory of his divinity. This duality is further evident in *On Perfection* in a passage on evangelical poverty. Here, as in the *Breviloquium*, Bonaventure identifies example and reward as the two factors that move the soul to desire. In or-der to cultivate a love for poverty, one should first contemplate the example of holy poverty presented through the humble life and gruesome death of Jesus, as well as through the lives of his exemplary followers, Francis and

Clare. And secondly, one should concentrate on the heavenly reward that awaits the person who shuns the comforts and riches of the world: "Voluntary poverty merits one to appear before the creator of glory, and to enter into the power of the Lord, in that eternal tabernacle, those illuminated mansions. They become citizens of that city whose artificer and sustainer is God."[24] The distinction between example and reward quickly collapses, however, when Bonaventure identifies this celestial dwelling as "nothing other than you, Lord Jesus Christ."[25] Jesus is both example and reward, and so to live according to the example of his life and death *is* to enter the mansions prepared for those who follow him.

The goal of entering into Christ as one's eternal dwelling is echoed in the treatise's discussion of Passion meditation. The genre of Passion meditation is often distinguished by the presence of rhetorical devices used to make the reader sensorially, imaginatively, and emotionally present to the events of Christ's Passion, as though the meditant were herself an eyewitness to the scene. Bonaventure explains the goal of meditating on the crucifixion, however, as a far deeper intimacy. The text appeals directly to the reader to

> draw near, O handmaid [*famula*], with the feet of your affection step
> to Jesus wounded, to Jesus crowned with thorns, to Jesus fixed to the
> gibbet of the cross, and with the blessed apostle Thomas, do not merely
> look upon the piercings of the nails in Jesus's hands; do not merely stick
> your finger into the place where the nails were; do not merely stick
> your hand into his side, but pass totally through the door in his side up
> to Jesus's very heart, and there, with the most ardent love of the cruci-
> fied one, you will be transformed into Christ.[26]

Here, the intense, sustained meditations on every aspect of Jesus's wounded body aim at more than compassion. But they neither leave behind nor rise above Jesus's humanity.[27] Rather, like the lover of poverty who longs to enter the heavenly city that is Christ, the meditant passes wholly into Jesus's wounded flesh until, fueled by love, she fully incorporates herself into Christ, taking the place of the Crucified. The text explains how this transformation comes about: "Fastened with the nails of holy fear, transfixed by the lance of the most deep-seated love [*praecordialis dilectionis*], penetrated [*transverberata*] by the sword of intimate compassion [*compassio*], seek for nothing else, desire nothing else, wish to be consoled by nothing else, than to be able to die with Christ on the Cross. And then, with the apostle Paul, you will cry out and say: In Christ I am nailed to the cross. I live, now not I; but Christ lives in me."[28] Fear, love, and compassion are the instruments of the reader's Passion, pious affections becoming-body in the soul's ecstatic transformation into Christ. The wound in Jesus's side is not simply a portal one passes through on the way from flesh to spirit, but an aporia, the gap in which affective dispossession, the ecstatic substitution of the lover for Christ, is embodied.[29] The incorporation, the becoming-body, of the lover into Christ is an affective transformation that displaces the "I" even as she testifies to her own crucifixion in the words of the Apostle.[30] An impossible testimony—the "I" who testifies to her crucifixion already "no longer"— the words of the Apostle are not the expression of the meditant's interior state but a kind of corpse, the body that remains in and after the *transitus*. Yet as the vacated "I" becomes at the same time the place in which "Christ lives," the body of her testimony, Christ's crucified body, is also Christ's resurrection body. The words of the meditant are witnesses to more than a transformation of the self; they are witnesses to the limits of what can be claimed for any self.

As Charles Stang has shown with regard to the Dionysian corpus, the twin, contradictory affirmations of Paul's words ("I live, now not I") amount to more than a simple self-denial. Instead, consistent with the dynamic of affirmation and negation developed throughout Dionysius's mystical theology, the apostle's words testify to the unknowing—the double movement of cataphasis and apophasis—of the self. As Stang concludes, Dionysius "offers an account of what it is to be properly human in relation to God—namely, no longer an 'I,' neither yourself nor someone else, because you are now both yourself *and* Christ."[31] In Bonaventure's hands, a devotional practice aiming at self-consuming love fueled by the remembrance of Jesus's bodily sufferings follows this double movement of Dionysian mystical theology: The meditant is urged to think over (variants of the term *cogitare* appear frequently in *De perfectione*), imagine, and feel Christ's body in pursuit of union, an incorporation more intimate than knowledge. The body of Christ is no longer an object of knowledge, but the place in which the lover dwells, united through love, fear, and compassion, in an attachment that transforms lover into Beloved. The pious affections proper to Passion meditation reveal themselves finally to be what they always already were—Dionysian, deifying *eros*.

Recall that in Bonaventure's early scholastic account of synderesis, the apex of the mind, he maintains that all knowledge is dependent on language and other external information in order to be realized, save for the affects of loving and fearing God. These affections proper to the divine are given innately and immediately to the soul. Thus they can be said to be "known," but the term is partly equivocal. The innate love and fear of God are set apart from everything else the soul is capable of knowing; that is to say, they are kept secret.

Because they require nothing external for their realization, these affections proper to God are in one sense that which is most fully claimed by the soul: "my secret is mine." It is a fitting coincidence, then, that the very same love and fear become, in the final passing over, the *arma Christi*, the instruments of the lover's passion. That which belongs to me utterly is thereby the means of my dispossession. The words that embody this dispossession—"In Christ I am nailed to the cross. I live, but now not I . . ."—are, to recur to the epigraph that opens this chapter, an imprint on the tongue, in which the tongue refers both to the body of the lover and to the discourse of Christian mystical theology. Just as Francis's seraphic vision dispossesses him and leaves his body marked, the lover's incorporation into Jesus unseats the "I" who testifies to that transformation, so that her words, said and unsaid, remain as a corporeal trace. The words of the lover are no more (and no less) *hers* than Francis's secret is his. To say that the lover's words *express* her interior affections, or to say that Francis's compassion is "externalized" in his flesh, would be to reinscribe in these scenes the selfsame subject that this devotional program aims to interrupt. A closer analog of what is occurring in this revelation can be found in Derrida's reflection on death and secrecy:

> And if my secret self, that which can be revealed only to the other, to the wholly other, to God if you wish, is a secret that I will never reflect on, that I will never know or experience or possess as my own, then what sense is there in saying that it is "my" secret, or in saying more generally that a secret *belongs*, that it is proper to or belongs to some "one," or to some *other* who remains some*one*? It is perhaps there that we find the secret of secrecy, namely, that it is not a matter of knowing and that it is there for no-one.[32]

What sense is there, after all? Only a sense peculiar to the place that Bonaventure reserves for the height of *affectus* in Christian mystical theology: an ecstatic inhabitation in which soul and body, possession and dispossession, crucifixion and resurrection, coincide.

ACKNOWLEDGMENTS

In taking account of the debts I owe in the making of this book, the line between the professional and personal is impossible to define, and for that overlap I consider myself fortunate. Clichéd as it is to say, I could write a book about Amy Hollywood's impact on my life and thinking. In a sense, that is just what I've done, though it still doesn't tell the half of it. Her hugely generous mentorship has enabled every step of my progress from master's student to assistant professor. Mark Jordan and Kevin Madigan have also been ideal guides throughout the initial formulation and count-less reformulations of this book's argument. Additionally, among many ex-cellent teachers at Harvard, I am particularly grateful to Beverly Kienzle and Sarah Coakley for teaching me, in different ways, how to read.

I am indebted to everyone who has contributed to the deeply affirm-ing and energizing environment of the Fordham Theology department, including Terrence Tilley, Patrick Hornbeck, Brad Hinze, Karina Hogan, and especially Brenna Moore, who has been an invaluable source of counsel and encouragement through the ups and downs of my early career. George Demacopoulos and Aristotle Papanikolaou, as well, have been wise and canny mentors. Christiana and Michael Peppard, Kathryn Reklis, Joshua Schapiro, John Seitz, Maureen O'Connell, and Sarit Kattan-Gribetz have enriched my life and work beyond measure these last few years as friends and conversation partners.

I have also been fortunate to land in the vibrant medievalist community at Fordham, for which I have to thank the unflagging work of Maryanne Kowaleski, Laura Morreale, and Susanna Hafner. The Center for Medi-eval Studies has provided me with some wonderfully supportive colleagues, including Susanna Barsella and Cristiana Sogno. Above all, I am grateful to Andrew Albin, who helped me see the stakes of this project in our first con-versation, and who has been expanding and sharpening my thinking ever since. Outside of theology and medieval studies, Samir Haddad, Jordan Stein, and Adam Fried have also helped me find my way at Fordham.

137

More than convention compels me to note that while I alone bear responsibility for this book's remaining vices, many others deserve credit for its virtues. Eleanor Johnson provided encouragement and incisive suggestions for how to frame and structure the argument. Lauren Mancia helped to inform my thinking on affective devotion, Niki Clements greatly expanded my understanding of and appreciation for affect theory, and Rachel Smith has enriched every aspect of my intellectual and academic life during the formation of this book . Julia Reed patiently and brilliantly talked me through the whole project (and much else besides) many times. I am enormously indebted to Constance Furey and Patricia Dailey for their encouraging, thorough, and insightful suggestions for revision. Patricia Dailey, in particular, saw the potential of the book's argument and provided painstaking feedback on how to articulate it more clearly and forcefully. From the beginning of my relationship with Fordham University Press, Richard Morrison has been an exemplary editor: professional, intelligent, and generous. Eric Newman and Nancy Rapoport provided valuable editorial guidance.

I am grateful for the friends and family who leavened the mostly self-imposed burdens of research and writing, including Anna Williams, Darcy Hirsh, Jacob Rhoads, Julia Reed, Margaret Gower, Mikael Haxby, and Natalie Williams. I have been nourished in many ways by the Dunning family: Steve and Roxy, Sarah and Charlie, Lucy, Kate, Frances, David, Monika, and Penny. Bob LaVelle's huge heart and energetic mind are an abiding source of inspiration, and both are abundantly evident in Lindsay. Vance LaVelle's love, playfulness, and very good advice saw me through many difficult passages in the writing process. The bedrock of this book is the unconditional and unmerited love of my grandmothers, Dorothy Davis and Laurine McKinney, and my parents, Glenn and Lynn Davis, *sine quibus non.*

I dedicate this book to Ben Dunning, who knows all too well now what it means to bear the weight of love. I owe him more than I know how to say, but I can start with the hours he spent reading the many drafts of this book. His incisive suggestions greatly improved the clarity and precision of my thoughts and words. I am also grateful to Billy, who routinely competed with my computer for my attention and almost always won.

An earlier version of Chapter 4 was previously published as "Hierarchy and Excess in Bonaventure's *Itinerarium mentis in Deum*," *Journal of Religion* 95.4 (2015): 433–53, © The University of Chicago. I am grateful for their permission to reprint this material here.

INTRODUCTION: WEIGHING AFFECT IN MEDIEVAL CHRISTIAN DEVOTION

1. Bonaventure, *Legenda Maior* 6.4 (*Doctoris seraphici S. Bonaventurae opera omnia*. Quaracchi: Ex Typographia Collegii S. Bonaventura, 1882–1902) XIII.520. Translations throughout this book are my own unless otherwise noted.

2. Ignatius Brady established the date of 1262 on the basis of several verbatim correspondences with Bonaventure's *Legenda Maior* of that same year, but this dating is not universally accepted. See Regis Armstrong, Wayne Hellmann, and William Short, eds., *Francis of Assisi: Early Documents*: vol. 2, *The Founder* (New York: New City Press, 2000), 718. J. F. Quinn argues for a dating of 1269 in "Chronology of St. Bonaventure's Sermons," *Archivum franciscanum historicum* 67 (1974),145–84. This sermon appears as the fourth sermon on St. Francis in the Quaracchi edition of Bonaventure's *Opera Omnia* (Collegium S. Bonaventura, 1882–1902) IX.585–90.

3. Quaracchi IX.589.

4. On the eschatological interpretation of Francis's wounds in this sermon see Zachary Hayes, "The Theological Image of St. Francis in the Sermons of St. Bonaventure," in *Bonaventuriana: Miscellanea in onore di Jacques Guy Bougerol, ofm* (Rome: Edizioni Anonianum, 1988), 1:333–34. On the eschatological significance of St. Francis for Bonaventure in general, see Joseph Ratzinger, *The Theology of History in St. Bonaventure*, trans. Zachary Hayes (Chicago: Franciscan Herald Press, 1971), 31–38. On the metaphor of Francis as book, see Richard Emmerson and Ronald Herzmann, *The Apocalyptic Imagination in Medieval Literature* (Philadelphia: University of Pennsylvania Press, 1992), 52–53, 70–72. On Francis's own contributions to the theology of ecstatic union and its cosmic dimensions, see Alessandro Vettori, *Poets of Divine Love: Franciscan Mystical Poetry of the Thirteenth Century* (New York: Fordham University Press, 2004), esp. 40–78.

5. On some of the meanings of *cor* and their importance in scholastic understandings of affectivity, see M.-D. Chenu, "Les catégories affectives au Moyen Âge," in *Du corps à l'esprit: Textes rassemblés et présentés par Jacques Durandeaux* (Desclée de Brouwer, 1989), 145–53. Bonaventure is also drawing

an analogy from contemporary medical knowledge in identifying heat as a property of the heart related to vigor. For a brief overview of medieval theories of *complexio* underlying this comparison, see Nancy G. Siraisi, *Medieval and Early Renaissance Medicine: An Introduction to Knowledge and Practice* (Chicago: University of Chicago Press, 1990), 101–6.

6. Thomas H. Bestul, *Texts of the Passion: Latin Devotional Literature and Medieval Society* (Philadelphia: University of Pennsylvania Press, 1996), 4.

7. Richard Southern, *The Making of Middle Ages* (New Haven: Yale University Press, 1992), 232.

8. See Thomas Bestul, "St. Anselm and the Continuity of Anglo-Saxon Devotional Traditions," *Annuale Medievale* 18 (1977), 20–41; Rachel Fulton, *From Judgment to Passion: Devotion to Christ and the Virgin Mary, 800–1200* (New York: Columbia University Press, 2002). Both Bestul and Fulton maintain, nevertheless, that the eleventh century marked a turning point in devotional attitudes and practices. For a more extensive critique of conventional narratives of an affective turn in high medieval spirituality, see Allen J. Frantzen, "Spirituality and Devotion in the Anglo-Saxon Penitentials," *Essays in Medieval Studies* 22 (2005), 117–28.

9. See Michelle Karnes, *Imagination, Meditation, and Cognition in the Middle Ages* (Chicago: University of Chicago Press, 2011), 15, and the similar critiques she cites there.

10. See, for example, Ewert Cousins, "The Humanity and the Passion of Christ" in *Christian Spirituality: High Middle Ages and Reformation*, ed. Jill Raitt (New York: Crossroad, 1987), 375–91; and Eric (Edmund) Colledge, ed., *The Medieval Mystics of England* (New York: Scribner, 1961), 3–55.

11. Fulton, 63 and 5.

12. Southern, 240.

13. Sarah Beckwith, *Christ's Body: Identity, Culture, and Society in Late Medieval Writings* (London: Routledge, 1993), 51–52.

14. Beckwith, *Christ's Body*, 53.

15. Beckwith, *Christ's Body*, 52.

16. Bestul, *Texts of the Passion*, 43.

17. Bestul, *Texts of the Passion*, 48.

18. Sarah McNamer, *Affective Meditation and the Invention of Medieval Compassion* (Philadelphia: University of Pennsylvania Press, 2010), 84.

19. McNamer, 90. In Bonaventure's *On the Perfection of Life Addressed to the Sisters*, McNamer recognizes the features of affective Passion meditation but notes that this text was written for a community of women and appears to reflect practices in which they were already engaged. I discuss this text further in the Conclusion.

20. Karnes, 5 and 65–70.

21. Karnes, 10.

22. For such studies, see Elizabeth Ann Dreyer, "Affectus in St. Bonaventure's Description of the Journey of the Soul to God" (Ph.D. dissertation, Marquette University, 1983); Franz P. Sirovic, *Der Begriff "Affectus" und die Willenslehre beim Hl. Bonaventura: Eine analytisch-synthetische Untersuchung* (Vienna: Missionsdruckerei St. Gabriel, 1965).

23. Ann Astell, *Eating Beauty: The Eucharist and the Spiritual Arts of the Middle Ages* (Ithaca, N.Y.: Cornell University Press, 2006), 104.

24. To put it another way, the becoming-body of Francis's desire is the absolute visibility of the secret of affect in the sight of God. In Jacques Derrida's analysis of secrecy in Jewish and Christian thought, secrecy is enabled by, paradoxically, the dissolution of secrecy in God's infinite and unlimited gaze, interiorized in the soul in conscience: "*There where, wherever,* or, since place no longer takes place one should say more precisely *as soon as* there is no longer any secret hidden from God or from the spiritual light that passes through every space, then a recess of spiritual subjectivity and of absolute interiority is constituted allowing secrecy to be formed within it." *The Gift of Death,* trans. David Wills (Chicago, University of Chicago Press, 1995), 100–1, emphasis original to translation.

25. For instances and a compelling critique of this enduring dichotomy, see Charlotte Radler, "'In Love I Am More God': The Centrality of Love in Meister Eckhart's Mysticism," *Journal of Religion* 90.2 (2010), 171–98.

26. Radler, 173.

27. See as representative Sarah Beckwith, "Passionate Regulation: Enclosure, Ascesis, and the Feminist Imaginary," *South Atlantic Quarterly* 93 (1994), 803–24; Amy Hollywood, *The Soul as Virgin Wife* (Notre Dame: University of Notre Dame Press, 1995); Sara S. Poor, *Mechthild of Magdeburg and Her Book: Gender and the Making of Textual Authority* (Philadelphia: University of Pennsylvania Press, 2011); Patricia Dailey, *Promised Bodies: Time, Language, and Corporeality in Medieval Women's Mystical Texts* (New York: Columbia University Press, 2013). Hollywood provides an indispensable overview of this scholarship in "Feminist Studies," in *The Blackwell Companion to Christian Spirituality,* ed. Arthur Holder (Blackwell, 2005), 363–86.

28. Caroline Walker Bynum, *Fragmentation and Redemption: Essays on Gender and the Human Body in Medieval Religion* (New York: Zone Books, 1991), 194.

29. See Amy Hollywood, "Inside Out: Beatrice of Nazareth and Her Hagiographer," in *Gendered Voices: Medieval Saints and their Interpreters,* ed. C. Mooney (Philadelphia: University of Pennsylvania Press, 1999), 78–98; "Feminist Studies," 366–74.

30. Patricia Dailey, "The Body and Its Senses," in *The Cambridge Companion to Christian Mysticism*, ed. Amy Hollywood and Patricia Z. Beckman (Cambridge: Cambridge University Press, 2012), 264–76 at 264.

31. Dailey, *Promised Bodies*, 117.

32. Dailey, *Promised Bodies*, 5.

33. Dailey, *Promised Bodies*, 70.

34. Karnes, 16.

35. Karnes, 16.

36. Dailey, *Promised Bodies*, 102.

37. See, for example, *Breviloquium* 2.9, where the basic division between the cognitive and the affective are indexed to the soul's relationship to truth and the good, respectively: "Rursus quia discretio veri est cognitio fuga et appetitus est affectio ideo tota anima dividitur in cognitivam et affectivam." While Bonaventure uses the language of *partes*, he maintains the position that, essentially speaking, the soul is not divided into parts. I discuss this distinction further, and the qualifications Bonaventure makes regarding it, in Chapter 2.

38. ". . . magis movetur affectus ad exempla quam ad argumenta magis ad promissiones quam ad ratiocinationes magis per devotiones quam per definitiones," *Breviloquium*, Prol. 5.

39. Damien Boquet, *L'ordre de l'affect au Moyen Age: Autour de l'anthropologie affective d'Aelred de Rievaulx* (Louvain: Brepols, 2005), 34–63.

40. Boquet, 91, my translation.

41. Cited in Boquet, 100.

42. Gordon Rudy, *The Mystical Language of Sensation in the Later Middle Ages* (New York: Routledge, 2002), 59.

43. Bernard McGinn, *The Growth of Mysticism: Gregory the Great through the 12th Century* (New York: Crossroad Herder, 1996), 501n212.

44. Michael Casey, *Athirst for God: Spiritual Desire in Bernard of Clairvaux's "Sermons on the Song of Songs"* (Cistercian Publications, 1986), 97.

45. See Thomas Davis's appendix to his translation of William of St. Thierry, *The Mirror of Faith* (Kalamazoo, Mich.: Cistercian Publications, 1979), 93.

46. Davis, 93.

47. William Reddy, *The Navigation of Feeling: A Framework for the History of Emotions* (Cambridge: Cambridge University Press, 2001).

48. Reddy defines an emotional regime as "the set of normative emotions and the official rituals, practices, and emotives that express and inculcate them," 129.

49. Reddy, 45.

50. Reddy, 54.

51. Niklaus Largier, "Inner Senses—Outer Senses: The Practice of Emotions in Medieval Mysticism," in *Codierung Von Emotionen Im Mittelalter (Emotions and Sensibilities in the Middle Ages)*, vol. 1, ed. C. Stephen Jaeger and Ingrid Kasten (Berlin and New York: de Gruyter, 2003), 3–15.

52. McNamer, 28. Compare also Fulton, *From Judgment to Passion*.

53. McNamer, 12.

54. Barbara Rosenwein, "Worrying About Emotions in History," *The American Historical Review* 107.3 (Jun. 2002), 821–45.

55. Rosenwein, "Worrying About Emotions," 842.

56. Sarah Ahmed, *The Cultural Politics of Emotion* (New York: Routledge, 2004), 3.

57. Thomas Dixon, *From Passions to Emotion: The Creation of a Secular Psychological Category* (Cambridge: Cambridge University Press, 2003).

58. Michel de Certeau, "The Freudian Novel: History and Literature," in *Heterologies: Discourse on the Other*, trans. Brian Massumi (Minneapolis: University of Minnesota Press, 2006), 17–34.

59. Cited in Dixon, 14.

60. In Chakrabarty's example, "*pani* in Hindi and *water* in English can both be mediated by H_2O." See Dipesh Chakrabarty, "The Time of History and the Times of Gods," in *The Politics of Culture in the Shadow of Capital*, ed. Lisa Lowe and David Lloyd (Durham, N.C.: Duke University Press, 1997), 35–60 at 38.

61. Brian Massumi, *Parables for the Virtual: Movement, Affect, Sensation* (Durham, N.C.: Duke University Press, 2002), 27.

62. Massumi, 28.

63. "An Inventory of Shimmers," in *The Affect Theory Reader*, ed. Gregg and Seigworth (Durham, N.C. and London: Duke University Press, 2010), 1 (emphasis original).

64. Ruth Leys, "The Turn to Affect: A Critique," *Critical Inquiry* 37:3 (Spring 2011), 434–72.

65. Eugenie Brinkema, *The Forms of the Affects* (Durham, N.C.: Duke University Press, 2014), xv.

66. Brinkema, xiii.

67. Brinkema, xii.

68. Massumi, 27.

69. Massumi, 27.

70. See Lauren Berlant, *Cruel Optimism* (Durham, N.C.: Duke University Press, 2011); Kathleen Stewart, *Ordinary Affects* (Durham, N.C.: Duke University Press, 2007).

71. Stewart, 4, my emphasis.

72. Massumi, 27.

73. Rei Terada, *Feeling in Theory: Emotion After the "Death of the Subject"* (Cambridge: Harvard University Press, 2003), 28.

74. Terada, 31.

75. Terada, 44.

76. Terada, 45.

1. THE SERAPHIC DOCTRINE: LOVE AND KNOWLEDGE
IN THE DIONYSIAN HIERARCHY

1. On post-Bonaventurean scholastic debates concerning the autonomy of the will, see Bonnie Kent, *Virtues of the Will: The Transformation of Ethics in the Thirteenth Century* (Washington: Catholic University of America Press, 1995).

2. Edward Mahoney's survey of the Dionysian conception of hierarchy in medieval philosophy, for example, makes no mention of Bonaventure (or Thomas Gallus, for that matter). See "Pseudo-Dionysius's Conception of Metaphysical Hierarchy and Its Influence on Medieval Philosophy," in *Die Dionysius-Rezeption im Mittelalter*, 429–75. Lees's study of the sources of the Cloud discusses Gallus at length, as well as Hugh of Balma who was undeniably and extensively influenced by Bonaventure, but she makes no mention of Bonaventure.

3. *Celestial Hierarchy (CH)* 205B–C, trans. Colm Lubheid, *Pseudo-Dionysius: The Complete Works* (Mahwah, N.J.: Paulist Press, 1987), 162. For the critical edition of the Greek text, see Beate Regina Suchla, Günter Heil, and Adolf Martin Ritter, *Corpus Dionysiacum*, 2 vols. (*Patristische Texte und Studien* bd. 33 and 36) (Berlin and New York: Walter de Gruyter, 1990–91).

4. *CH* 165A (Lubheid, 154).

5. *CH* 301B (Lubheid, 177).

6. Here the term "mediate" is misleading to the extent that it implies hierarchical ranks standing "between" God and the lower orders. Hierarchy does not separate one level from another; it is, on the contrary, the reason all things are united to and filled with God. For a thorough and precise analysis of this dynamic, see Eric D. Perl, *Theophany: The Neoplatonic Philosophy of Dionysius the Areopagite* (Albany, N.Y.: SUNY Press, 2007), 65–81. Perl's phrase for this aspect of Dionysian thought, "immediate mediation," captures the simultaneous necessity and difficulty of using the term "mediate" to describe the activity of hierarchy.

7. *CH* 305A (Lubheid, 179). John Sarrazen's Latin translation reads, "Ad intelligibilem visorum sursumagebatur cognitionem"; see Sarrazen's and other Latin translations edited in P. Chevallier, ed., *Dionysiaca: Recueil donnant l'ensemble des traductions latines des ouvrages attribués au Denys de l'Aréopage*, 2 vols. (Bruges 1937–50), I.966.

8. Rorem, "The Early Latin Dionysius: Eriugena and Hugh of St. Victor," in *Re-thinking Dionysius the Areopagite*, ed. Sarah Coakley and Charles M. Stang (Oxford: Wiley-Blackwell, 2009), 71–84. In fact, the association of the Seraphim with a sublime circular movement resonates with ancient descriptions of the circular movement of heavenly bodies. More specifically, Gregory of Nyssa in his *Songs* commentary connects the "immovable movement" of the Seraphim with *epektasis*. See Maurice de Gandillac, *La hiérarchie céleste*, *Sources Chrétiennes* 58 (Paris: Éditions du cerf, 1958), 107n1.

9. Though Gregory mentions Dionysius the Areopagite by name in this homily, his knowledge of the *Celestial Hierarchy*—and thus his direct debt to Dionysius for his own angelic hierarchy—remains disputed. Joan Petersen argues that given the discrepancies between Gregory and Dionysius's list of angelic ranks, Gregory may have derived his rank either directly from the relevant biblical passages or from earlier Latin authors. See Petersen, "'Homo omnino Latinus?' The Theological and Cultural Background of Pope Gregory the Great," *Speculum* 62.3 (1987), 529–51. In the *Moralia in Iob*, Gregory provides an alternative ordering for the angelic hierarchy (Book 32, Chapter 23).

10. "And there are some who are enkindled with the fire of heavenly contemplation, and they burn with desire for their creator alone. They want nothing from this world, but are fed only with love for eternity. Abandoning every earthly thing, they transcend all temporal things with their minds. Loving and burning, and resting in their ardor, they burn with love. They inflame others by speaking, and those whom they touch with their words immediately begin to burn with love for God. What can I call them but Seraphim, whose hearts, which have been turned into fire, shine and burn?" *Homiliae in euangelia* 34.7, *Corpus Christianorum Series Latina* (*CCSL*) 141, ed. R. Etiax (Turnhout: Brepols, 1999), 311.

11. *Hom. in euan.* 34.10.

12. *Sermones super Cantica Canticorum* (*Bernardi opera*, vols. 1–2), I.111.

13. Associations of the Seraphim with love are widespread in twelfth- and thirteenth-century Cistercian writing. Isaac of Stella's *Epistola de anima*, for example, connects the Seraphim with the desire for and love of God, which Isaac calls hope (in a passage that was included in the Pseudo-Augustinian *De spiritu et anima*, and thus familiar to Parisian theologians in the thirteenth century). Additionally, William of St. Thierry's *De Natura et dignitate amoris* (discussed in Chapter 3) uses the image of the Seraph to describe those who are surrounded with such *affectus* that they ignite one another in the love of God. On the question of influence of the Dionysian corpus on Cistercian authors see McGinn, "Pseudo-Dionysius and the Early Cistercians," in *One Yet Two: Monastic Tradition East and West*, ed. M. Basil Pennington (*Cistercian Studies* 29) (Kalamazoo: Cistercian Publications, 1973), 200–41.

14. For an overview of the theological orientation of Hugh's commentary, see David Luscombe, "The Commentary of Hugh of Saint-Victor on the Celestial Hierarchy," in *Die Dionysius-Rezeption im Mittelalter*, ed. T. Boiadjiev, et al. (Turnhout: Brepols, 2000), 159–75, esp. 164–72. For an analysis of the ways in which Hugh revises and contests Eriugena's interpretation, see Csaba Németh, "The Victorines and the Areopagite," in *L'ecole de Saint-Victor de Paris*, ed. Dominique Poirel (Bibliotheca Victorina 22) (Turnhout: Brepols, 2010), 333–83 at 337–41.

15. *Expositiones in Ierarchiam Coelestem*, ed. J. Barbet, *Corpus Christianorum Continuatio Mediaeualis (CCCM)* 31 (Turnhout: Brepols, 1975). The relevant passages of Eriugena's commentary include Cap V, ln 139–40 ("angeli sunt Seraphim, quia feruore caritatis caleficantur a superioribus et se inferiores caleficant"); VII.26–29 ("Et quidem, inquit, qui sciunt hebraicarum uocum proprias significationes, sanctum nomen Seraphim aut incedentes, aut calefacientes manifestare; hic subauditur dicunt; est enim EKLEIPSIC uerbi"); VII.90–145 (on the warm motion of the Seraphim); VII.164–211 (on the relation of the Seraphic warmth to love, for example, lines 170–73: "Ipsa etiam ignea celestis Seraphim uirtus incircumuelata et inextinguibilis, incircumuelata uidelicet, quia totam se inferioribus reuelat, inextinguibilis uero, quoniam semper in ea diuinus ardet amor"); et al. Chapter XIII treats Dionysius's discussion of the Seraph who visited Isaiah.

16. On the relationship between the thought of Richard of St. Victor and Thomas Gallus, see Robert Javelet, "Thomas Gallus et Richard de Saint-Victor mystiques," *Recherches de théologie ancienne et médiévale* 29 (1962), 206–33. As Rosemary Lees notes, "Gallus' concept of the unitive experience is thus emphatically super intellectual, and in his *Spectacula Contemplationis* he underlines his divergence in this respect from traditional Victorine contemplative theory as it was formulated by Richard, which envisages union through the higher function of the intellect, the *intelligentia*," The Negative Language of the Dionysian School of Mystical Theology: An Approach to the Cloud of Unknowing, vol. 1 (Salzburg: Institut für Anglistik ind Amerikanistik, 1983), 280.

17. See Lawell, "Thomas Gallus's Method as Dionysian Commentator: A Study of the *Glose super Angelica Ierarchia* (1224), with Considerations on the *Expositio librorum beati Dionysii*," in *Archives d'histoire doctrinale et littéraire du Moyen Âge*, 76.1 (2009), 89–117 at 91.

18. Németh, 381–83. Among other hallmarks, Németh notes the shift in emphasis from the *Celestial Hierarchy* to the *Mystical Theology* as the central text of the corpus.

19. On the Dionysian corpus in thirteenth-century Paris, see H. F. Dondaine, *Le Corpus Dionysien de l'Université de Paris au XIIIe Siècle* (Rome:

Edizioni di storia e letteratura, 1953), and Németh, "The Victorines and the Areopagite," 334. For a study of one particular thirteenth century manuscript, see D. E. Luscombe, "Venezia, Bibl. Naz. Marziana, Latini Classe II, 26 (2473) and the Dionisian Corpus of the University of Paris in the Thirteenth Century," *Recherches de théologie ancienne et médiévale* 52 (1985), 224–27. Regarding the translations available to Bonaventure, Dondaine cites evidence from *De scientia Christi* and *De mysterio Trinitatis* that Bonaventure had access at least to the translations of Hilduin, Sarrazen, and Eriugena (Dondaine, 114n121).

20. Additionally, Gallus also refers to his own *Exposicio* on the *Mystical Theology* and a *glose* on the *Celestial Hierarchy*. James McEvoy translated and published what he believes to be Gallus's *Expositio* in *Mystical Theology: The Glosses by Thomas Gallus and the Commentary of Robert Grosseteste on* De Mystica Theologia, ed. and trans. James McEvoy, Dallas Medieval Texts and Translations 3 (Leuven: Peeters, 2003). Lawell disputes this attribution and regards this work as a later gloss influenced by Gallus ("Thomas Gallus's Method," 111–17). Lawell has edited the *Glose super Angelica Ierarchia* in *CCCM*, vol. 223A (Turnhout: Brepols, 2011).

21. Coolman, "The Medieval Affective Dionysian Tradition," in Coakley and Stang, 91; the passage to which Coolman refers is in Gallus's *Extractio* on the Mystical Theology, Chapter 1 (Chevallier, I.710).

22. "... principalis affectio, et ipsa est scintilla sinderesis que sola unibilis est spiritui diuino ..." *Explanatio MT* I, *CCCM* 223, ed. Declan Lawell (Turnhout: Brepols, 2011), 4. See Lawell, "Affective Excess: Ontology and Knowledge in the Thought of Thomas Gallus," *Dionysius* 26 (2008), 147. As Lawell explains, however, Thomas distinguishes synderesis as a *vis animae* from the *scintilla*, which is not a power of the soul, but something produced in the contact of synderesis with the divine Other and thus not properly belonging to the soul. See also Lawell, *"Ne de ineffabili penitus taceamus*: Aspects of the Specialized Vocabulary of the Writings of Thomas Gallus," *Viator* 40.1 (2009), 151–84, esp. 154–57.

23. Jacques de Vitry, *The Life of Marie D'Oignies* 1.22, trans. Margot H. King (Toronto: Peregrina Publishing, 1993), 54.

24. On the possible evidence for direct influence, see Sarah McNamer, *Affective Meditation and the Invention of Medieval Compassion* (Philadelphia: University of Pennsylvania Press, 2010), 86, 236n3; and King's introduction to de Vitry's *Vita*, 8.

25. The original attribution of this title is generally credited to the Dominican friar Raynor of Pisa, who used the epithet for Bonaventure in his 1333 *Pantheologia*.

26. Here I am interested primarily in the Seraph as an image of fire, love, and hierarchy, though these significations are not the only functions of the Seraph image. For example, Ewert Cousins examines the six-winged Seraph image as a meditative image or mandala representing an "organized totality." See Cousins, "Mandala Symbolism in the Theology of Bonaventure," *University of Toronto Quarterly* 40 (1971), 185–201.

27. Wayne Hellmann, "The Seraph in Thomas of Celano's *Vita Prima*," in *That Others May Know and Love: Essays in Honor of Zachary Hayes, OFM*, ed. Michael F. Cusato and F. Edward Coughlin (Franciscan Studies 34) (St. Bonaventure: Franciscan Institute, 1997), 23–41.

28. Thomas of Celano, *Uita prima sancti Francisci*, in *Legendae S. Francisci Assisiensis saeculis XIII et XIV conscriptae*, ed. PP. Collegii S. Bonaventurae (*Analecta Franciscana*, X, 1926–41), 2.94.

29. Thomas of Celano, *Uita prima*, 2.114.

30. Thomas of Celano, *Uita prima*, 2.114.

31. Thomas of Celano, *Uita prima*, 2.115.

32. Hellmann contends that Thomas would have been aware of the Dionysian and monastic theological associations of the Seraph image from his education at Monte Cassino. Whatever Thomas's education had or had not exposed him to, however, what is evident is that his discussion of the Seraph does not at any point in his *Vita* exploit the association of the Seraph with fire. Moreover, Thomas's Seraph-like figure is not depicted as performing the same purifying function as the biblical Seraph. Its significance is limited to its cruciform posture, its six wings outlining the virtues, and its flight symbolizing Francis's ascent to Christ. For a discussion of the differences in the Seraph imagery in Thomas and Bonaventure's respective accounts, see Hellmann, "The Seraph in Thomas of Celano and Bonaventure: The Victorine Transition," in *Bonaventuriana I*, ed. Chevero Blanco (Rome: Edizioni Antonianum, 1988), 347–56. On the development of the legend of the Seraph in Francis's vision, see Chiara Frugoni, *Francesco e l'invenzione delle stimmate: Una storia per parole e immagini fino a Bonaventura e Giotto* (Turin: Einaudi, 1993).

33. ". . . corroborato itinere, et sensus desere et intellectuales operationes et sensibilia et invisibilia et omne non ens et ens, et ad unitatem, ut possibile est, inscius restituere ipsius, qui est super omnem essentiam et scientiam," *Itinerarium mentis in Deum* 7.5. Translations are my own; I refer throughout to the page numbers in the reprinting of the Quaracchi edition (with facing-page English translation) in Philotheus Boehner and Zachary Hayes, *Works of St. Bonaventure*, vol. 2 (St. Bonaventure, N.Y.: Franciscan Institute, 2002).

34. *Itin.* 7.4. (Boehner and Hayes, 36). Compare the similar statement in the *Breviloquium* 5.6 (Quaracchi V.260), in which Bonaventure characterizes

the *excessus* as "learned ignorance" and paradoxically identifies darkness as a form of illumination: "Quo quidem desiderio ferventissimo ad modum ignis spiritus noster non solum efficitur agilis ad ascensum, verum etiam quadam ignorantia docta supra se ipsum rapitur in caliginem et excessum, ut non solum cum sponsa dicat: In odorem unguentorum tuorum curremus, verum etiam cum Propheta psallat: Et nox illuminatio mea in deliciis meis. Quam nocturnam et deliciosam illuminationem nemo novit nisi qui probat, nemo autem probat nisi per gratiam divinitus datam, nemini datur, nisi ei qui se exercet ad illam."

35. See also *Collationes in Hexaemeron* 2.30, where Bonaventure describes the "suprema unitio per amorem" as a state in which "affect alone keeps vigil and imposes silence on all the other powers" (*sola affectiva vigilat et silentium omnibus aliis potentiis imponit*), Quaracchi V: 341.

36. Etienne Gilson, *The Philosophy of St. Bonaventure*, trans. Dom Illtyd Trethowan and Frank J. Sheed (New York: Sheed and Ward, 1938), 458–64.

37. George Tavard, *Transiency and Permanence: The Nature of Theology According to St. Bonaventure* (St. Bonaventure, N.Y.: Franciscan Institute, 1954), 244–45.

38. Joseph Ratzinger, *The Theology of History in St. Bonaventure*, trans. Zachary Hayes (Chicago: Franciscan Herald Press, 1971), 90.

39. *Commentarius in Ecclesiasten* (*Comm. in Eccl.*) 7 (Quaracchi IV.54).

40. Coolman, 86.

41. "Et dici potest secundum quod hid accipitur amor: ineffable quondam feuds armonicum creators et create uniuersitatis . . ." *Explanatio in libros Dionysii*, ed. D. Lawell, *CCCM* 223 (Turnhout: Brepols, 2011), 248:1718–20. As Denys Turner writes with regard to Thomas Gallus: "In the last resort the true point of Gallus' dependence on neo-platonic *eros* is there, where Bernard's or Denys the Carthusian's is to be found: in their enthusiastic espousal of a general world-view in which erotic love, or love modeled on the erotic, is the prime mover, the moved, and the end of all motion, whether in the orders of nature, of the human, or of grace," *Eros and Allegory: Medieval Exegesis on the Song of Songs* (Cistercian Studies 156) (Kalamazoo, Mich.: Cistercian Publications, 1995), 73.

42. Hilduin translates *eros* as *cupiditas*. But Bonaventure favors the translation of *eros* as *amor* found in both Eriugena and John Sarrazen's translations.

43. Denys Turner, *Eros and Allegory: Medieval Exegesis on the Song of Songs* (Kalamazoo, Mich.: Cistercian Publications, 1995), 47.

44. *Divine Names* (*DN*) 709D (Lubheid, 81). See Turner's lucid discussion of Dionysian *eros* in *Eros and Allegory*, 47–70.

45. *Divine Names* (*DN*) 709D (Lubheid, 81).

46. On Dionysian *eros* and its relation to ecstatic union in the context of ancient Greek and Hellenistic thought, see Charles M. Stang, *Apophasis and Pseudonymity in Dionysius the Areopagite: "No Longer I"* (Oxford: Oxford University Press, 2012), 170–81.

47. *DN* 712A (Lubheid, 82). Sarrazen's translation reads: "Est autem faciens exstasim divinus amor, non dimittens sui ipsorum esse amatores, sed amatorum" (Chevallier, I.215).

48. "Amorem dicimus vim unitivam," *Commentarius in Secundum Librum Sententiarum* (2 *Sent.*), d. 39, dub 1 (Quaracchi II.916). This is a paraphrase of *DN* 713A–B (Lubheid, 83), in which Dionysius credits his teacher Hierotheus with this definition of *eros*: "When we speak of yearning [*ton erōta*], whether this be in God or an angel, in the mind [*noeron*] or in the spirit [*psychikon*] or in nature [*physikon*], we should think of a unifying [*enōtikēn*] and co-mingling [*synkratikēn*] power [*dynamin*] . . ." Sarrazen's translation of this passage reads, "Amorem sive divinum sive angelicum sive intellectualem sive animalem sive naturalem dicamus, unitivam quamdam et concretivam intelligemus virtutem . . ." (Chevallier I.225–26). See Chapter 3 for further discussion of Bonaventure's interpretation of this passage.

49. *Commentarius in Evangelium Lucae* 13.46 (Quaracchi VII.349).

50. "Excessivum autem modum cognoscendi dico, non quo cognoscens excedat cognitum, sed quo cognoscens fertur in obiectum excedens excessivo quodam modo, erigendo se supra se ipsum," *Quaestiones disputatae de scientia Christi*, q. 7, concl. (Quaracchi VII.40). In his *Sentences* commentary, Bonaventure makes similar distinctions within knowledge. 3 *Sent.* d. 24, dub. 4 (Quaracchi III.531): "God is known through vestiges, through images, through the effects of grace, and through intimate union of God and the soul [*animae*], just as the Apostle says, 'Whoever adheres to God is one spirit with him.' And this is the most excellent knowledge [*cognitio*], which Dionysius teaches. This knowledge consists in ecstatic love and is above the knowledge of faith [*elevat supra cognitionem fidei*] according to its common state."

51. *De scientia Christi*, q. 7, concl. (Quaracchi VII.40).

52. 1 *Sent.* d. 32, a. 2, q. 1, ad.1, 2, 3. (Quaracchi I.562): "Certain acts refer to a motion from a thing to the soul, such as wisdom, while others refer to the motion from the soul to the thing, such as loving [*amare*]." In his much later *Collationes in Hexaemeron*, Bonaventure discusses ecstasy as a *sapientia nulliformis*, but this passage from the *Sentences* indicates that *sapientia* is not necessarily an ecstatic movement any more than *cognitio* is.

2. AFFECT, COGNITION, AND THE NATURAL MOTION OF THE WILL

1. The most extended treatment of the development of the concept of synderesis is D. Odon Lottin, *Psychologie et morale au xii⁻ et xii⁻ siècles*. Tome

II: Problèmes de morale, part 1 (Louvain: 1948), 101–349. Lottin edits many
of the relevant texts and provides a clear analysis. For a brief summary, with
emphasis on the spiritual and unitive sense of the term, see Aimé Solignac,
"Syndérèse," *Dictionnaire de Spiritualité: ascétique et mystique, doctrine et histoire*
(*DS*), vol. 14.2, ed. Marcel Viller, et al. (Paris: G. Beauchesne, 1932–95),
1407–12.

    2. See, for example, Romans 7:15 and 2:15, respectively.

    3. See de Blic, "Syndérèse ou conscience?" *Revue d'ascetique et de mystique*
25 (1949), 146–57.

    4. Douglas Kries, "Origen, Plato, and Conscience (*Synderesis*) in Jerome's
Ezekiel Commentary," *Traditio* 57 (2002), 69. Kries argues convincingly
that Jerome's reference to followers of Plato who posit the fourth part of
the soul as *syneidesis* refers directly to Origen. In his commentary on Romans,
Origen identified *syneidesis*, mentioned in 2 Corinthians 1:12, with the
pneuma of 1 Corinthians 2:11 and Romans 8:16. All of these Pauline passages
would reappear as *auctoritates* in medieval discussions of synderesis. See also
Michael B. Crowe, "The Term *Synderesis* and the Scholastics," *Irish Theological Quarterly* 23 (1956), 151–64, 228–45.

    5. ". . . quartumque ponunt quae super haec et extra haec tria est, quam
Graeci uocant *syneidesin*—quae scintilla conscientiae in Cain quoque pec-
tore, postquam eiectus est de paradiso, non extinguitur, et, uicti uoluptati-
bus uel furore, ipsaque interdum rationis decepti similitudine, nos peccare
sentimus—, quam proprie aquilae deputant, non se miscentem tribus sed tria
errantia corrigentem, quam in scripturis interdum uocari legimus spiritum,
qui *interpellat pro nobis gemitibus ineffabilibus. Nemo enim scit ea quae hominis
sunt, nisi spiritus qui in eo est,* quem et Paulus ad Thessalonicenses scribens
cum anima et corpore seruari integrum deprecatur. Et tamen hanc quoque
ipsam conscientiam, iuxta illud quod in Pouerviis scriptum est: *Impius cum
uenerit in profundum peccatorum, contemnit,* cernimus praecipitari apud quos-
dam et suum locum amittere, qui ne pudorem quidem et uerecundiam habent
in delictis et merentur audire: *Facies meretricis facta est tibi, nescis erubescere,*"
Commentarii In Ezechielem, ed. F. Glorie, *CCSL* 12 (Turnhout, 1964) 12.

    6. Though the theory that *synderesis* was a mistranscription of *syneidesis*
is the most widely accepted, there have been other theories put forward to
explain the term's appearance in Jerome's commentary. At the end of the
nineteenth century, H. Siebeck argued that the term *synteresis* derives from
tereo and signifies a principle of conservation or maintenance. See Siebeck,
"Noch einmal die Synderesis," *Archiv für Geschichte der Philosophie* 10 (1897),
520–29. Also see Oscar Brown, *Natural Rectitude and Divine Law in Aquinas*
(Toronto: Pontifical Institute of Mediaeval Studies, 1981), 175–77; Jean
Rohmer, "Syndérèse," in *Dictionnaire Théologie Catholique,* vol. 14.2 (Paris,

1941), 2992–96; Gerard Verbeke maintains that the medieval concept of synderesis is fundamentally related to the Stoic conception of *oikeiosis*, a term that "refers to the basic impulse of a being, especially of man, toward himself, toward his own nature and condition, toward what is suitable and connatural for him, in a word, toward whatever is appropriate for him," *The Presence of Stoicism in Medieval Thought* (Washington: Catholic University of America Press, 1983), 55.

7. "The Spark of Conscience: Bonaventure's View of Conscience and Synderesis," *Franciscan Studies* 53 (1993), 93.

8. *Conscience and Other Virtues: From Bonaventure to MacIntyre* (University Park: Pennsylvania State University Press, 2001), 36.

9. See, for example, 2 *Sent.* d. 24, a. 2, q. 1 (Quaracchi II.559), in which he characterizes the question of the distinction between reason and will as one more of "curiosity than utility." Nevertheless, while Bonaventure refuses an essential distinction between the faculties, he establishes a clear basis for differentiation in terms of operation.

10. Timothy Potts, *Conscience in Medieval Philosophy* (Cambridge: Cambridge University Press, 1980),

11. Joseph Ratzinger, *On Conscience: Two Essays* (San Francisco: Ignatius Press, 2007), 30.

12. Ratzinger, 22.

13. Augustine refers to the higher part of reason or the *ratio sublimior* throughout *De Trinitate* XII. For a helpful discussion of the sources and subsequent development of this concept, see R. W. Mulligan, "Ratio Superior and Ratio Inferior: The Historical Background," *The New Scholasticism*, 29 (1955), 1–32.

14. *Speculum Speculationum*, ed. Rodney M. Thomson (Auctores Britannici Medii Aevi XI) (Oxford University Press, 1988), 405.

15. *Questiones magistri Rolandi super quattuor libros Sententiarum* (Paris Maz. 795), ed. Lottin, 130–34.

16. For Philip, the disposition that informs synderesis is what distinguishes it from the natural will. The natural will, in turn, is no more than a simple potentiality in the soul, undetermined to any particular end.

17. See *Philippi Cancellarii Parisiensis Summa de bono*, 2 vols., ed. Nikolaus Wicki (Corpus philosophorum Medii Aevi) (Bernae: Francke, 1985).

18. Thomas Aquinas treats synderesis and conscience as distinct as well. He expresses their relationship as one of habit to act, both belonging to the practical intellect (*STh* I.79.12–13). Aquinas discusses many of the traditional questions about synderesis at greater length in the sixteenth question of his *De veritate*, but the basic definition is the same. For a comparison of Bonaventure and Thomas Aquinas's conceptions of synderesis, see Eduard Lutz,

Die Psychologie Bonaventuras, in Beitrage zur Geschicte der Philosophie des Mittelalters VI, 4–5 (Munster, 1909), 180–90).

19. *Summa Theologica* II.73.1.1 (Quaracchi: Ex Typographia Collegii St. Bonaventurae, 1924), 417. Alexander died before completing his *Summa Theologica*. What is known as his *Summa*—or the *Summa Fratris Alexandri*—was compiled in its completed form by Alexander's students, including Bonaventure. See V. Doucet, "The History of the Problem of the Authenticity of the Summa," *Franciscan Studies* 7 (1947), 26–42, 274–312.

20. *Summa* II.73.1.2 (Quaracchi II.418).

21. *Summa* II.73.2.3 (Quaracchi II.423).

22. *Summa* II.73.2.6 (Quaracchi II.426).

23. Lottin II.1, 199n1.

24. Latin text of Gallus's commentary ed. G Théry, "Commentaire sur Isaïe de Thomas de Saint-Victor," *La vie spirituelle* 47 (1936), 146–62.

25. *Explanatio MT* I (Lawell, 4).

26. Lawell, "Specialized Vocabulary," 153.

27. Peter Lombard, *Sententiae in iu libris distinctae* 2. d. 39, c. 3, ed. I. Brady, *Spicilegium Bonaventurianum* 4–5 (Grottaferrata: Editiones Collegii S. Bonaventurae Ad Claras Aquas, 1971–81).

28. Peter Lombard, *Sent.* 2. d. 39, c. 3.

29. Bonaventure, 2 *Sent.* d. 39 (Quaracchi II.897).

30. 2 *Sent.* d. 39 (Quaracchi II.897).

31. 2 *Sent.* d. 39, a. 1, q. 1, fund. 5 (Quaracchi II.898).

32. 2 *Sent.* d. 39, a. 1, q. 1, fund. 3 (Quaracchi II.898).

33. 2 *Sent.* d. 39, a. 1, q. 1, concl. (Quaracchi II.899).

34. 2 *Sent.* d. 39, a. 1, q. 1, concl. (Quaracchi II.899).

35. In his response to an objection, Bonaventure qualifies this definition a bit, noting that conscience can also be understood as a *potentia*. Though it is tempting to see here a parallel to his definition of synderesis as a *potentia habitualis*, he appears to be making a very different point about conscience. A *potentia habitualis* is a power that is perfected or determined to a particular end by a habit. By naming conscience as a power *and* a habit simultaneously, however, Bonaventure is gesturing toward its indeterminacy. See 2 *Sent.* a. 1, q. 1, ad 1 (Quaracchi II.900): "Since an acquired habit is able to purify and stain the soul, thus it is that conscience is called pure and impure, right and not right. Still, these differences pertain more to conscience as power than conscience as habit."

36. In a response to an article by Cary Nederman, Marcia Colish lays out clearly the two competing senses of *habitus* in twelfth- and thirteenth-century scholastic theology. See "*Habitus* Revisited: A Reply to Cary Nederman," *Traditio* 48 (1993), 77–92.

37. 2 *Sent.* d. 39, a. 1, q. 2, concl. (Quaracchi II.902).

38. 2 *Sent.* d. 39, a. 1, q. 2, resp. (Quaracchi II.903), citing *Posterior Analytics* II.19.

39. *De Trin.* XII.24.

40. 2 *Sent.* d. 39, a. 1, q. 2, resp. (Quaracchi II.903).

41. According to Timothy Potts, from the perspective of contemporary ethical theory, Bonaventure's distinction between innate and acquired knowledge thus becomes "a logical and no longer a psychological criterion for basic deontic propositions and is independent of whether we have any intuition about the truth of a deontic proposition." As a result, Potts argues, Bonaventure fails to provide "an appropriate method for determining the truth-values of *a priori* deontic propositions; thinking it complete, he turned to *synderesis.*" *Conscience in Medieval Philosophy* (Cambridge: Cambridge University Press, 1980), 41–42.

42. 2 *Sent.* d. 39, a. 1, q. 2, resp. (Quaracchi II.904).

43. More precisely, synderesis is an orientation not simply to God but to the Good as it exists in others. Yet the significance of this distinction is tempered somewhat by Bonaventure's contention that every good is desirable only with reference to the supreme good, as in *De Scientia Christi* IV, fund. 29 (Quaracchi VII.20) (my emphasis): "Just as the affect holds itself to the good, so the intellect holds itself to the true, and as every good comes from the highest goodness, so every truth comes from the highest truth. *But it is impossible for our affect to be drawn directly to a good without in some way touching the highest good.*" Similarly, *Itinerarium* III.4 (Boehner and Hayes, 88): "Desire is principally concerned with that which moves it the most. And that which moves it the most is that which is loved the most. And that which is loved the most is to be happy. But happiness is attained only by reaching the best and ultimate end. Therefore, human desire wants nothing but the supreme Good, or that which leads to it or in some way reflects that Good."

44. By "secret," I mean an interiority that is both the limit of representability and, in a sense, its possibility, the space or interval that constitutes conscience as (never fully achievable) self-presence. I elaborate on this dynamic (as well as the philosophical debts that inform my thinking here) in the Conclusion.

45. Following the familiar framework of the scholastic disputed question, the particular difficulty arises from seemingly conflicting authorities: On the one hand, Jerome calls synderesis a fourth power distinct from the rational, irascible, and concupiscible parts. On the other hand, the pseudo-Augustinian *De spiritu et anima* posits only the threefold division of powers (*vires*). See 2 *Sent.* d. 39, a. 2, q. 1 (Quaracchi II.909).

46. Langston, "Spark of Conscience," 93.

47. 2 *Sent.* d. 39, a. 2, q. 1, resp. (Quaracchi II.910).

48. 2 *Sent.* d. 39, a. 2, q. 1 (Quaracchi II.911).

49. 2 *Sent.* d. 39, a. 2, q. 1, resp. (Quaracchi II.910). On the cognitive and affective aspects of *liberum arbitrium* see also 2 *Sent.* d. 25, p. 1, art. un., q. 1, concl. (Quaracchi II.592), and q. 3, concl. (Quaracchi II.598). I discuss these passages further in Chapter 5.

50. "hinc est, quod dicitur super alias volare . . . " 2 *Sent.* d. 39, a. 2, q. 1 (Quaracchi II.911).

51. 2 *Sent.* d. 39, a. 2, q. 1, ad 3. (Quaracchi II.910).

52. 2 *Sent.* d. 39, a. 2, q. 2, resp. (Quaracchi II.912).

53. 2 *Sent.* D. 39, a. 2, q. 2, concl. (Quaracchi II.912).

54. See 2 *Sent.* d. 39, a. 1, q. 3, concl. (Quaracchi II.906): "All conscience either binds one to do what it dictates, or it binds one to change his conscience if it is in error."

55. 2 Sent. d. 39, a. 2, q. 2, ad 3 (Quaracchi II.913).

56. See, for example, 2 Sent. d. 39, a. 1, q. 2; and d. 16, a. 2, q. 3.

57. See 2 *Sent.* d. 39, a. 2, q. 3, ad 4 (Quaracchi II.915).

58. 2 *Sent.* d. 39, a. 2, q. 3 (Quaracchi II.914).

59. 2 *Sent.* d. 39, a. 2, q. 3, ad 6 (Quaracchi II.915).

60. 2 *Sent.* d. 39, a. 2, q. 3, ad 6 (Quaracchi II.915).

61. 2 *Sent.* d. 39, a. 2, q. 3, ad 6 (Quaracchi II.915).

62. See 2 *Sent.* d. 24, a. 2, q. 1 (Quaracchi II.559).

63. 2 *Sent.* d. 39, a. 2, q. 3 (Quaracchi II.913).

64. 2 *Sent.* d. 39, a. 2, q. 3, ad 4 (Quaracchi II.915).

65. 2 *Sent.* d. 39, a. 2, q. 3, ad 4 (Quaracchi II.915).

66. 2 *Sent.* d. 39, a. 2, q. 3, ad 4 (Quaracchi II.915).

67. 2 *Sent.* d. 39, a. 2, q. 3, ad 4 (Quaracchi II.915).

68. 2 *Sent.* d. 39, a. 2, q. 3, ad 4 (Quaracchi II.915).

69. See 2 *Sent.* d. 39, a. 2, q. 1 ad 1 (Quaracchi II.910): ". . . just as Gregory said concerning the first chapter of Job, we speak to God not only through thoughts [*cogitationibus*] and exterior words, but even through affects and desires [*affectibus et desideriis*]." Thus, Bonaventure reasons, synderesis is not cognitive even though it is described as "speaking."

3. ELEMENTAL MOTION AND THE FORCE OF UNION

1. 2 *Sent.* d. 39, a. 2, q. 1 (Quaracchi II.909).

2. 2 *Sent.* d. 39, a. 2, q. 1, resp. (Quaracchi II.910).

3. Alexander of Hales, 2 *Sent.* d. 40 (Lottin 2.1, 176).

4. See the discussion of ancient theories of affect in the Introduction, as well as Simo Knuuttila, *Emotions in Ancient and Medieval Philosophy* (Oxford: Clarendon Press, 2004), 5–110.

5. Lottin, 198.

6. 2 *Sent.* d. 14, p. 1, a. 1, q. 2, ad 2, 3 (Quaracchi II.340).

7. See also 2 *Sent.* d. 24, p. 1, a. 2, q. 1, ad 7 (Quaracchi II.562), in which, in the process of arguing for the distinction of reason and will as different powers, Bonaventure suggests that the sun heats and illumines by means of different powers.

8. There is no modern edition; J. P. Migne includes the work in the appendix to the works of Augustine (under uncertain authorship) in the *Patrologia Latina* 40:779–832. Bernard McGinn's English translation appears in *Three Treatises on Man: A Cistercian Anthropology* (Kalamazoo, Mich.: Cistercian Publications, 1977), 179–288.

9. Peter Lombard, *Sent.* 2. d. 39.

10. 2 *Sent.* d. 30, dub. 2 (Quaracchi II.916).

11. 2 *Sent.* d. 30, dub. 2 (Quaracchi II.916).

12. 2 *Sent.* d. 30, dub. 2 (Quaracchi II.916).

13. 2 *Sent.* d. 30, dub. 2 (Quaracchi II.917).

14. "Dicendum, quod bonitas voluntatis inchoatur in appetitu naturali et consummatur in virtute deliberativa; nec est voluntas simpliciter bona et recta, nisi sit recta, in quantum movetur deliberative, et in quantum movetur naturaliter," 2 *Sent.* d. 39, dub. 2 (Quaracchi II.917).

15. See 4 *Sent.* d. 49, p. 2, s. 1, a. 3, q. 2, fund. 1 (Quaracchi IV.1020): "All cognition is motion to the soul . . . " and 1 *Sent.* d. 32, a. 2, q. 1, ad.1, 2, 3. (Quaracchi I.562): "Certain acts refer to a motion from a thing to the soul, such as wisdom, while others refer to the motion from the soul to the thing, such as loving [*amare*]." Here Bonaventure explains that while intelligence or understanding conveys a form, an act of love conveys to the soul both a form and an effect.

16. "Amorem dicimus vim unitivam," 2 *Sent.* d. 39, dub. 1 (Quaracchi II.916). On the Dionysian reference, see the introduction, nn. 38–39.

17. See also 2 *Sent.* d. 16, a. 1., q. 1 (Quaracchi 2.393–94), where Bonaventure deploys this definition of love to demonstrate that man is truly an image of God: "Likewise, what is most bound to be united to the other is most bound to be configured and conformed to it—for love [*amor*], because it unites, is said 'to transform the lover into the one loved,' just as Hugh of St. Victor says [in *De arrha anima*]—but a rational creature, such as a human being, is most bound to be united to God and to tend to Him through love: therefore he is most bound to be configured and assimilated to Him. If, therefore, image names an expressed similitude, it is clear that etc."

18. "Amor enim dicit affectionis adhaesionem respectu amati," 1 *Sent.* d. 10, dub. 1 (Quaracchi I.205).

19. 2 *Sent.* d. 39, a. 2, q. 3, ad 4 (Quaracchi II.915).

20. *2 Sent.* d. 39, a. 1, q. 1, concl. (Quaracchi II.899).

21. *2 Sent.* d. 39, a. 2, q. 1, ad 3 (Quaracchi II.910).

22. "Thus, it is no surprise that the two things that seem to be productive of movement are desire and practical thinking. It is because of the movement started by the object of desire that the thinking produces its movement, that which is desired being its point of departure. And even imagination, whenever it produces movement, does not do so without desire." Trans. Hugh Lawson-Tancred (New York: Penguin, 1986), 213.

23. Though several passages are relevant for this problem (see especially *Physica* VIII.4), the difficulty is readily apparent in *De anima* III.10: "In form, then, that which produces movement is a single thing, the faculty of desire as such. But first of all is the object of desire, which, by being thought or imagined, produces movement while not itself in motion. In number, however, there is more than one thing that produces movement" (Lawson-Tancred, 215).

24. Furley suggests that the contradiction can be resolved by holding (as he believes Aristotle implicitly held) that the objects of animal desire are in some way intentional objects—that is, are in some sense internal to perceiving and thinking beings. See David Furley, "Self-Movers," in *Aristotle on Mind and the Senses* (Proceedings of the Seventh Symposium Aristotelicum), ed. G. E. R. Lloyd and G. E. L. Owens (Cambridge: Cambridge University Press, 1978), 165–80. Furley's argument has been the subject of a significant amount of debate, much of it collected in the volume (in which Furley's original essay is reprinted) *Self-Motion: From Aristotle to Newton*, ed. Mary Louise Gill and James G. Lennox (Princeton, N.J.: Princeton University Press), 1994.

25. "The change of anything that is changed by itself is natural; this is the case with all animals, for example. For animals are self-movers, and we say that everything which has its own inner source of change is changed naturally." Trans. Robin Waterfield (Oxford: Oxford University Press, 1996), 196.

26. Waterfield, 33.

27. Waterfield, 199.

28. *De caelo* IV.1, in *The Basic Works of Aristotle*, trans. Richard McKeon (New York: Random House, 1941), 454. In the first complete Latin translation of the work (William of Moerbeke c. 1260), the terms are "grave" and "leve." Robert Grosseteste produced an incomplete translation of the work several years earlier, but this did not include Book 4.

29. *De Caelo* 4.3 (McKeon, 459).

30. *De Caelo* 4.3 (McKeon, 459).

31. *De Caelo* 4.3 (McKeon, 460).

32. *De Caelo* 4.3 (McKeon, 460).

33. The Aristotelian concept of natural place as a theological theme can also be found in Meister Eckhart's notion of *abegescheidenheit* or detachment. In Eckhart's formulation, however, it is God who is inexorably and necessarily moved. "And I prove that detachment compels God to come to me in this way; it is because everything longs to achieve its own natural place. Now God's own natural place is unity and purity, and that comes from detachment. Therefore God must of necessity give himself to a heart that has detachment," *On Detachment*, trans. Edmund Colledge, in *Meister Eckhart: The Essential Sermons, Commentaries, Treatises, and Defense* (Mahwah, N.J.: Paulist Press, 1981), 286.

34. *Confessiones* XIII.9. Latin text ed. James O'Donnell, *Confessions: Introduction and Text* (vol. 1) (Oxford: Clarendon Press, 1992), 187.

35. *Confessiones* XIII.9 (O'Donnell, 187).

36. "Si essemus lapides, aut fluctus, aut uentus, aut flamma, uel quid eiusmodi, sine ullo quidem sensu atque uita, non tamen nobis deesset quasi quidam nostrorum locorum atque ordinis appetitus. Nam velut amores corporum momenta sunt ponderum, siue deorsum grauitate, siue sursum leuitate nitantur. Ita enim corpus pondere, sicut animus amore fertur, quocumque fertur." *De civitate Dei* XI.28.

37. The precision of this understanding of *pondus* distinguishes Augustine's elaboration of the theme from other metaphorical descriptions of the soul rising to God. Cf., for example, John Cassian, *Conf.* 9:4–5.

38. For an overview of this theme in Augustine's writings, see C. Harrison, "Measure, Number and Weight in Saint Augustine's Aesthetics," *Augustinianum* 28 (1988), 591–602. See also Olivier du Roy, *L'intelligence de la foi en la Trinité selon saint Augustin: genèse de sa théologie jusqu'en 391* (Paris: Études augustiniennes, 1966), 279–81.

39. *De Genesi ad litteram* IV.3, *CCSL*, vol. 47, ed. B. Dombart (Turnhout: Brepols, 1955), 99.

40. *De Genesi ad litteram* IV.4 (Dombart, 100).

41. *De Genesi ad litteram* IV.3 (Dombart, 100).

42. ". . . pondus sine pondere est, quo referuntur ut quiescant, quorum quies purum gaudium est, nec illud jam refertur ad aliud," *De Genesi ad litteram* IV.3 (Dombart, 100).

43. ". . . quomodo dicam de pondere rupiditatis in abruptam abyssum, et de sublevatione charitatis per Spiritum tuum, qui superferebatur super aquas?" *Conf.* XIII.7.

44. ". . . in potestate non habet lapis cohibere motum quo fertur inferius, animus uero dum non uult non ita mouetur ut superioribus desertis inferiora diligat. et ideo lapidi naturalis est ille motus, animo uero iste uoluntarius," *De libero arbitrio* III.1, *CCSL* 29, ed. W. M. Green (Turnhout: Brepols, 1970) 211–321 at 260.

45. William of St. Thierry, *De natura et dignitate amoris* n. 1, CCCM 88, ed. P. Verdeyen (Turnhout: Brepols, 2003), 177.

46. *De natura et dignitate amoris* n. 4 (Verdeyen, 177).

47. *De natura et dignitate amoris* n. 4 (Verdeyen, 177).

48. *De natura et dignitate amoris* n. 4 (Verdeyen, 177).

49. *De natura et dignitate amoris* n. 4 (Verdeyen, 180).

50. *De natura et dignitate amoris* n. 12 (Verdeyen, 186).

51. See Thomas Davis's discussion of William's notion of *affectus* in *The Mirror of Faith*, 93–95.

52. *De natura et dignitate amoris* n. 14 (Verdeyen, 188).

53. *De natura et dignitate amoris* n. 44 (Verdeyen, 211).

54. *Breviloquium* 2.1 (Quaracchi V.219).

55. *Breviloquium* 2.1 (Quaracchi V.219).

56. In 1 *Sent.* d. 3, p. 1, dub. 3 (Quaracchi I.79), Bonaventure correlates the triad of measure, number, and weight with Dionysius's triad of *substantia*, *virtus* and *operatio* and Peter Lombard's triad of *unitas, speciem*, and *ordinem*.

57. *Brev.* 2.1 (Quaracchi V.219).

58. *Brev.* 5.8 (Quaracchi V.273).

59. *Brev.* 5.1 (Quaracchi V.252).

60. "Deus non concdescendit per sui essentiam incommutabilem, sed per influentiam ab ipso manantem," *Brev.* 5.1 (Quaracchi V.252).

61. ". . . illud non potest esse per habitum aliquem naturaliter insertum sed solum per donum divinitus gratis infusum . . . " *Brev.* 5.1 (Quaracchi V.253).

62. 1 *Sent.* d. 37, p. 1, a. 1, q. 1, concl. (Quaracchi I.639).

63. For a concise and helpful presentation of Bonaventure's conception of *vanitas*, see Christopher Cullen, *Bonaventure* (Great Medieval Thinkers), New York: Oxford University Press, 2006), 107–8.

64. *Brev.* 5.2 (Quaracchi V.253), citing Augustine, *Enchiridion* 32.9.

65. *Brev.* 5.8 (Quaracchi V.262).

66. "Et caritas ipsa est radix forma et finis virtutum iungens omnes cum ultimo fine et ligans omnia ad invicem simul et ordinate; ideo ipsa est pondus inclinationis ordinatae et vinculum colligationis perfectae," *Brev.* 5.8 (Quaracchi V.262).

67. On Bonaventure's notion of "hierarchization," see Chapter 4.

68. *Brev.* 5.8 (Quaracchi V.262). This bond of charity is also the principle of unity of the *ecclesia* as the mystical body of Christ. See Peter Fehlner, *The Role of Charity in the Ecclesiology of St. Bonaventure* (Rome: Miscellanea Francescana, 1965).

69. As Jay Hammond notes, Bonaventure invokes the concept of *pax* frequently in his works to mean "right order." See Jay Hammond's essay "Order in the *Itinerarium*," in his translation and edition of J. A. Wayne Hellmann's *Divine and Created Order in Bonaventure's Theology* (St. Bonaventure, N.Y.:

Franciscan Institute, 2001), 202. Hammond also argues, with respect to the
Itinerarium, that Bonaventure's "universal analogy" is in fact an affirmation
of the univocity of God's being throughout all creation, a presence which is
at the same time God's all-pervading love drawing all things potentially to
union (Hammond, Order in the *Itinerarium*, 209).

70. "Dicitur autem transire figura huius mundi non quantum ad destruc-
tionem totalem huius mundi sensibilis sed quia per actionem illius ignis
omnia elementaria inflammantis consummentur vegetabilia et animalia, purgabuntur et innovabuntur elementa, maxime aër et terra, purgabuntur iusti et
adurentur reprobi; quibus factis, cessabit etiam motus caeli, ut sic, completo
numero electorum, fiat quodam modo innovatio et praemiatio corporum
mundanorum," *Brev.* 7.4 (Quaracchi V.284).

71. See Cicero's discussion in *De natura deorum* 2.118, Loeb Classical
Library 19, trans. H. Rackham (Cambridge: Cambridge University Press,
1967). Macrobius also discusses this theory in his *Commentarii in Somnium
Scipionis* 2.10, a major source for ancient natural philosophy for twelfth-
century Latin theologians. On the influence of these theories in the thought
of Origen, see Alan Scott, *Origen and the Life of the Stars: The History of an
Idea* (Oxford: Clarendon Press, 1991), esp. 115–17.

72. *Brev.* 7.2 (Quaracchi V.282). See also Aelred of Rivaulx's discussion of
corporeal fire in hell (which collects a number of late ancient authorities) in
Dialogue on the Soul 3.

73. *Brev.* 7.6 (Quaracchi V.287), citing Rev 14.11.

74. ". . . necesse est, illos spiritus evolare, in quibus est caritatis ignis
sursum levans, et nihil retardans ex parte impuritatis animae vel reatus." *Brev.*
7.2 (Quaracchi V.283).

75. See, for example, the account of Diogenes Laërtius 7.156–57, trans.
Brad Inwood and Lloyd P. Gerson in *The Stoics Reader: Selected Writings and
Testimonials* (Cambridge: Hackett Publishing Company, 2008), 57.

76. See Cicero, *De natura deorum* 2.118, Loeb Classical Library 268, ed.
Jeffrey Henderson, trans. H. Rackam (Cambridge: Harvard University Press,
1933): "ita relinqui nihil praeter ignem, a quo rursum animante ac deo reno-
vatio mundi fieret atque idem ornatus oreretur."

77. 2 *Sent.* d. 39, dub. 1 (Quaracchi II.916).

78. 2 *Sent.* d. 25, p. 1, art. un., q. 1, ad 4 (Quaracchi II.594). For further
discussion of this argument, see Chapter 4.

79. *Brev.* 2.9 (Quaracchi V.227).

4. HIERARCHY AND EXCESS IN THE *ITINERARIUM MENTIS IN DEUM*
  1. *Itinerarium* Prol.2. (Boehner and Hayes, 36).
  2. *Itin.* Prol.2 (Boehner and Hayes, 36).

3. The *Itinerarium* is one of a number of treatises dated to within a few years of Bonaventure's appointment as Minister General of the Franciscan order in 1257. In the case of the *Itinerarium*, Bonaventure himself provides the date. If his dating can be taken literally, then the composition, or at least the conception, of the *Itinerarium* took place in September or October of 1259, around the thirty-third anniversary of Francis's death on October 4, 1226. See the excellent recent analysis of evidence for Bonaventure's chronology in Jay M. Hammond, "Dating Bonaventure's Inception as Regent Master," *Franciscan Studies* 67 (2009), 179–226. For a general (though in some cases disputed) chronology of Bonaventure's works, see Jacques Bougerol, *Introduction to the Works of Bonaventure*, trans. José de Vinck (Paterson, N.J.: St. Anthony Guild Press, 1963), 171–82; also Joseph F. Quinn, "The Chronology of St. Bonaventure (1217–1257)," *Franciscan Studies* 32 (1972), 168–86. Whether or not Bonaventure's own dating of the work is reliable, however, it would be a mistake to take it *only* literally, given its multifaceted allegorical significance. The *Itinerarium* is, in a sense, an exegesis of Francis's Seraphic vision at Mount La Verna and of the stigmata he received with that vision. Accordingly, the Christological significance is underscored by the number thirty-three, which recalls the traditional age of Jesus at the time of his crucifixion. Furthermore, the wording, "circa Beati ipsius transitum," connects the death (*transitus*) of Francis with the "passing over" (also *transitus*) that is the goal and summit of the *itinerarium*. The dating, then, should be understood as part of the strategy of the prologue, which frames the journey described in the treatise in a richly significant spiritual time and place, whatever else it might indicate about the historical circumstances of the writing.

4. Bonaventure's account of Francis's vision at La Verna is in *Legenda Maior* 13 (Quaracchi XIII.543ff).

5. On Bonaventure's conception of *transitus* see Werner Hülsbusch, "Die Theologie des Transitus bei Bonaventura," in *S. Bonaventura 1274–1974* (Grottaferrata: Collegio S. Bonaventura, 1973), 4:533–65 and André Ménard, "Spiritualité du Transitus," *S. Bonaventura 1274–1974*, 4:607–35.

6. *Itin.* Prol.3 (Boehner and Hayes, 36).

7. On *ecstasis* and the related term *raptus* in Bonaventure's writings, see Karl Rahner, "Der Begriff der ecstasis bie Bonaventura." *Zeitschrift fur Aszese und Mystik* 9 (1934), 1–18, and J. Beumer, "Zwei schwierige Begriffe in der mystischen Theologie Bonaventuras ('raptus' und 'ecstasis')," in *Franziskanische Studien* 56 (1974), 249–62.

8. Gregory LaNave, "Knowing God through and in All Things: A Proposal for Reading Bonaventure's *Itinerarium mentis in Deum*," *Franciscan Studies* 67 (2009), 267–99, and Jay Hammond's "Respondeo" to LaNave's essay in the same volume, 301–21.

9. For a comparison of the two works, and a discussion of Richard's influence on Bonaventure, see Stephen Brown, "Reflections on the Structural Sources of Bonaventure's *Itinerarium Mentis in Deum*," in *Medieval Philosophy and Modern Times*, ed. G. Homström-Hintikka, vol. 1–16 (Netherlands: Kluwer, 2000), 1–15.

10. Karnes, 83.

11. *Itin.* Prol.3 (Boehner and Hayes, 38).

12. *Itin.* 1.1 (Boehner and Hayes, 44).

13. *Itin.* 1.1 (Boehner and Hayes, 44).

14. Jay Hammond, "An Historical Analysis of the Concept of Peace in Bonaventure's *Itinerarium mentis in Deum*" (Ph.D. dissertation, Saint Louis University, 1998), 21. Hammond seeks to place the *Itinerarium*, and specifically its call for peace, in the historical context of the rifts developing in the Franciscan order during Bonaventure's first years as Minister General. Thus "order" resonates as both a political and theological ideal. For more on the notion of *ordo* in the *Itinerarium*, see also Jay Hammond, "Order in the *Itinerarium*" in J. A. Wayne Hellmann, *Divine and Created Order in Bonaventure's Theology*, trans. and ed. Jay M. Hammond (St. Bonaventure, N.Y.: The Franciscan Institute, 2001).

15. The multivalence of the term *mens* suggests "soul" as a better translation than "mind." At times, Bonaventure clearly uses it to mean the higher part of the soul—the memory, understanding, and will by which the soul is the image of God (see especially *Itin.* 3). In this usage, the term could be translated as "mind." Yet Bonaventure is also clear that the soul as a unity is the subject of ascent, and not simply the higher mind alone, making "mind" a misleading translation for the subject of the *Itinerarium*. While Bonaventure does at times recognize some distinction between *mens* and *anima*, it is clear that by "mind," he does not mean the "superior reason" or higher intellect. Thus, in order to avoid overemphasizing the cognitive aspects of ascent, and to signify that Bonaventure's subject is the entire soul, I have generally followed recent scholarly convention in translating *mens* as "soul," except where context suggests that the term refers restrictively to the higher powers or the triad of memory, understanding, and will.

16. Denys Turner insists rightly that Bonaventure's notion of hierarchy is one in which each step contains within it all of the previous stages. However, as I will argue later in this chapter, what makes Bonaventure's "hierarchy" truly dynamic is the way in which each stage also contains its superior stage. See Turner, "Hierarchy Interiorised: Bonaventure's *Itinerarium mentis in Deum*" in *The Darkness of God: Negativity in Christian Mysticism* (Cambridge: Cambridge University Press, 1995), 102–34.

17. *Itin.* Prol.3 (Boehner and Hayes, 38).

18. *Itin.* 7.4 (Boehner and Hayes, 136).

19. *Itin.* 1.6 (Boehner and Hayes, 50).

20. Augustine discusses this triad as the image of God in *mens* at length in *De Trinitate* Book 10, in a reflection on the Delphic oracle and Ciceronian injunction, *nosce te* (know thyself).

21. *Itin.* 3.2 (Boehner and Hayes, 82).

22. *Itin.* 3.4 (Boehner and Hayes, 88).

23. "Desiderium autem principaliter est illius quod maxime ipsum movet. Maxime autem movet quod maxime amatur; maxime autem amatur esse beatum; beatum autem esse non habetur nisi per optimum et finem ultimum: nihil igitur appetit humanum desiderium nisi quia summum bonum, vel quia est ad illud, vel quia habet aliquam effigiem illius," *Itin.* 3.4 (Boehner and Hayes, 88).

24. As J. Bougerol explains, *desiderium* for Bonaventure is "more than a force or impulsion—it is a tendency," one that does not require cognitively certain judgment regarding the object, but rather only that the soul "taste the power, the beauty, and the fruit of the attraction" ("L'aspect original de l'Itinerarium mentis in Deum et son influence sur la spiritualite de son temps," *Antonianum* 52 [1977], 311). See also *Comm. in Eccl.* 7 (Quaracchi IV.54): "When something is desired, it is not necessary that a certain cognition precede it. For desire follows estimation alone" (*Quod aliquid desideratur, non necesse est, quod praecedat cognitio certitudinis; desiderium enim sequitur solam aestimationem*). Bonaventure makes a similar claim for *dilectio* in 2 Sent. d. 23, a. 2, q. 3, ad. 4 (Quaracchi II.545–46), in response to the objection that, if Adam loved God in Paradise, he must have had a preceding vision of God. Refuting this argument, Bonaventure cites William of St. Thierry (misidentified as Bernard of Clairvaux) that *dilectio* "extends itself further than vision," since "*dilectio* sometimes follows estimation alone."

25. *Itin.* 4.3 (Boehner and Hayes, 100).

26. *Itin.* 2.3 (Boehner and Hayes, 64).

27. See *Brev.* 5.6 (Quaracchi V.259).

28. This point is also made clearly by Thomas Aquinas in the *Summa Theologiae*, I.78.3. The standard critical edition is the *Opera Omnia, iussu Leonis XIII O.M, edita cura et studio fratrum praedictorum* (Rome: 1882–1996), vols. 4–11.

29. Trans. in Denys Turner, *Eros and Allegory: Medieval Exegesis of the Song of Songs* (Kalamazoo, Mich.: Cistercian Publications), 326.

30. For a more thorough account of Bonaventure's teachings on the spiritual senses, see Karl Rahner, "The Doctrine of the Spiritual Senses in the Middle Ages," in *Theological Investigations* vol. 16, trans. Cornelius Ernst (Baltimore: Helicon Press, 1961), 109–28; and Gregory LaNave, "Bonaven-

ture," ch. 9 of *The Spiritual Senses: Perceiving God in Western Christianity*, ed.
Paul Gavrilyuk and Sarah Coakley (Cambridge: Cambridge University Press,
2012), 159–73.

31. *STh* I.78.3.

32. Thomas notes, however, that in sensible creatures, the effect an object
has on the perceiver is never merely natural. That is, it is never entirely without an intellectual response; otherwise the sense of touch would have to be
extended to even inanimate objects, which are also naturally affected by external agents. John Milbank and Catherine Pickstock point out that for Thomas,
touch is the basest of the senses both in being the most bodily and the most
extensive, and insofar as all sense perception is based on or understood on the
model of touch. In fact, Milbank and Pickstock understand touch for Thomas
as not only not opposed to intellect, but also as the mode (or model?) of intelligence, both human and divine. See John Milbank and Catherine Pickstock,
Truth in Aquinas (New York: Routledge, 2001), 71.

33. *Itin.* 4.3 (Boehner and Hayes, 100).

34. *Itin.* 4.3 (Boehner and Hayes, 100).

35. *Itin.* 4.3 (Boehner and Hayes, 100).

36. The same triad appears in Bonaventure's *De perfectione vitae ad sorores*
5.6–9. On contemplation and the overthrow of reason in the *Beniamin
Maior*, see Stephen Jaeger, "Richard of St. Victor and the Medieval Sublime,"
in Stephen Jaeger, ed., *Magnificence and the Sublime in Medieval Aesthetics:
Art, Architecture, Literature, Music* (New York: Palgrave Macmillan, 2010),
157–78.

37. Richard of St. Victor, *Beniamin Maior* 5.11; trans. Grover A. Zinn
as *The Mystical Ark*, in *Richard of St. Victor*, Classics of Western Spirituality
(Mahwah, N.J.: Paulist Press, 1979), 325.

38. On Bonaventure's elaboration of the Dionysian triad of purification-
illumination-perfection in his *Triplex Via*, see J. Bougerol, "Le perfection
chrétienne et la structuration des trois voies," *Etudes Franciscaines* 19 (1969),
397–409.

39. *Itin.* 4.4 (Boehner and Hayes, 100).

40. *Comm. in Luc.* 10.62 (Quaracchi VII:271).

41. *Itin.* 4.3 (Boehner and Hayes, 98).

42. *Itin.* 4.8 (Boehner and Hayes, 106).

43. The verb "hierarchizare" and related forms appear in Bonaventure's
work only later, and most frequently in the *Collationes in Hexaemeron*, but
his frequent use of the phrase *efficitur hierarchicus* in the *Itinerarium* suggests
the same: being made into a hierarchy. For a thorough study of the uses and
senses of *hierarchia* and related terms, see Romano Guardini and Werner
Dettloff, *Systembildene Elemente in der Theologie Bonaventuras: die Lehren vom*

lumen mentis, von der gradatio entium, und der influentia sensus et motus (Leiden: E. J. Brill, 1964), 146–75.

44. *Brev.* 2.12 (Quaracchi V.230).

45. *Itin.* 7.1 (Boehner and Hayes, 132).

46. See especially Jay Hammond, "Order in the *Itinerarium*" and "Respondeo." Note that Steven Brown also sees a correlation in Richard between *sensibilia* and vestiges, *intelligibilia* and images, and *intellectibilia* and— rather than similitudes—the divine reality itself. See Brown, "Structural Sources," 5.

47. See 1 *Sent.* d. 3, p. 1, art. un., q. 2, ad. 4 (Quaracchi I.72–73), where Bonaventure distinguishes the *umbra* as another mode distinct from the *vestigium*.

48. The term *similitudo*, and the triad *vestigium, imago*, and *similitudo*, require, I think, a slightly different elaboration, and will be considered later in this chapter.

49. 1 *Sent.* d. 3, p. 1, art. un., q. 2 (Quaracchi I:71–74.)

50. In fact, Bonaventure himself seems to take this position in the first of his *Disputed Questions on the Trinity*, 1.2, concl (Quaracchi V.54): "Every creature is either only a vestige of God—as is corporeal nature—or an image of God, as is the intellectual creature."

51. Etienne Gilson, *Philosophy of St. Bonaventure*, 185–214.

52. *Brev.* 2.12 (Quaracchi V.230).

53. In the first chapter, Bonaventure refers only to the distinction of vestige and image: "In accordance with our condition, the totality of things [*rerum universitas*] is a ladder for ascending to God. And among things, some are vestiges, others images; some corporeal, others spiritual; some temporal, others, everlasting; some things are outside us, and some within us" (Boehner and Hayes, 46).

54. "Secundus modus distinguendi est, quod imago est in *naturalibus*, et similitudo in *gratuitis*, qui similiter habet ortum ex illa *prima* differentia. Quia enim *imago* dicit *configurationem*; et illa attenditur ex parte naturalium potentiarum animae, scilicet memoriae, intelligentiae et voluntatis: hinc est, quod imago est in naturalibus. Quia vero *similitudo* dicit convenientiam, quae ortum habet a *qualitate*; et qualitas, in qua anima similatur Deo, haec est gratia: ideo *similitudo* dicitur in gratuitis esse," 2 *Sent.* d. 16, a. 2, q. 3, concl. (Quaracchi II.405).

55. Turner maintains, though in a carefully qualified way, that the passage from stages three to four is the hinge of nature and grace in the movement of ascent. Here his qualification is that, in keeping with the nature of *hierarchia*, the fourth stage does not exclude the operations of nature as seen in the first three stages, but takes them up and transforms them. While I do not disagree

with this basic point, I maintain, as noted previously, that the distinction between the operations of nature and the operations of grace is complicated not only by the non-linear nature of the *itinerarium*, but by the excess that structures each of its stages. See Turner, *Darkness of God*, 112–13; and *Eros and Allegory*, 145–49.

56. *Itin.* 7.1 (Boehner and Hayes, 132).

57. For an analysis of the temple motif that structures the *Itinerarium*, see Bernard McGinn, "Ascension and Introversion in the Itinerarium Mentis in Deum," in *S. Bonaventura 1274–1974*, vol. 3 (Rome: Grottaferrata, 1974), 535–52; Lillian Turney, "The Symbolism of the Temple in St. Bonaventure's *Itinerarium mentis in Deum*," unpublished Ph.D. dissertation (Fordham University, 1968).

58. *Itin.* 6.3 (Boehner and Hayes, 126).

59. *Itin.* 7.1 (Boehner and Hayes, 132).

60. *Itin.* Prol.1 (Boehner and Hayes, 34).

61. *Itin.* 7.1 (Boehner and Hayes, 132).

62. *Itin.* Prol.2 (Boehner and Hayes, 36).

63. Boehner's notes to the *Itinerarium* draw many of these lexical connections. See *Works* vol. 2, 146nn6–7.

64. "Suspendium elegit anima mea, et mortem ossa mea," *Itin.*, 138.

65. Bonaventure's last work, *Collationes in Hexaemeron*, just as frankly posits the necessity of death, and its connection to ascent and to love: "quia oportet hominem mori per illum amorem, ut sursum agatur," *Col. Hex*, Princ.2.31 Ed. Ferdinand Delorme, Bibl. Franciscana Scholastica Medii Aevi, vol. 8 (Ad Claras Aquas: Florentiae ex typographia Collegii S. Bonaventurae, 1934). On Bonaventure's conception of mystical death see Alois M. Haas, *Sermo Mysticus: Studien zu Theologie und Sprache der Deutschen Mystik* (Universitätsverlag Freiburg Schweiz, 1979), 406–9. Haas rightly insists that *mors* for Bonaventure is not merely metaphorical, but expresses a reality as physical as the crucified incarnation of the Word.

66. *Itin.* 7.6 (Boehner and Hayes, 138).

67. ". . . non lucem, sed ignem totaliter inflammantem et in Deum excessivis unctionibus et ardentissimis affectionibus transferentem," *Itin.* 7.6 (Boehner and Hayes, 138).

68. 2 *Sent.* d. 39, a. 2, q. 2, concl. (Quaracchi II.910).

69. "In hoc autem transitu, si sit perfectus, oportet quod relinquantur omnes intellectuales operationes, et apex affectus totus transferatur et transformetur in Deum," *Itin.* 7.4 (Boehner and Hayes, 136).

70. "sensus desere et intellectuales operationes et sensibilia et invisibilia et omne non ens et ens, et ad unitatem, ut possibile est, inscius restituere ipsius, qui est super omnem essentiam et scientiam." *Itin.* 7.5 (Boehner and Hayes, 136).

71. On this Latin interpretive tradition see, most recently, two complementary essays: Paul Rorem, "The Early Latin Dionysius: Eriugena and Hugh of St. Victor," and Boyd Coolman, "The Medieval Affective Dionysian Tradition," in *Re-thinking Dionysius the Areopagite*, ed. Sarah Coakley and Charles M. Stang (Oxford: Wiley-Blackwell, 2009), 71–84 and 85–102.

72. On fire as the active, motive element, see 2 *Sent.* d. 15 (Quaracchi II.379–81).

73. *Itin.* 7.6 (Boehner and Hayes, 138). On Bonaventure's use of the term *passio*, see Erich Auerbach, "Excursus: *Gloria Passionis*," in *Literary Language and Its Public in Late Antiquity and in the Middle Ages*, trans. Ralph Manheim (New York: Pantheon, 1965), 67–81.

74. See also Thomas Gallus's account of the *hierarchia mentis*: "The lowest hierarchy of mind consists in its very own nature; the middle in what it can do by effort, which incomparably exceeds nature; the highest in ecstasy (*excessus mentis*). At the lowest, only nature is at work; at the highest, only grace; at the middle, both grace and effort work together" (trans. Turner, *Eros and Allegory*, 321).

5. THE EXEMPLARY BODIES OF THE *LEGENDA MAIOR*

1. On the development of the concept of *voluntas* more generally in Latin Christian theology, see Albrecht Dihle, *The Theory of the Will in Classical Antiquity* (Berkeley: University of California Press, 1982), and N. Gilbert, "The Concept of the Will in Early Latin Philosophy," *Journal of the History of Philosophy* 11 (1973), 299–317. On the concept of *voluntas* and its relation to the intellect and free choice in the later middle ages, see Kent, *Virtues of the Will*.

2. See J. Korolec, "Free Will and Free Choice," in *The Cambridge History of Later Medieval Philosophy*, ed. Norman Kretzmann, et al. (Cambridge: Cambridge University Press, 1988), 630: "The will itself was defined as the rational appetite, or the desire for the good apprehended by reason, and not in terms of a capacity for choosing between alternatives." See also discussion in Kent, *Virtues of the Will*, 98. Kent notes, however, that after 1270, though *liberum arbitrium* remained a common topic of inquiry, some masters began to discuss the problem of *voluntas libera* or *libertas voluntatis*.

3. The modern association of "rational" with "intellectual" or "cognitive" is also a misleading approach to medieval theological uses of the adjective *rationalis*, whose range of meaning for Bonaventure I discuss below. *Rationalis* and *intellectualis*, though not entirely discrete terms for Bonaventure, nevertheless are not synonymous, as I will suggest.

4. "Augustinus de Quinque Responsionibus 4 'Cum de libero arbitrio loquimur, non de parte animae loquimur, sed de tota': ergo non tantummodo comprehendit cognitivam, immo etiam affectivam," 2 *Sent.* d. 25, p. 1,

art. un., q. 3, fund. 1 (Quaracchi II.597). The common definition of *liberum arbitrium* as a "faculty of will and reason" was taken from Lombard's *Sentences* II.25, though it was commonly misattributed to Augustine.

5. Brev. II.9 (Quaracchi V.226).

6. 2 *Sent.* d. 25, p. 1, art. un., q. 1, concl. (Quaracchi II.592); and q. 3, concl. (Quaracchi II.598).

7. "Quod enim obiicitur, quod non comprehendit totam rationem, nec totam voluntatem; dicendum, quod verum est; sed comprehendit solum ipsam potentiam cognitivam, in quantum iuncta est affectivae, et affectivam, in quantum iuncta est cognitivae; unde dicit affectum deliberativum, vel deliberationem voluntariam. Et propterea, quia ratio nominat ipsam potentiam cognitivam ut ordinatam ad affectivam, et voluntas ipsam affectivam ut regulatam et ratiocinatam a cognitiva; hinc est, quod liberum arbitrium potius dicitur facultas voluntatis et rationis quam intellectus et affectus" (2 *Sent.* 25, p. 1, art. un., q. 3, ad 2, 3 [Quaracchi II.599]).

8. 2 Sent. d. 25, p. 1, art. un., q. 3, contr. 3 (Quaracchi II.598).

9. "Concedendum est igitur, quod naturalis voluntas et deliberativa potest esse eadem potentia, quae quidem secundum alium et alium modum movendi sic et sic appellatur. Eadem enim est potentia, qua appeto beatitudinem, et qua appeto virtutem, sive facere hoc bonum vel illud ad beatitudinem ordinatum; quae, ut appetit beatitudinem, dicitur naturalis, quia immutabiliter appetitus eius ad beatitudinem inclinatur; ut vero appetit hoc vel illud bonum facere, deliberativa dicitur, et secundum iudicium rationis potest ad contrarium inclinari," 2 *Sent.* d. 24, p. 1, a. 2, q. 3, concl. (Quaracchi II.566).

10. *Metaphysics* IX, 3 and 10.

11. Thus, free choice can only choose evil insofar as free choice itself is deficient, as Bonaventure explains in 2 *Sent.* d. 25, p. 2, art. un., q. 3, concl. (Quaracchi II.614).

12. See *Itin.* 3.4, and discussion in previous chapter.

13. 2 *Sent.* d. 24, p. 1, a. 2, q. 3 (Quaracchi II.565).

14. See Richard Sorabji, "The Concept of the Will from Plato to Maximus the Confessor," in Thomas Pink and M. W. F. Stone, eds., *The Will and Human Action: From Antiquity to the Present Day* (New York: Routledge, 2004), 20–22. Sorabji argues that Maximus's conception of the natural will (*thelema phusikon*) is directly related to this Stoic idea. See also Sorabji, *Animal Minds and Human Morals* (Ithaca, N.Y.: Cornell University Press, 1995), chs. 12 and 13.

15. 2 *Sent.* d. 24, p. 1, a. 2, q. 3 (Quaracci II.566).

16. 2 *Sent.* d. 24, p. 1, a. 2, q. 3 (Quaracci II.566).

17. Bonaventure neither endorses nor refutes the notion of the natural will of animals as a self-preservation instinct.

18. 2 *Sent.* d. 24, p. 1, a. 2, q. 3, ad. 2 (Quaracchi II.566).

19. "Si autem sic esset determinata ad unum quod nullo modo posset in opposita, sicut est potentia calefaciendi et illuminandi in igne, tunc esset pure naturalis, et non esset deliberativa sive rationalis," 2 *Sent.* d. 24, p. 1, a. 2, q. 3, ad 2 (Quaracchi II.566).

20. 2 *Sent.* d. 25, p. 2, art. un., q. 2, concl. (Quaracchi II.596).

21. *Brev.* II.9 (Quaracchi V.227).

22. 2 *Sent.* d. 25, p. 1, art. un, q. 1, concl. (Quaracchi II.593).

23. 2 *Sent.* d. 25, p. 1, art. un, q. 1, concl. (Quaracchi II.593).

24. 2 *Sent.* d. 25, p. 1, art. un, q. 1, ad 4 (Quaracchi II.594). See also 1 *Sent.* 1, dist 37, p. 2, a. 2, q. 1, ad. 3 (Quaracchi I.658), where in response to the question of whether the fact that angels move indicates imperfection, Bonaventure distinguishes natural and voluntary movements—voluntary movements do not indicate any sort of lack in the one moving, whereas natural movement is always from lack or imperfection, because perfection in nature is a state of rest: "To the objection that all that is moved is moved on account of indigence, this must be admitted to be true in natural motion [*in motu naturali*], in which a nature moves only through an appetite for something. And this appetite stands as an imperfection in that nature, since a nature, once it attains its perfection, is at rest. But this is not true in the case of voluntary motion [*in motu voluntario*], in which something is moved either for the purpose of acquiring something, or to demonstrate its virtue, just as a gladiator is moved in the stadium. Or it must be said that it is true in every motion, insofar as 'indigence' can be taken generally . . . For in this way indigence can be posited either to a being whose privation indicates an imperfection, or to a being whose privation is not an imperfection, but a limitation, and the latter is case in Angels."

25. 2 *Sent.* d. 25, p. 1, art. un, q. 1, concl. (Quaracchi II.593).

26. 2 *Sent.* d. 25, p. 1, art. un, q. 1, concl. (Quaracchi II.593).

27. *Liber de Causis* XV.124, ed. Adriaan Pattin, in *Tijschrift voor filosofie* 28 (1966), 90–203 at 167): "Every knower who knows its own essence returns to its essence in a complete reversion" (*Omnis sciens qui scit essentiam suam est rediens ad essentiam suam reditione completa*).

28. 2 *Sent.* d. 25, p. 1, art. un, q. 1 (Quaracchi II.592).

29. Denys Turner makes a similar point in analyzing Pseudo-Dionysius's conception of *eros*: "Erotic love is necessity lived in the mode of freedom and freedom lived in the mode of necessity," *Eros and Allegory*, 59.

30. Note the similarity to the account of reason's abandonment to ecstasy in Richard of St. Victor's *Beniamin Minor*.

31. This paradox of interiority and exteriority is an echo of Dionysius's own understanding of God as ecstatic love, as Perl characterizes it: "In God

as Love, therefore, pure interiority coincides with pure exteriority" (Perl, *Theophany*, 46).

32. *Legenda Maior* XIII.10 (Quaracchi XIII.545). Translations are my own, but I have referred to the translation and notes by Ewert Cousins (Mahwah, N.J.: Paulist Press, 1978), 177–327. For an analysis of the major themes and structure of the *Legenda*, see Regis J. Armstrong, "The Spiritual Theology of the *Legenda Major* of Saint Bonaventure (PhD dissertation, Fordham University, 1978). Armstrong argues that the entire work is laid out according to the threefold pattern of purgation, illumination, and perfection (52–54).

33. As Ann Astell puts it well, the *Itinerarium* and the *Legenda* provide "a kind of commentary on one another" (*Eating Beauty*, 104).

34. I agree with Richard Emmerson and Ronald Herzmann's contention that a careful reading of the *Legenda* reveals its "close connection with several of Bonaventure's theological works, particularly with those emphasizing Christology, mysticism, and the meaning of salvation history." See Emmerson and Herzmann, *The Apocalyptic Imagination in Medieval Literature*, 44.

35. In his introduction to the text, Cousins provides a list of the material that is original to Bonaventure's *Legenda*, and gives detailed notes throughout his translation for Bonaventure's earlier sources (Cousins, *Bonaventure*, 39n74).

36. See Cousins's introduction to his translation for a sketch of the historical circumstances of the *Legenda*'s composition (Cousins, *Bonaventure*, 37–42). Some historians in the twentieth century, interested in recovering the primitive Franciscan ideal, have criticized Bonaventure's version as unreliable, unoriginal, and less a historical document than a political intervention in the growing schism within the order. When it was approved as the official biography by the General Chapter of Paris in 1266, all earlier *vitae* were suppressed. Astell wryly suggests that the evident failure of the *Legenda* to produce that unity constitutes an argument for its historical veracity (Astell, *Eating Beauty*, 100n4). These debates are important but, for the present study, the relation of the *Legenda* to Bonaventure's other writings is more relevant than its relation to the needs of the order in the thirteenth century.

37. ". . . angelico deputatus officio incendioque seraphico totus ignitus et ut vir hierarchicus curru igneo sursum vectus." *Legenda* Prol.1 (Quaracchi XIII.504).

38. Nor are the angelic associations limited to the Dionysian hierarchy. In the prologue, Bonaventure writes that Francis is symbolized by the "angel who ascends from the sunrise bearing the seal of the living God" depicted in Rev. 6.12. See analysis of this symbol and its apocalyptic resonances in Emmerson and Herzman, *The Apocalyptic Imagination*, 36–75.

39. *Legenda* Prol.2 (Quaracchi XIII.504).

40. *Legenda* 1.1 (Quaracchi XIII.506).

41. *Legenda* 8.5 (Quaracchi XIII.543). This section is original to Bonaventure's *vita*.

42. "Pietas vera, quae secundum Apostolum ad omnia valet, adeo cor Francisci repleverat ac penetraverat viscera, ut totum videretur virum Dei in suum dominium vindicasse. Haec est, quae ipsum per devotionem sursum agebat in Deum, per compassionem transformabat in Christum, per condescensionem inclinabat ad proximum et per universalem conciliationem ad singula refigurabat ad innocentiae statum," *Legenda* 8.1 (Quaracchi XIII.526).

43. *Legenda* 1.5 (Quaracchi XIII.507).

44. *Legenda* 5.8 (Quaracchi XIII.518).

45. *Legenda* 5.8 (Quaracchi XIII.518).

46. ". . . nondum didicerat contemplari caelestia nec assueverat degustare divina. Et quia spirituali auditui dat intellectum inflicta vexatio, facta est super eum manus Domini et immutatio dexterae Excelsi, diutinis languoribus ipsius corpus affligens, ut coaptaret animam ad sancti Spiritus unctionem," *Legenda* 1.2 (Quaracchi XIII.506).

47. *Legenda* 1.2 (Quaracchi XIII.506).

48. *Legenda* Prol.4 (Quaracchi XIII.505).

49. *Legenda* Prol.3 (Quaracchi XIII.504).

50. *Legenda* Prol.3 (Quaracchi XIII.504).

51. *Legenda* 2.1 (Quaracchi XIII.507–8).

52. *Legenda* 2.1 (Quaracchi XIII.508).

53. *Legenda* 3.4 (Quaracchi XIII.510).

54. *Legenda* 10.2 (Quaracchi XIII.533).

55. *Legenda* 10.2 (Quaracchi XIII.533).

56. *Legenda* 10.4 (Quaracchi XIII.534).

57. *Legenda* 10.4 (Quaracchi XIII.534).

58. *Legenda* 13.2 (Quaracchi XIII.542).

59. *Legenda* 13.3 (Quaracchi XIII.543).

60. *Legenda* 13.3 (Quaracchi XIII.543). Jill Bennett suggests that this passage reveals the close association between sensory vision and affective transformation in medieval psychology, "Stigmata and Sense Memory: St. Francis and the Affective Image," *Art History* 24.1 (February 2001), 1–16.

61. On Francis as another Christ, and medieval critics of this form of veneration, see Lester K. Little, "*Imitatio Francisci*: The Influence of Francis of Assisi on Late Medieval Religious Life," in *Defenders and Critics of Franciscan Life: Essays in Honor of John V. Fleming*, ed. Michael F. Cusato and Guy Geltner (Leiden: Brill, 2009), 195–218 at 196.

62. By calling Francis's body a martyr, I intend to draw attention to its function as a witness to Francis's love and as a victim of it. On Francis's

wounds as a visible "index of *affectus*," see Bennett, "Stigmata and Sense
Memory," 14.

63. *Legenda* 6.4 (Quaracchi XIII.520).

64. *Legenda* 9.2, 9.4, and 9.6, respectively (Quaracchi XIII.530–32).

65. Elsewhere, Bonaventure characterizes obedience as a matter of being
moved by grace. See *Comm. in Eccl.* 2 (Quaracchi VI.25): "It must be said that
to follow God through being equal to God is not given to any creature. And
since Satan wanted this, he fell. But one can also follow through subjection
and obedience, and this is possible for human beings: not whoever wishes, but
those to whom it is given by God through grace, and whom he draws. And
thus no one through themselves is able to follow without God's help."

66. "Et quia affectus ad exempla quam ad argumenta, magis ad promissiones quam ad ratiocinationes, magis per devotiones quam per definitions . . ." *Breviloquium*, Prol.5.2. (Quaracchi V.206). That the affect is
moved both to examples and to promised rewards amounts, according to a
standard scholastic account of human motivation, to the same thing. In both
cases, the example and the reward, it is a matter of an *end* moving the soul
to act—in the first case, perfect imitation of Francis, which is imitation of
Christ, is the end to which the example moves the soul. In the second case,
the promised reward is nothing other than Christ, the beloved with whom
the soul is united in spiritual perfection. See also *Collationes de decem praeceptis*
1.1 (Quaracchi V.507): "And this is the proper order, that the end moves the
agent, so that agent might work to the proper end."

67. *Legenda* 10.2 (Quaracchi XIII.533).

68. For a comprehensive study of the animal stories and their context, see
Edward Armstrong, *Saint Francis: Nature Mystic: The Derivation and Signifi-
cance of the Nature Stories in the Franciscan Legend* (Berkeley and Los Angeles:
University of California Press, 1973).

69. *Legenda* 8.6 (Quaracchi XIII.527).

70. *Legenda* 8.6 (Quaracchi XIII.527).

71. *Legenda* 8.10 (Quaracchi XIII.529).

CONCLUSION: A CORPUS, IN SUM

1. Trans. John P. Leavey, Jr., in *On the Name*, ed. Thomas Dutoit (Stanford: Stanford University Press, 1995), 55.

2. *Legenda* 13.4 (Quaracchi XIII.543).

3. *Legenda* 13.4 (Quaracchi XIII.543). Given the dispossession of Francis
in Christ through his spiritual martyrdom, these words are anything but a
straightforward declaration of possession by Francis. In light of the scriptural
provenance, they can themselves be understood as, paradoxically, an ecstatic
utterance.

4. *Legenda* 13.4 (Quaracchi XIII.543).

5. *Legenda* 13.8 (Quaracchi XIII.544).

6. Derrida repeatedly appears to deny this structure of absolute secrecy to Christian apophatic discourse, as for example in "How to Avoid Speaking: Denials," trans. Ken Frieden, in *Derrida and Negative Theology*, ed. Harold Coward and Toby Foshay (Albany, N.Y.: SUNY Press, 1992). The question is not so much whether Derrida is right or wrong about the Dionysian tradition, but rather, whether it is possible to read that tradition otherwise. For analysis of this possibility and a convincing attempt to realize it in the text of the thirteenth-century beguine Hadewijch, see Amy Hollywood, "Derrida's Noble Unfaith, or What Reading Hadewijch Can Teach You about Reading Derrida," *Minnesota Review* 80 (2013), 95–105.

7. *Legenda* 14.1 (Quaracchi XIII.545).

8. See, for example, *Legenda* 5.6 (Quaracchi XIII.518).

9. *Legenda* 14.6 (Quaracchi XIII.547).

10. *Legenda* 15.3 (Quaracchi XIII.548).

11. On the *agilitas* of the glorified resurrection body, see *Brev.* VII.7, n. 1 (Quaracchi V.289).

12. *Legenda* 15.2 (Quaracchi XIII.547).

13. *Legenda* 15.4 (Quaracchi XIII.548). The episode of the knight echoes a scene before Francis's death when a doubting follower put his fingers in the wounds (*Legenda* 13.8 [Quaracchi XIII.544]). This suggests, perhaps, that Francis's body should be understood as a resurrection body both before and after his literal death, and that this passing is less decisive than the death he undergoes in his vision of the Seraph. The post-death appearance of this second Thomas figure is original to Bonaventure's *vita*. The addition is consistent with Bonaventure's intensification of biblical patterns in his presentation of Francis's life and death, even as it confirms, specifically, the identification of Francis's corpse with Christ's resurrection body.

14. *Legenda* 15.3 (Quaracchi XIII.548).

15. Karnes, 112.

16. *Lignum vitae*, Prol. 1 (Quaracchi XIII.66).

17. *Lignum vitae*, Prol. 1 (Quaracchi XIII.66).

18. See Karnes, 130–35; Patrick F. O'Connell, "The Lignum vitae of Saint Bonaventure and the Medieval Devotional Tradition" (unpublished PhD Dissertation, Fordham University, 1985).

19. On the dating, context, and themes of the work, Lezlie S. Knox, *Creating Clare of Assisi: Female Franciscan Identities in Later Medieval Italy* (Leiden: Brill, 2008), 64–69.

20. McNamer, 90–92.

21. This consistency has been recognized by scholars. See, for example, Knox, 66. On the threefold scheme in Bonaventure's works, see Bougerol, "Le perfection chrétienne."

22. *De perfectione vitae ad sorores* 6.1 (Quaracchi VIII.120).

23. *De perfectione* 5.5 (Quaracchi XIII.119).

24. *De perfectione* 4.10 (Quaracchi XIII.115).

25. *De perfectione* 4.10 (Quaracchi XIII.115).

26. *De perfectione* 6.2 (Quaracchi XIII.120).

27. Karnes, on the contrary, reads this passage as emphasizing "not sharing Christ's pain but rising with Christ to bliss," a journey from Jesus's humanity to Christ in heaven. Yet Bonaventure's language seems to resist any such disjunction—the kingdom of God that the meditant enters is, for Bonaventure, Jesus's tortured body. See Karnes, 135–37.

28. *De perfectione* 6.2 (Quaracchi XIII.120).

29. I am indebted here to Catherine Keller's insightful meditation on the aporetic nature of mystical writing as an opening toward rethinking embodiment in the medieval Christian *via negativa*. See "The Cloud of the Impossible: Embodiment and Apophasis," in *Apophatic Bodies: Negative Theology, Incarnation, and Relationality*, ed. Chris Boesel and Catherine Keller (New York: Fordham University Press, 2010).

30. Dionysius glosses Paul's words in Galatians 2:20 as the confession of the lover in ecstatic union in *Divine Names* 4 (Lubheid, 82). For an interpretation of the Dionysian corpus in light of it, see Stang, *Apophasis and Pseudonymity*, and especially the analysis of this passage in 161–70.

31. Stang, 205.

32. Derrida, *The Gift of Death*, 92.

PRIMARY SOURCES

Alexander of Hales. *Summa theologica*. 4 vols. Quaracchi: Ex Typographia
Collegii S. Bonaventura, 1951.

Anselm of Canterbury. *Opera Omnia*. 6 vols. Edited by F. S. Schmitt. Edin-
burgh: Thomas Nelson and Sons Publishers, 1940–61.

Aristotle. *The Basic Works of Aristotle*. Translated by Richard McKeon.
New York: Random House, 1941.

———. *On the Soul*. Edited by Hugh Lawson-Tancred. New York: Penguin,
1986.

———. *Physics*. Translated by Robin Waterfield. Oxford: Oxford University
Press, 1996.

Armstrong, Regis, Wayne Hellmann, and William Short, eds. *Francis of Assisi:
Early Documents*. Vol. 2, *The Founder*. New York: New City Press, 2000.

Augustine, *Confessiones*. Edited by James O'Donnell. Vol. 1, *Confessions: Introduction and Text*. Oxford: Clarendon Press, 1992.

———. *De Genesi ad litteram. Corpus Christianorum Series Latina*. Vol. 47.
Edited by B. Dombart. Turnhout: Brepols, 1955.

———. *De libero arbitrio. Corpus Christianorum Series Latina*. Vol. 29. Edited
by W. M. Green. Turnhout: Brepols, 1970.

Bernard of Clairvaux. *Bernardi opera*. 8 vols. Edited by J. Leclercq, C. H.
Talbot, and H. M Rochais. Rome: Editiones Cisterciensis, 1957–77.

Bonaventure. *Collationes in Hexaemeron*. Edited by Ferdinand M. Delorme.
Volume 8, Bibliotheca Franciscana Scholastica Medii Aevi. Quaracchi:
Ex Typographia Collegii S. Bonaventura, 1934.

———. *Doctoris seraphici S. Bonaventurae opera omnia*. 10 vols. Quaracchi:
Ex Typographia Collegii S. Bonaventura, 1882–1902.

———. *Itinerarium mentis in Deum*. Translated by Zachary Hayes. With
notes by Philotheus Boehner. *Works of St. Bonaventure* II. Saint Bonaventure, N.Y.: Franciscan Institute Publications, 2002.

———. *The Life of St. Francis*. Translated by Ewert Cousins. Classics of Western Spirituality. Mahwah, N.J.: Paulist Press, 1978.

Chevallier, P., ed. *Dionysiaca: Recueil donnant l'ensemble des traductions latines des ouvrages attribués au Denys de l'Aréopage.* 2 vols. Bruges 1937–50.

Cicero. *De natura deorum; Academica.* Loeb Classical Library. Works of Cicero, vol. 19. H. Rackham. Cambridge, Mass.: Cambridge University Press, 1967.

Eckhart, Meister. *The Essential Sermons, Commentaries, Treatises, and Defense.* Translated by Edmund Colledge, O.S.A. and Bernard McGinn. Mahwah, N.J.: Paulist Press, 1981.

———. *Teacher and Preacher.* Edited by Bernard McGinn. Mahwah, N.J.: Paulist Press, 1986.

Eriugena, John Scotus. *Expositiones in Ierarchiam Coelestem.* Edited by J. Barbet. Vol. 31, *Corpus Christianorum Continuatio Mediaeualis.* Turnhout: Brepols, 1975.

Furley, David. "Self-Movers." In *Aristotle on Mind and the Senses.* Proceedings of the Seventh Symposium Aristotelicum, edited by G.E.R. Lloyd and G.E.L. Owens, 165–80. Cambridge: Cambridge University Press, 1978.

de Gandillac, Maurice. *La hiérarchie céleste. Sources Chrétiennes* 58. Paris: Éditions du cerf, 1958.

Gerson, Lloyd, ed. *The Stoics Reader: Selected Writings and Testimonials.* Cambridge: Hackett Publishing Company, 2008.

Gregory the Great. *Homiliae in euangelia. Corpus Christianorum Series Latina.* Vol. 141. Edited by R. Etiax. Turnhout: Brepols, 1999.

Hugh of St. Victor. *Commentarii in Hierarchiam Coelestem.* Edited by J. P. Migne. *Patrologia Latina.* Vol. 175: 923–1154.

Jerome. *Commentarii In Ezechielem.* Edited by F. Glorie. Vol. 12, *Corpus Christianorum Series Latina.* Turnhout: Brepols, 1964.

Lottin, Odon, trans. *Psychologie et morale aux XIIe et XIIIe siècles.* 6 vols. Louvain: Abbaye du Mont César, 1942–60.

McGinn, Bernard, trans. *Three Treatises on Man: A Cistercian Anthropology.* Kalamazoo, Mich.: Cistercian Publications, 1977.

Nequam, Alexander. *Speculum speculationum.* Edited by Rodney M. Thomson. Auctores Britannici Medii Aevi XI. Oxford University Press, 1988.

Peter Lombard, *Sentences.* 4 vols. Translated by Giulio Silano. Toronto: Pontifical Institute of Mediaeval Studies, 2007–10.

Philip the Chancellor. *Philippi Cancellari Parisiensis Summa de bono.* 2 vols. Edited by Nikolaus Wicki. Corpus philosophorum Medii Aevi. Bernae: Francke, 1985.

Plato. *The Collected Dialogues.* Edited by Edith Hamilton and Huntington Cairns. Princeton, N.J.: Princeton University Press, 1961.

Pseudo-Aristotle. *Liber de Causis.* Adriaan Pattin, ed. *Tijschrift voor filosofie* 28 (1966): 90–203.

Pseudo-Dionysius. *Corpus Dionysiacum*. 2 vols. Edited by Regina Suchla, Günter Heil, and Adolf Martin Ritter. *Patristische Texte und Studien* bd. 33 and 36. Berlin and New York: Walter de Gruyter, 1990–91. English translation in *Pseudo-Dionysius: The Complete Works*. Translated by Colm Lubheid. Mahwah, N.J.: Paulist Press, 1987.

Richard of St. Victor. *Benjamin Major*. Translated by Grover A. Zinn. Classics of Western Spirituality. Mahwah, N.J.: Paulist Press, 1979.

Thomas Aquinas. *Quaestiones disputatae de vertitate. Sancti Thomae Aquinatis, doctoris angelici Opera Omnia iussu Leonis XIII*, vol 22. *O.M. edita, cura et studio fratrum praedictorum*. Rome: 1882–1996.

———. *Summa Theologiae. Sancti Thomae Aquinatis, doctoris angelici Opera Omnia iussu Leonis XIII*, vols. 4–11. *O.M. edita, cura et studio fratrum praedictorum*. Rome: 1882–1996.

Thomas Gallus. *Commentaire sur Isaïe de Thomas de Saint-Victor*. Edited by G. Théry. *La vie spirituelle* 47 (1936): 146–62.

———. *Explanatio in libros Dionysii*. Vol. 223, *Corpus Christianorum Continuatio Mediaeualis*. Edited by Declan Lawell. Turnhout: Brepols, 2011.

———. *Exposicio Vercellensis* of *De Mystica Theologia*. Edited and translated by James McEvoy in *Mystical Theology: The Glosses by Thomas Gallus and the Commentary of Robert Grosseteste on* De Mystica Theologia. Dallas Medieval Texts and Translations 3. Peeters, 2003.

de Vitry, Jacques, *The Life of Marie D'Oignies*. Translated by Margot King. Toronto: Peregrina Publishing, 1993): 35–171.

William of St. Thierry. *De natura et dignitate amoris*. Vol. 88, *Corpus Christianorum Continuatio Mediaeualis*. Edited by P. Verdeyen. Turnhout: Brepols, 2003.

———. *The Mirror of Faith*. Translated by Thomas Davis. Cistercian Fathers Series 15. Kalamazoo, Mich.: Cistercian Publications, 1979.

SECONDARY WORKS

Ahmed, Sarah. *The Cultural Politics of Emotion*. New York: Routledge, 2004.

Anderson, C. Colt. *A Call to Piety: Saint Bonaventure's Collations on the Six Days*. Quincy, Ill.: Franciscan Press, 2003.

Armstrong, Edward. *Saint Francis: Nature Mystic: The Derivation and Significance of the Nature Stories in the Franciscan Legend*. Berkeley and Los Angeles: University of California Press, 1973.

Armstrong, Regis. "The Spiritual Theology of the *Legenda Major* of Saint Bonaventure." PhD dissertation, Fordham University, 1978.

Astell, Ann. *Eating Beauty: The Eucharist and the Spiritual Arts of the Middle Ages*. Ithaca, N.Y.: Cornell University Press, 2006.

Auerbach, Erich. *Literary Language and Its Public in Late Antiquity and in the Middle Ages*. Translated by Ralph Manheim New York: Pantheon, 1965.

Beckwith, Sarah. *Christ's Body: Identity, Culture, and Society in Late Medieval Writings*. London: Routledge, 1993.

———. "Passionate Regulation: Enclosure, Ascesis, and the Feminist Imaginary." *South Atlantic Quarterly* 93 (1994): 803–24.

Beirnaert, Louis. "Le symbolisme ascensionnel dans la liturgie et la mystique chrètiennes." In *Eranos-Jahrbuch* 19 (1950): 43–44.

Bennett, Jill. "Stigmata and Sense Memory: St. Francis and the Affective Image." *Art History* 24.1 (February 2001): 1–16.

Berlant, Lauren. *Cruel Optimism*. Durham, N.C.: Duke University Press, 2011.

Bestul, Thomas H. "St. Anselm and the Continuity of Anglo-Saxon Devotional Traditions. *Annuale Medievale* 18 (1977): 20–41.

———. *Texts of the Passion: Latin Devotional Literature and Medieval Society*. Philadelphia: University of Pennsylvania Press, 1996.

Bettoni, Efrem. *Saint Bonaventure*. Translated by Angelus Gambatese. Westport, Conn.: Greenwood Press, 1981.

Beumer, J. "Zwei schwierige Begriffe in der mystischen Theologie Bonaventuras ('raptus' und 'ecstasis')." *Franziskanische Studien* 56 (1974): 249–62.

de Blic, J. "Synderèse ou conscience?" *Revue d'ascetique et de mystique* 25 (1949): 146–57.

Bissen, J.-M. *L'Exemplarisme divin selon Saint Bonaventure*. Paris: Librairie Philosophique J. Vrin, 1929.

Boquet, Damien. *L'ordre de l'affect au Moyen Age: Autour de l'anthropologie affective d'Alred de Rievaulx*. Louvain: Brepols, 2005.

Bougerol, J. Guy. "L'aspect original de *l'Itinerarium mentis in Deum* et son influence sur la spiritualite de son temps." *Antonianum* 52 (1977): 309–25.

———. *Introduction to the Works of Bonaventure*. Translated by José de Vinck. Paterson, N.J.: St. Anthony Guild Press, 1963.

———. "Le perfection chrétienne et la structuration des trois voies." *Etudes Franciscaines* 19 (1969): 397–409.

———. *Saint Bonaventure: études sur les sources de sa pensée*. Northampton: Variorum Reprints, 1989.

Bowman, Leonard J. "The Cosmic Exemplarism of Bonaventure." *Journal of Religion* 55:2 (April 1975): 181–98.

———. "*Itinerarium*: The Shape of the Metaphor." In *Itinerarium: The Idea of a Journey*. Leonard Bowman, ed. Salzburg: Institut für Anglistik und Amerikanistik, 1983. 3–33.

Brown, Oscar. *Natural Rectitude and Divine Law in Aquinas*. Toronto: Pontifical Institute of Medieval Studies, 1981.

Brown, Stephen. "Reflections on the Structural Sources of Bonaventure's *Itinerarium Mentis in Deum*." In *Medieval Philosophy and Modern Times*, edited by G. Homström-Hintikka, vol. 1–16 (Netherlands: Kluwer, 2000): 1–15.

Brinkema, Eugenie. *The Forms of the Affects.* Durham, N.C.: Duke University Press, 2014.

Bynum, Caroline Walker. *Fragmentation and Redemption: Essays on Gender and the Human Body in Medieval Religion.* New York: Zone Books, 1991.

Casey, Michael. *Athirst for God: Spiritual Desire in Bernard of Clairvaux's "Sermons on the Song of Songs."* Cistercian Publications, 1986.

Chakrabarty, Dipesh. "The Time of History and the Times of Gods." In *The Politics of Culture in the Shadow of Capital,* edited by Lisa Lowe and David Lloyd, 35–60. Durham, N.C.: Duke University Press, 1997.

Chenu, M.-D. "Les catégories affectives au Moyen Âge." *Du corps à l'esprit: Textes rassemblés et présentés par Jacques Durandeaux.* Desclée de Brouwer, 1989, 145–53.

———. "Spiritus, le vocabulaire de l'âme au xiie siècle." *Revue des sciences philosophiques et theologiques* 41 (1957): 209–32.

Coakley, Sarah, and Charles M. Stang, eds. *Re-thinking Dionysius the Areopagite.* Oxford: Wiley-Blackwell, 2009.

Colish, Marcia. "*Habitus* Revisited: A Reply to Cary Nederman." *Traditio* 48 (1993): 77–92.

———. *Remapping Scholasticism.* Toronto: Pontifical Institute of Medieval Studies, 1983.

Colledge, Eric (Edmund), ed. *The Medieval Mystics of England.* New York: Scribner, 1961.

Coolman, Boyd Taylor. "The Medieval Affective Dionysian Tradition." In *Re-thinking Dionysius the Areopagite,* edited by Sarah Coakley and Charles M. Stang, 85–102. Malden, Mass.: Wiley-Blackwell, 2009.

Conger, George. *Theories of Macrocosms and Microcosms in the History of Philosophy.* New York: Russell and Russell, 1922.

Corbin, Michel. *L'inoui de Dieu: Six Etudes Christologiques.* Paris: Desclée de Brouwer, 1979.

Cousins, Ewert H. *Bonaventure and the Coincidence of Opposites.* Chicago: Franciscan Herald Press, 1978.

———. "The Humanity and the Passion of Christ." In *Christian Spirituality: High Middle Ages and Reformation,* edited by Jill Raitt, 375–91. New York: Crossroad, 1987.

———. "Mandala Symbolism in the Theology of Bonaventure." *University of Toronto Quarterly* 40 (1971): 185–201.

Crowe, Michael. *The Changing Profile of the Natural Law.* The Hague: Nijhoff, 1977.

———. "The Term *Synderesis* and the Scholastics." *Irish Theological Quarterly* 23 (1956): 151–64; 228–45.

Cullen, Christopher M. *Bonaventure. Great Medieval Thinkers*. Oxford: Oxford University Press, 2006.

Dailey, Patricia. "The Body and Its Senses." In *The Cambridge Companion to Christian Mysticism*, edited by Amy Hollywood and Patricia Z. Beckman, 264–76. Cambridge: Cambridge University Press, 2012.

———. *Promised Bodies: Time, Language, and Corporeality in Medieval Women's Mystical Texts*. New York: Columbia University Press, 2013.

de Certeau, Michel. "The Freudian Novel: History and Literature." In *Heterologies: Discourse on the Other*, translated by Brian Massumi, 17–34. Minneapolis: University of Minnesota Press, 2006.

Delio, Ilia. *Simply Bonaventure: An Introduction to His Life, Thought, and Writings*. Hyde Park, N.Y.: New City Press, 2001.

Derrida, Jacques. *The Gift of Death*. Translated by David Wills. Chicago: University of Chicago Press, 1995.

———. "How to Avoid Speaking: Denials." In *Derrida and Negative Theology*, edited by Harold Coward and Toby Foshay. Albany, N.Y.: SUNY Press, 1992.

———. "*Sauf le nom (Post-Scriptum)*." Translated by John P. Leavey, Jr. In *On the Name*, edited by Thomas Dutoit, 34–85; 144–47. Stanford: Stanford University Press, 1995.

Dihle, Albrecht. *The Theory of the Will in Classical Antiquity*. Berkeley: University of California Press, 1982.

Dixon, Thomas. *From Passions to Emotion: The Creation of a Secular Psychological Category*. Cambridge: Cambridge University Press, 2003.

Dondaine, H. F. *Le Corpus Dionysien de l'Université de Paris au XIIIe Siècle*. Rome: Edizioni di storia e letteratura, 1953.

Doucet, V. "The History of the Problem of the Authenticity of the Summa." *Franciscan Studies* 7 (1947): 26–42, 274–312.

Dreyer, Elizabeth Ann. "Affectus in St. Bonaventure's Description of the Journey of the Soul to God." PhD dissertation, Marquette University, 1983.

Duba, William. "Seeing God: Beatitude and Cognition in the Thirteenth Century." PhD dissertation, University of Iowa, 2006.

Emery, Kent, Jr. "Reading the World Rightly and Squarely: Bonaventure's Doctrine of the Cardinal Virtues." *Traditio* 39 (1983): 183–218.

Emmerson, Richard, and Ronald Herzmann. *The Apocalyptic Imagination in Medieval Literature*. Philadelphia: University of Pennsylvania Press, 1992.

Evans, G. R., ed. *Mediaeval Commentaries on the Sentences of Peter Lombard: Current Research*. Vol. 1. Leiden: Brill, 2002.

Fehlner, Peter. *The Role of Charity in the Ecclesiology of St. Bonaventure*. Rome: Miscellanea Francescana, 1965.

Foshee, C. N. "St. Bonaventure and the Augustinian Concept of *Mens*." *Franciscan Studies* 27 (1967): 163–75.

Frantzen, Allen J. "Spirituality and Devotion in the Anglo-Saxon Penitentials." *Essays in Medieval Studies* 22 (2005): 117–28.

Frugoni, Chiara. *Francesco e l'invenzione delle stimmate: Una storia per parole e immagini fino a Bonaventura e Giotto*. Turin: Einaudi, 1993.

Fulton, Rachel. *From Judgment to Passion: Devotion to Christ and the Virgin Mary, 800–1200*. New York: Columbia University Press, 2002.

Gavrilyuk, Paul, and Sarah Coakley, eds. *The Spiritual Senses: Perceiving God in Western Christianity*. Cambridge: Cambridge University Press, 2012.

Gendreau, B. A. "The Quest for Certainty in Bonaventure." *Franciscan Studies* 21 (1961): 104–227.

Gersh, Stephen. *From Iamblichus to Eriugena: An Investigation of the Prehistory and Evolution of the Pseudo-Dionysian Tradition*. Leiden: Brill, 1978.

Gilbert, N. "The Concept of the Will in Early Latin Philosophy." *Journal of the History of Philosophy* 11 (1973): 299–317.

Gill, Mary Louise, and James G. Lennox. *Self-Motion: From Aristotle to Newton*. Princeton, N.J.: Princeton University Press, 1994.

Gilson, Etienne. *The Philosophy of St. Bonaventure*. Translated by Dom Illtyd Trethowan and Frank J. Sheed. Paterson, N.J.: St. Anthony Guild Press, 1965.

Greene, Robert A. "Instinct of Nature: Natural Law, Synderesis, and the Moral Sense." *Journal of the History of Ideas* 58:2 (April 1997): 173–98.

———. "Synderesis, the Spark of Conscience, in the English Renaissance." *Journal of the History of Ideas* 52:2 (April–June 1991): 195–219.

Gregg, Melissa, and Gregory Seigworth, eds. *The Affect Theory Reader*. Durham, N.C.: Duke University Press, 2010.

Guardini, Romano, and Werner Dettloff. *Systembildene Elemente in der Theologie Bonaventuras: die Lehren vom lumen mentis, von der gradatio entium, und der influentia sensus et motus*. Leiden: E. J. Brill, 1964.

Haas, Alois. *Sermo Mysticus: Studien zu Theologie und Sprache der Deutschen Mystik*. Universitätsverlag Freiburg Schweiz, 1979.

Hammond, Jay. "Bonaventure's *Itinerarium*: A *Respondeo*." *Franciscan Studies* 67 (2009): 301–21.

———. "Dating Bonaventure's Inception as Regent Master." *Franciscan Studies* 67 (2009): 179–226.

———. "An Historical Analysis of the Concept of Peace in Bonaventure's *Itinerarium mentis in Deum*." PhD dissertation, Saint Louis University, 1998.

Harrison, C. "Measure, Number and Weight in Saint Augustine's Aesthetics." *Augustinianum* 28 (1988): 591–602.

Hayes, Zachary. "Christology and Metaphysics in the Thought of Bonaventure." *Journal of Religion* 58, Suppl. ("Celebrating the Medieval Heritage.") (1978): 82–96.

———. *The Hidden Center: Spirituality and Speculative Christology in St. Bonaventure.* Mahwah, N.J.: Paulist Press, 1981.

———. "The Theological Image of St. Francis in the Sermons of St. Bonaventure." *Bonaventuriana: Miscellanea in onore di Jacques Guy Bougerol, ofm.* Rome: Edizioni Antonianum, 1988.

Heinrichs, Maurus. "Synderesis und Apatheia: Ein Beitrag zur Theologie Bonaventuras im östilchen Raum." In *S. Bonaventura 1274–1974.* Vol. 3. Grottaferrata: Collegio S. Bonaventura, 1973, 623–95.

Hellmann, J. A. Wayne, *Divine and Created Order in Bonaventure's Theology.* Translated by J. M. Hammond. St. Bonaventure, N.Y.: Franciscan Institute, 2001.

———. "The Seraph in the Legends of Thomas of Celano and St. Bonaventure: The Victorine Transition." In *Bonaventuriana I,* edited by Chevero Blanco, 347–56. Rome: Edizioni Antonianum, 1988.

———. "The Seraph in Thomas of Celano's *Vita Prima.*" In *That Others May Know and Love: Essays in Honor of Zachary Hayes, OFM,* edited by Michael F. Cusato and F. Edward Coughlin, 23–41 (Franciscan Studies 34). St. Bonaventure, N.Y.: Franciscan Institute, 1997.

Hollywood, Amy. "Derrida's Noble Unfaith, or What Reading Hadewijch Can Teach You about Reading Derrida." *Minnesota Review* 80 (2013): 95–105.

———. "Feminist Studies." In *The Blackwell Companion to Christian Spirituality,* edited by Arther Holder, 363–86. West Sussex: Blackwell Publishing, 2005.

———. "Inside Out: Beatrice of Nazareth and Her Hagiographer." In *Gendered Voices: Medieval Saints and Their Interpreters,* edited by C. Mooney, 78–98. Philadelphia: University of Pennsylvania Press, 1999.

———. *The Soul as Virgin Wife.* Notre Dame: University of Notre Dame Press, 1995.

Hollywood, Amy, and Patricia Z. Beckman, eds. *The Cambridge Companion to Christian Mysticism.* Cambridge: Cambridge University Press, 2012.

Hülsbusch, Werner. "Die Theologie des Transitus bei Bonaventura." *S. Bonaventura 1274–1974,* vol. 4, 533–65. Grottaferrata: Collegio S. Bonaventura, 1974.

Ivánka, Endree V. *Plato Christianus: Übernahme und Umgestaltung des Platonismus durch die Väter.* Johannes Verlag Einsiedeln, 1964.

Jaeger, Stephen, ed. *Magnificence and the Sublime in Medieval Aesthetics: Art, Architecture, Literature, Music.* New York: Palgrave Macmillan, 2010.

Javelet, Robert. "Thomas Gallus et Richard de Saint-Victor mystiques." *Recherches de théologie ancienne et médiévale* 29 (1962): 206–33.

Johnson, Timothy, "Prologue as Pilgrimage: Bonaventure as Spiritual Cartographer." *Miscellanea Francescana*, 106–7 (2006–2007): 445–64.

———. *The Soul in Ascent: Bonaventure on Poverty, Prayer, and Union with God.* Quincy, Ill.: Franciscan Press, 2000.

Jordan, Mark D. "The Intelligibility of the World and the Divine Ideas in Aquinas." *The Review of Metaphysics* 38:1 (September 1984): 17–32.

Karnes, Michelle. *Imagination, Meditation and Cognition in the Middle Ages.* Chicago: University of Chicago Press, 2011.

Kent, Bonnie. *Virtues of the Will: The Transformation of Ethics in the Late Thirteenth Century.* Washington: Catholic University Press, 1995.

Kitanov, S. "Bonaventure's Understanding of Fruitio." *Picenum Seraphicum*, n.s., 20 (2001): 137–81.

Knowles, David. "The Influence of Pseudo-Dionysius on Western Mysticism." In *Christian Spirituality: Essays in Honor of Gordon Rupp*, edited by Peter Brooks, 79–94. London: SCM Press, 1975.

Knox, Lezlie S. *Creating Clare of Assisi: Female Franciscan Identities in Later Medieval Italy.* Leiden: Brill, 2008.

Knuuttila, Simo. *Emotions in Ancient and Medieval Philosophy.* Oxford: Oxford University Press, 2004.

Korolec, J. "Free Will and Free Choice." In *The Cambridge History of Later Medieval Philosophy*, edited by Norman Kretzmann, et al. Cambridge: Cambridge University Press, 1988.

Kries, Douglas. "Origen, Plato, and Conscience (*Synderesis*) in Jerome's Ezekiel Commentary." *Traditio* 57 (2002): 67–83.

Ladner, Gerhardt. "Medieval and Modern Understanding of Symbolism: A Comparison." In *Images and Ideas in the Middle Ages: Selected Studies in History and Art.* Rome: Edizioni di storia e letteratura, 1983, 239. Reprinted from *Speculum* 54 (1979): 223–56.

LaNave, Gregory. "Knowing God through and in All Things: A Proposal for Reading Bonaventure's *Itinerarium mentis in Deum*." *Franciscan Studies* 67 (2009): 267–99.

———. *Through Holiness to Wisdom: The Nature of Theology According to St. Bonaventure.* Rome: Istituto storico dei Cappuccini, 2005.

Langston, Douglas C. *Conscience and Other Virtues: From Bonaventure to MacIntyre.* University Park, Pa.: Pennsylvania State University Press, 2001.

Largier, Niklaus. "Inner Senses-Outer Senses: The Practice of Emotions in Medieval Mysticism." In *Codierung Von Emotionen Im Mittelalter (Emotions and Sensibilities in the Middle Ages*), vol. 1, edited by C. Stephen Jaeger and Ingrid Kasten, 3–15. Berlin and New York: de Gruyter, 2003.

Lawell, Declan. "Affective Excess: Ontology and Knowledge in the Thought of Thomas Gallus." *Dionysius* 26 (Dec. 2008): 139–74.

———. "*Ne de ineffabili penitus taceamus*: Aspects of the Specialized Vocabulary of the Writings of Thomas Gallus." *Viator* 40.1 (2009): 151–84.

———. "Thomas Gallus's Method as Dionysian Commentator: A Study of the *Glose super Angelica Ierarchia* (1224), with Considerations on the *Expositio librorum beati Dionysii*." *Archives d'histoire doctrinale et littéraire du Moyen Âge*, 76.1 (2009): 89–117.

Lees, Rosemary Ann. Vol. 1, *The Negative Language of the Dionysian School of Mystical Theology: An Approach to the Cloud of Unknowing*. Salzburg: Institut für Anglistik ind Amerikanistik, 1983.

Little, Lester K. "*Imitatio Francisci*: The Influence of Francis of Assisi on Late Medieval Religious Life." In *Critics of Franciscan Life: Essays in Honor of John V. Fleming*, edited by Michael F. Cusato and Guy Geltner, 195–218. Leiden: Brill, 2009.

Lottin, Odon. "Le premier Commentaire connu des Sentences de Pierre Lombard." *Recherches de théologie ancienne et médiévale* 11 (1939): 64–71.

Luscombe, David. "The Commentary of Hugh of Saint-Victor on the Celestial Hierarchy." In *Die Dionysius-Rezeption im Mittelalter*, edited by T. Boiadjiev, et al. Turnhout: Brepols, 2000, 159–75.

———. "Venezia, Bibl. Naz. Marziana, Latini Classe II, 26 (2473) and the Dionisian Corpus of the University of Paris in the Thirteenth Century." *Recherches de théologie ancienne et médiévale* 52 (1985): 224–27.

Lutz, Eduard. *Die Psychologie Bonaventuras. Beitrage zur Geschicte der Philosophie des Mittelalters* VI, 4–5. Munster, 1909. 180–90.

Marthaler, Berard. *Original Justice and Sanctifying Grace in the Writings of Saint Bonaventure, Excerpta ex Dissertatione ad Lauream*. Rome: Editrice "Miscellanea Francescana," 1965.

Massumi, Brian. *Parables for the Virtual: Movement, Affect, Sensation*. Durham, N.C.: Duke University Press, 2002.

McEvoy, Jan. "Microcosm and Macrocosm in the Writings of St. Bonaventure." In *S. Bonaventura 1274–1974*, vol. 2, 309–43. Grottaferrata: Collegio S. Bonaventura, 1974.

McGinn, Bernard. "Ascension and Introversion in the *Itinerarium Mentis in Deum*." In *S. Bonaventura 1274–1974*, vol. 3, 535–52. Grottaferrata: Collegio S. Bonaventura, 1974.

———. *The Flowering of Mysticism: Men and Women in the New Mysticism, 1200–1350 (The Presence of God: A History of Western Christian Mysticism*. Vol. 3). New York: Crossroad Herder, 1998.

———. *The Golden Chain: A Study in the Theological Anthropology of Isaac of Stella*. Washington: Cistercian Publications, 1972.

———. *The Growth of Mysticism: Gregory the Great through the 12th Century* (*The Presence of God: A History of Western Christian Mysticism*, Vol. 2). New York: Crossroad Herder, 1996.

———. "Love, Knowledge and Mystical Union in Western Christianity: Twelfth to Sixteenth Centuries." *Church History* 56, no. 1 (March 1987): 7–24.

———. "Pseudo-Dionysius and the Early Cistercians." *One Yet Two: Monastic Tradition East and West*. Edited by M. Basil Pennington. *Cistercian Studies* 29 (Kalamazoo: Cistercian Publications, 1973): 200–41.

———. "Thomas Gallus and Dionysian Mysticism." *Studies in Spirituality* 8 (Louvain, 1994): 81–96.

McNamer, Sarah. *Affective Meditation and the Invention of Medieval Compassion*. Philadelphia: University of Pennsylvania Press, 2009.

Ménard, André. "Spiritualité du Transitus." In *S. Bonaventura* 1274–1974, vol. 4, 607–35. Grottaferrata: Collegio S. Bonaventura, 1974.

Miethe, Terry L. "Natural Law, the Synderesis Rule, and St. Augustine." *Augustinian Studies* 11 (1980): 92–98.

Milbank, John, and Catherine Pickstock. *Truth in Aquinas*. New York: Routledge, 2001.

Miner, Robert. *Thomas Aquinas on the Passions: A Study of* Summa Theologiae *1a2ae 22–48*. Cambridge: Cambridge University Press, 2009.

Minnis, A. J. *Medieval Theory of Authorship: Scholastic Literary Attitudes in the Later Middle Ages*. 2nd ed. Aldershot: Scolar Press, 1988.

Mulligan, R. W. "Ratio Superior and Ratio Inferior: The Historical Background." *The New Scholasticism* 29 (1955): 1–32.

Narcisse, Gilbert. *Les raisons de Dieu: Arguments de convenance et esthétique théologique selon St. Thomas d'Aquin et Hans Urs von Balthasar*. Fribourg: Editions Universitaires Fribourg Suisse, 1997.

Németh, Csaba. "The Victorines and the Areopagite." In *L'ecole de Saint-Victor de Paris*, edited by Dominique Poirel, 333–83. Bibliotheca Victorina 22. Turnhout: Brepols, 2010.

O'Connell, Patrick. "The Lignum vitae of Saint Bonaventure and the Medieval Devotional Tradition." PhD dissertation, Fordham University, 1985.

Perl, Eric. *Theophany: The Neoplatonic Philosophy of Dionysius the Areopagite*. Albany, N.Y,: SUNY Press, 2007.

Petersen, Joan. "'Homo omnino Latinus?' The Theological and Cultural Background of Pope Gregory the Great." *Speculum* 62.3 (1987): 529–51.

Pink, Thomas, and M. W. F. Stone, eds. *The Will and Human Action: From Antiquity to the Present Day*. London: Routledge, 2003.

Poor, Sara S. *Mechthild of Magdeburg and Her Book: Gender and the Making of Textual Authority.* Philadelphia: University of Pennsylvania Press, 2011.

Potts, Timothy J. *Conscience in Medieval Philosophy.* Cambridge: Cambridge University Press, 1980.

Prentice, Robert. *The Psychology of Love According to St. Bonaventure.* St. Bonaventure, N.Y.: Franciscan Institute, 1950.

Quinn, John F. "Chronology of St. Bonaventure (1217–1257)." *Franciscan Studies* 32 (1972): 168–86.

———. "Chronology of St. Bonaventure's Sermons." *Archivum franciscanum historicum* 67 (1974): 145–84.

———. *The Historical Constitution of St. Bonaventure's Philosophy.* Toronto: Pontifical Institute of Mediaeval Studies, 1973.

———. "The Moral Philosophy of St. Bonaventure." *The Southwestern Journal of Philosophy* 5 (1974): 39–70.

———. "St. Bonaventure's Fundamental Conception of Natural Law." In *S. Bonaventura 1274–1974.* Vol. 3, 571–98. Grottaferrata: Collegio S. Bonaventura, 1973.

Radler, Charlotte. "'In Love I Am More God': The Centrality of Love in Meister Eckhart's Mysticism." *Journal of Religion* 90.2 (2010): 171–98.

Rahner, Karl. "Der Begriff der ecstasis bie Bonaventura." *Zeitschrift fur Aszese und Mystik,* 9 (1934): 1–18.

———. "The Doctrine of the Spiritual Senses in the Middle Ages." In *Theological Investigations,* vol. 16, translated by Cornelius Ernst, 109–28. Baltimore: Helicon Press, 1961.

Ratzinger, Joseph. *On Conscience: Two Essays.* San Francisco: Ignatius Press, 2007.

———. *The Theology of History in St. Bonaventure.* Translated by Zachary Hayes. Chicago: Franciscan Herald Press, 1971.

Reddy, William. *The Navigation of Feeling: A Framework for the History of Emotions.* Cambridge: Cambridge University Press, 2001.

Reynolds, Philip. "Analogy of Divine Names in Bonaventure." *Mediaeval Studies* 65 (2003): 117–62.

Rohmer, Jean. "Syndérèse." *Dictionnaire Théologie Catholique.* Vol. 14.2, 2992–96. Paris, 1941.

Rorem, Paul, "The Early Latin Dionysius: Eriugena and Hugh of St. Victor." In *Re-thinking Dionysius the Areopagite,* edited by Sarah Coakley and Charles M. Stang, 71–84. Malden, Mass.: Wiley-Blackwell, 2009.

———. *Pseudo-Dionysius: A Commentary on the Texts and an Introduction to their Influence.* Oxford: Oxford University Press, 1993.

Rosemann, Phillipp W. *The Story of a Great Medieval Book: Peter Lombard's Sentences.* Rethinking the Middle Ages, vol. 2. Toronto: Broadview Press, 2007.

Rosenwein, Barbara. *Emotional Communities in the Early Middle Ages*. Ithaca, N.Y.: Cornell University Press, 2006.

———. "Worrying About Emotions in History." *The American Historical Review* 107.3 (June 2002): 821–45.

de Roulers, L. "Le rôle du mot 'habitus' dans la theologie bonaventurienne." *Collectanea Franciscana* 26 (1956): 225–50, 337–72.

du Roy, Olivier. *L'intelligence de la foi en la Trinité selon saint Augustin: genèse de sa théologie jusqu'en 391*. Paris: Études augustiniennes, 1966.

Rudy, Gordon. *The Mystical Language of Sensation in the Later Middle Ages*. New York: Routledge, 2002.

Scafi, Alessandro. *Mapping Paradise: A History of Heaven on Earth*. Chicago: University of Chicago Press, 2006.

Schaefer, Alexander. "The Position and Function of Man in the Created World According to Saint Bonaventure." *Franciscan Studies* 20 (1960): 261–316.

Schlosser, Marianne. *Cognitio et amor: Zum kognitiven und voluntativem Grund der Gotteserfahrung nach Bonaventura*. Ferdinand Schöningh, 1990.

Scott, Alan. *Origen and the Life of the Stars: The History of an Idea*. Oxford: Clarendon Press, 1991.

Siebeck, H. "Noch einmal die Synderesis." *Archiv für Geschichte der Philosophie* 10 (1897): 520–29.

Siraisi, Nancy G. *Medieval and Early Renaissance Medicine: An Introduction to Knowledge and Practice*. Chicago: University of Chicago Press, 1990.

Sirovic, P. Franz. *Der Begriff "Affectus" und die Willenslehre beim Hl. Bonaventura: Eine analytisch-synthetische Untersuchung*. Vienna: Missionsdruckerei St. Gabriel, 1965.

Solignac, Aimé. "Syndérèse." In *Dictionnaire de Spiritualité: ascétique et mystique, doctrine et histoire*, vol. 14.2, edited by Marcel Viller, et al., 1407–12. Paris: G. Beauchesne, 1932–95.

Sorabji, Richard. *Animal Minds and Human Morals*. Ithaca, N.Y.: Cornell University Press, 1995.

Southern, Richard. *The Making of the Middle Ages*. New Haven: Yale University Press, 1992.

Spago, Emma Jane Marie. *The Category of the Aesthetic in the Philosophy of Saint Bonaventure*. St. Bonaventure, N.Y.: Franciscan Institute, 1953.

Stang, Charles M. *Apophasis and Pseudonymity in Dionysius the Areopagite: "No Longer I."* Oxford: Oxford University Press, 2012.

Stewart, Kathleen. *Ordinary Affects*. Durham, N.C.: Duke University Press, 2007.

Tavard, George H. *Transiency and Permanence: The Nature of Theology According to St. Bonaventure*. St. Bonaventure, N.Y.: The Franciscan Institute, 1954.

Terada, Rei. *Feeling in Theory: Emotion After the "Death of the Subject."* Cambridge: Harvard University Press, 2003.

Tomasic, Thomas Michael. "Neoplatonism and the Mysticism of William of St.-Thierry." In *An Introduction to the Medieval Mystics of Europe: Fourteen Original Essays*, edited by Paul E. Szarmach, 53–75. Albany, N.Y.: SUNY Press, 1984.

Tracy, David, ed. *Celebrating the Medieval Heritage: A Colloquy on the Thought of Aquinas and Bonaventure*. Chicago: University of Chicago Press, 1978.

Turner, Denys. *The Darkness of God: Negativity in Christian Mysticism*. Cambridge: Cambridge University Press, 1995.

———. *Eros and Allegory: Medieval Exegesis on the Song of Songs*. Cistercian Studies 156. Kalamazoo, Mich.: Cistercian Publications, 1995.

Turney, Lillian. "The Symbolism of the Temple in St. Bonaventure's *Itinerarium mentis in Deum*." PhD dissertation, Fordham University, 1968.

Van Steenberghen, Ferdinand. *Aristotle in the West: The Origins of Latin Aristotelianism*. Translated by Leonard Johnston. New York: Humanities Press, 1955.

Verbeke, Gerard. *The Presence of Stoicism in Medieval Thought*. Washington: Catholic University of America Press, 1983.

Vettori, Alessandro. *Poets of Divine Love: Franciscan Mystical Poetry of the Thirteenth Century*. New York: Fordham University Press, 2004.

Werner, Karl. *Die Psychologie und Erkenntnislehre des Johannes Bonaventura*. Reprint. New York: Burt Franklin, 1973. Originally published 1876.